BRIGHT STAR
GREEN LIGHT

*The RSC Shakespeare: Collaborative Plays
by Shakespeare and Others (co-editor)*

The Public Value of the Humanities

*The RSC Shakespeare: Individual Works
(with Eric Rasmussen, 34 volumes)*

*The RSC Shakespeare: Complete Works
(with Eric Rasmussen)*

John Clare: Selected Poems

*Shakespeare: An Illustrated Stage History
(with Russell Jackson)*

Green Romanticism: Studies in Romanticism Special Issue

The Romantics on Shakespeare

Charles Lamb: Elia and The Last Essays of Elia

INTRODUCTIONS

The Folio Poets: Lord Byron

The Tempest: A Film by Julie Taymor

*Andrew Marvell: The Complete Poems
(Penguin Classics)*

Titus: A Film by Julie Taymor

CREATIVE WORKS

The Shepherd's Hut (poems)

Being Shakespeare (a one-man play for Simon Callow)

The Cure for Love (novel)

BRIGHT STAR
GREEN LIGHT

THE BEAUTIFUL WORKS AND DAMNED LIVES
OF JOHN KEATS AND F. SCOTT FITZGERALD

JONATHAN BATE

Yale

UNIVERSITY PRESS

NEW HAVEN AND LONDON

First published in 2021 in the United States by Yale University Press
and in Great Britain by William Collins.

Copyright © Jonathan Bate 2021

Jonathan Bate asserts the moral right to be identified as the author of this
work in accordance with the Copyright, Designs and Patents Act 1988.

Yale University Press books may be purchased in quantity for
educational, business, or promotional use. For information, please e-mail
sales.press@yale.edu (U.S. office) or sales@yaleup.co.uk (U.K. office).

Typeset in Sabon LT Std by Palimpsest Book Production Ltd,
Falkirk, Stirlingshire.

Printed in the United States of America.

Library of Congress Control Number: 2021930600

ISBN 978-0-300-25657-4 (hardcover : alk. paper)

This paper meets the requirements of ANSI/NISO Z39.48-1992
(Permanence of Paper).

10 9 8 7 6 5 4 3 2 1

For

Philip Davis, boat against the current

&

Kelvin Everest, Keatzian

& in memory of Miriam Allott

CONTENTS

LIST OF ILLUSTRATIONS

1. Scott Fitzgerald's editions of Keats's works and Colvin's biography (author's collection)
2. Scott Fitzgerald posing cross-dressed for the Princeton Triangle theatricals (Photo 12 / Alamy Stock Photo)
3. Ginevra King, *Town and Country Magazine*, July 1918 (public domain)
4. Guy's Hospital in Keats's time (public domain)
5. Leigh Hunt (author's collection)
6. Engraving after Nicolas Poussin's *The Realm of Flora* (public domain)
7. Zelda Sayre, 1917 (public domain)
8. Fitzgerald in his prime (Pictorial Press Ltd / Alamy Stock Photo)
9. Rupert Brooke (author's collection)
10. Newspaper clipping regarding the novelist and the flapper (public domain)
11. Title page of Fitzgerald's edition of the works of Keats (author's collection)
12. Benjamin Robert Haydon (author's collection)
13. The sea at Margate in Keats's time (public domain)
14. Advertisement for *The Chorus Girl's Romance* (public domain)
15. Jacket of *Flappers and Philosophers* (public domain)

Biography is the falsest of the arts. That is because
there were no Keatzians before Keats
(F. Scott Fitzgerald, undated notebook entry)

I have lov'd the principle of beauty in all things
(John Keats, letter to Fanny Brawne, February 1820)

Beauty of great art, beauty of all joy, most of all the
beauty of women
(F. Scott Fitzgerald, *This Side of Paradise*)

I think I shall be among the English Poets after
my death
(John Keats, letter of 14 October 1818)

thinking of my ambitions so nearly achieved of being
part of English literature
(F. Scott Fitzgerald, letter of summer 1930)

The artist is the creator of beautiful things. To reveal
art and conceal the artist is art's aim.
The critic is he who can translate into another manner
or a new material his impression of beautiful things.
(Oscar Wilde, preface to
The Picture of Dorian Gray, 1890)

1

THE PARALLEL

A little before Christmas 1818, John Keats wrote from the village of Hampstead, just outside London, to his brother and sister-in-law George and Georgiana. They were 4,000 miles away in the log cabin of the ornithologist John James Audubon in Henderson, Kentucky. They had a wild turkey nesting on the roof, a household of children and a boisterous pet swan called Trumpeter to keep them company. Keats was alone with his grief, writing with the news about their other brother that they had been dreading for months: 'The last days of poor Tom were of the most distressing nature.' Tuberculosis had taken him.

Keats comforted himself with the thought that he had 'scarce a doubt of immortality of some nature of other'. 'Of other' was a slip of the pen for 'or other', but perhaps a telling one in that Keats conceived of immortality as a connection to others rather than something to do with God and heaven. 'That will be one of the grandeurs of immortality,' he continued, 'there will be no space and consequently the only commerce between spirits will be by their intelligence of each other.' The immortals 'will completely understand each other – while we in this world merely comprehend each other in different degrees'. Mutual comprehension, he suggests, is the measure of love and friendship. He did not feel so very distant from George and Georgiana, despite their emigration to America, because he could remember every detail of their manner of thinking and feeling, the shaping of their joys and sorrows, their ways of walking, standing, sauntering, sitting down, laughing and joking.

In order to demonstrate their connection, he proposed that he should read a passage of Shakespeare every Sunday morning at ten o'clock and that they should do so at the same time. Shakespeare would bring them 'as near each other as blind bodies can be in the same room'. This experiment in quasi-telepathy via shared simultaneous reading would, presumably, have been stymied by the difference in time zone, of which Keats was not aware. But that would not have mattered. Whether the time difference is six hours, as it was for the Keats siblings, or 200 years, as divided Keats from Shakespeare and divides us from Keats, the act of reading creates a community across time. Keats described the great writers of the past as 'the mighty dead'. Their 'charactered language', he said, 'show like the hieroglyphics of beauty'; his ambition was to join them in what he called 'an immortal freemasonry'. The endurance of great art was the only immortality of which he was certain.

George and Georgiana had eight children, including a son named John Keats, who became a civil engineer in Missouri. He lived until 1917. A report in a Minnesota newspaper had once predicted that 'the name of Keats will probably die with him'. But by 1917 the name of Keats was truly among the immortals. It lived through those who read and loved his work, such as a Princeton student from St Paul, Minnesota, who that very year was immersing himself in poetry, beginning his first novel, and yearning for a green light from the girl of his dreams.

*

Biographers and critics have noted that John Keats was F. Scott Fitzgerald's favourite author. Academic essays have been written about particular passages in his novels where the relationship becomes apparent. But the full extent of the influence, its pervasiveness across Fitzgerald's career, the sense that he saw himself as the prose Keats, remains underappreciated.

The parallels between their lives are uncanny. Each of them established themselves as authors in the aftermath of a long and devastating war. Each lived in a time of freedom and experimentation that came to an abrupt end with a financial crisis: the stock-market panic of 1825 and the Wall Street crash of 1929. Each sought to supplement the work that was their vocation – poetry in Keats's case, prose fiction in Fitzgerald's – by trying to make money in the more lucrative arena of the performing arts: Keats writing for the London stage, Fitzgerald for the Hollywood screen.

Keats's last years were shadowed by his unconsummated love for Fanny Brawne, for whom he wrote his most famous sonnet, 'Bright Star'. Fitzgerald's writing was shadowed by his unconsummated love for Ginevra King, who inspired the character of Daisy Fay in *The Great Gatsby*. In their literary taste, both were borne back ceaselessly into the past: Keats to the romance of the Middle Ages and to the English poetry that he loved (Milton, Shakespeare); Fitzgerald, to Keats.

Keats's imagination was fired to life by Shakespeare, but he failed when he tried to write pseudo-Shakespearean blank-verse drama. He succeeded, triumphantly, when he took the spirit of Shakespeare and infused it into a different form, that of lyric poetry – the ode, above all. F. Scott Fitzgerald's imagination was fired to life by Keats, but he failed when he tried to write pseudo-Keatzian lyric poetry. He succeeded, triumphantly, when he took the spirit of Keats and infused it into a different form, that of the lyrical novel – *The Great Gatsby*, above all.

They were both cursed by tuberculosis. Fitzgerald was further damned by chronic alcoholism. Had Keats lived longer, he might have taken a less sanguine view of the pleasures of intoxication than that expressed in one of his incomparable letters:

> whenever I can have Claret I must drink it. – 'tis the only palate affair that I am at all sensual in. Would it not be a good Speck to send you some vine roots – could it be done? I'll enquire – If you could make some wine like Claret to drink on summer evenings in an arbour! For really 'tis so fine – it fills the mouth one's mouth with a gushing freshness – then goes down cool and feverless – then you do not feel it quarrelling with your liver.

'O for a beaker full of the warm south . . . That I might drink, and leave the world unseen', he would write a few months later, in the poem that gave Fitzgerald the title *Tender is the Night*.

Keats is the epitome of the Romantic poet; Fitzgerald the epitome of the Romantic novelist.

*

The notion of 'parallel lives' has a long history. Many of the foundations for the art of biography were laid 2,000 years ago by Plutarch in the book that Shakespeare read in an English translation entitled *The Lives of the Noble Grecians and Romans Compared*. Plutarch thought that biography was the most interesting part of history because it offered immense riches of narrative and character: 'stories are fit for every place, reach to all persons, serve for all times, teach the living, revive the dead, so far excelling all other books'. His technique was to pair up figures from Greece and Rome – for example, the soldiers Alexander the Great and Julius Caesar, the political orators Demosthenes and Cicero. He told the stories of their lives, with a particular emphasis on anecdotes and incidents that were revelatory of their character, and then he offered a 'parallel' between the pair.

This book is a revival of the experiment of paralleling two similar but different geniuses: one of them English, a poet, and of the early nineteenth century; the other, American, a novelist, and of the early twentieth. The lives of Keats and Scott Fitzgerald were short, but many biographies of them have been very long. Instead of replicating the detailed 'cradle to grave' narratives of their admirable biographers, I have sought to bring them back to life in the Plutarchan style: in parallel and by means of a highly selective series of anecdotes, moments and scenes that seem to me to come to their essence and to reveal the wellsprings of their art. My theme is the gestation of Keats's mature poems and the making of Fitzgerald's novels. Readers should go elsewhere if they are in search of a day-by-day account of Keats through his letters or an enumeration of Fitzgerald's every short story and drunken escapade.

Without assuming the reader's prior knowledge of the work of either author – beyond, perhaps, *The Great Gatsby* or the odes of Keats – the book accordingly seeks to offer lovers of Keats a brief life of F. Scott Fitzgerald, lovers of Fitzgerald a brief life of John Keats, and, at the same time, an account of the two writers' shared commitment to words that evoke and create beauty. To put it another way, here is a reading of Keats through the eyes of Fitzgerald and a Keatzian* reading of Fitzgerald.

---

* Fitzgerald's idiosyncratic spelling (both his and Keats's misspellings are retained in quotations from their letters).

2

'GREEN FELICITY'

Scott Fitzgerald learned about the life of John Keats from a 600-page biography bound in dark green board with gold debossed type on the front: 'JOHN KEATS – SIDNEY COLVIN'. Published in New York by Charles Scribner's Sons in 1917 to mark the centenary of Keats's first volume of poetry, its full title was *John Keats: His Life and Poetry, His Friends, Critics and After-Fame*. The author was a distinguished figure in English cultural life. He had been Slade Professor of Fine Art at Cambridge University and a close friend of the renowned Robert Louis Stevenson prior to the latter's premature death. He had then become Keeper of Prints and Drawings at the British Museum.

Colvin explained in his preface that his was the first book to give a full and connected account of Keats's life and poetry. Thirty years earlier, he had written the slender volume on the poet for a series of popular biographies called English Men of Letters, but now, too old for war service, he had 'found solace and occupation' through the 'soul-shaking years' of 1914 to 1917 in researching and writing the first comprehensive biography, based on a full examination of published and unpublished sources. By bringing together the reminiscences of Keats's friends, the evidence of reviews and press coverage, and above all the poet's own extraordinarily self-revelatory letters, Colvin was able to recreate both the everyday and the inner life of his subject with a fullness and authority rarely accorded to the literary biographer. There have been many excellent biographies of Keats since Colvin's, rich in psychological, literary critical and historical contextual insight, but surprisingly few new facts have been added to his narrative. He can be our guide, as he was Fitzgerald's.

*

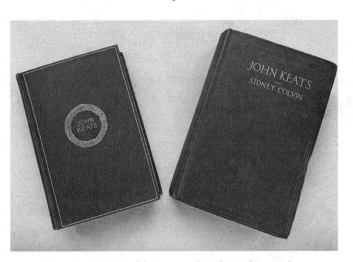

Keats's poems and letters, and Colvin's biography:
the editions owned by Scott Fitzgerald

Thomas Keats or Keates came out of the west. His family belonged to Devon or Cornwall, the counties in the far south-west of England, bordering on the Atlantic Ocean. As American westerners a century later would go east to New York to seek their fortune, so he headed for London. Being a countryman, he knew horses. By the time he was twenty, he had become head ostler in a livery stable providing horses for hire at an inn called the Swan and Hoop overlooking Moorfields, in the east of the

city. In October 1794, he married Frances, the lively and impul-
sive nineteen-year-old daughter of his employer, John Jennings.

Their first son, John Keats, was born a year later. The notion
of him being cradled in a stable like some latter-day Jesus would
fuel the romantic idea of his humble genius, though in reality
his place of birth is not known for certain (and records differ
as to whether he was born on 29 or 31 October 1795). When
he was three, the family moved from their rooms above the
inn to a house just off the busy City Road. By then, Johnny
had a brother, George. Another boy, Thomas, followed a year
later and three years after that, they moved back to the Swan
and Hoop. Jennings had decided to retire, and Thomas Keats
took over as manager. Horses could now be purchased from
'Keates's Livery Stable'. The following summer, in June 1803,
Frances Keats gave birth to her only daughter, Fanny.

Colvin recorded two anecdotes about the young John Keats.
According to an old lady who was a neighbour when they were
living near the City Road, when he first learned to speak,
'instead of answering sensibly, he had a trick of making a rime
to the last word people said and then laughing'. He was also
said to be fiercely devoted to his mother. Once, when she was
ill and the doctor had ordered rest, he stood guard at the door
with an old sword and refused to let anybody in. The artist
Benjamin Robert Haydon, who would play a major part in
Keats's story and who loved to embroider a tale, heightened
the force of the anecdote:

> He was when an infant a most violent and ungovernable child.
> At five years of age or thereabouts, he once got hold of a naked
> sword and shutting the door swore nobody should go out. His
> mother wanted to do so, but he threatened her so furiously she
> began to cry, and was obliged to wait till somebody through
> the window saw her position and came to the rescue.

Keats would one day write that 'A Man's life of any worth is a continual allegory – and very few eyes can see the Mystery of his life – a life like the scriptures, figurative.' True poets such as Shakespeare, he continued, live lives of allegory upon which their works are a commentary. By the same account, the literary biographer infers the writer's character from their works and finds incidents in the life that allegorize it. Thus Keats the born rhymester, the child with an innate sense of humour, the boy of strong passion.

In April 1804, when Keats was eight years old, his father was riding home late at night when his horse stumbled and he was thrown. He cracked his head on the ground. A watchman found him at one o'clock in the morning and he was dead soon after dawn. Just two months later, Frances Keats remarried and her new husband was installed as manager of the Swan and Hoop. Her father, old Mr Jennings, died the following spring, leaving substantial legacies to his family. But the terms of the will were unclear and Frances, who felt herself excluded, challenged it in the Court of Chancery. The action failed, but it delayed the possibility of an inheritance for the Keats children. Around the time of the court judgment, her second marriage broke up and for a time she disappeared from the family, perhaps into alcoholism.

John, George, Tom and Fanny were now effectively orphans. They clung closely to each other. Henceforth, his siblings would be among the most important people in Keats's life. They moved in with their grandmother, Mr Jennings' widow, who lived in Edmonton, a village a few miles to the north of London, close to another village, Enfield, where John and George had been enrolled at a small but excellent school.

Clarke's Academy offered a formidable education in the 'dissenting' tradition. In contrast to the ancient 'public' boarding schools for gentlemen, where the curriculum was confined almost entirely to the Greek and Latin classics, John Clarke offered more varied fare: Latin remained a staple part of the daily diet, but there was also French translation, English history, mathematics, science (mechanics, optics, even astronomy), botany and gardening – pupils were given little plots for growing and tending plants. This was a practical education, preparing lower-middle-class boys for working lives in trade, but there was also a message that they should take pride in the hard-won English traditions of liberty, freedom of thought and religion, and a mixed political constitution. Those who had fought and written in the middle of the seventeenth century against the old regime of monarchical absolutism were regarded as heroes, none more than the poet and pamphleteer John Milton. John Clarke was a kindly and liberal figure, who became a substitute father for the Keats boys.

In bringing back to life the image of John Keats as a schoolboy, Colvin quoted three witnesses. Brother George wrote of his goodness of heart mingled with fierceness of temper: 'we loved, jangled, and fought alternately'. A fellow pupil, Edward Holmes, who grew up to become a famous music critic and the author of the first properly researched English biography of Mozart, elaborated on the theme of the future poet's fierce temper. He recalled that Keats was in childhood not attached to books: 'His *penchant* was for fighting. He would fight any one – morning, noon, and night, his brother among the rest. It was meat and drink to him.' Holmes claimed that he won Keats's friendship only by fighting with him. Keats was 'in every way the creature of passion':

> In all active exercises he excelled . . . This violence and vehe-
> mence – this pugnacity and generosity of disposition – in passions
> of tears or outrageous fits of laughter – always in extremes – will
> help to paint Keats in his boyhood. Associated as they were

with an extraordinary beauty of person and expression, these
qualities captivated the boys, and no one was more popular.

Reading this, the equally pugnacious and beautiful Scott
Fitzgerald could as well have been looking into a self-portrait
– save that it took him a while to cultivate the persona that
would make him popular among his peers. They shared a self-
dramatizing quality.

The theatrical side of Keats's personality is wonderfully
captured in the reminiscences of Colvin's third witness, Charles
Cowden Clarke, son of the headmaster. Eight years older than
Keats, he treated him with great affection and indulgence, as
if he were a histrionic younger brother. Johnny's gift for imitation, along with his 'terrier courage', made him a favourite
among the boys:

> One of the transports of that marvellous actor, Edmund Kean
> – whom, by the way, he idolized – was its nearest resemblance;
> and the two were not very dissimilar in face and figure. Upon
> one occasion, when an usher [junior teacher], on account of
> some impertinent behaviour, had boxed his brother Tom's ears,
> John rushed up, put himself into the received posture of offence,
> and, it was said, struck the usher – who could, so to say, have
> put him in his pocket.

When he was in a temper, his much taller and stronger brother
George sometimes had to hold him down. 'It was all, however,
a wisp-of-straw conflagration; for he had an intensely tender
affection for his brothers, and proved it upon the most trying
occasions.'

Charles Cowden Clarke loved him for his 'utter unconsciousness of a mean motive, his placability, his generosity'. He went
on to explain that it was only towards the end of his time at

school that Keats became an ardent reader. He credited himself with introducing the younger boy to the joys of poetry, notably by way of Edmund Spenser's *The Faerie Queene*, an Elizabethan wonderland of magical imagery and chivalric adventure. Clarke remembered how Keats, upon returning the copy of Spenser that Clarke had lent him, hoisted himself up, looking burly and dominant as he said, singling out one of Spenser's characteristic compound epithets, 'What an image that is – *sea-shouldering whales*!'

Keats's very first poem would be an 'Imitation of Spenser'. Instead of a sea-shouldering whale, it had a gliding swan, oaring himself along, with 'jetty eyes', while 'on his back a fay [fairy] reclined voluptuously'. Words often drift, swan-like, into a writer's unconscious. In *The Great Gatsby*, a Fay would recline voluptuously on a sofa and eyes would look with longing towards a jetty.

*

Keats's mother reappeared in the summer of 1809, coming to live with the family in Edmonton, but she died of a 'decline' – almost certainly consumption – the following spring. John was the most devoted of her sons; he is said to have cooked her food, administered her medicine, and sat up all night reading novels to her; after her death, he grieved so deeply that he took to hiding in a nook under the desk of his schoolmaster. Her demise led to further complications in the family finances, as grandmother Jennings appointed new executors to handle the estate and serve as legal guardians to the Keats children. The leading role was taken by a tea merchant called Richard Abbey, who came from her original home village in the north. He withdrew John from school and apprenticed him to the apothecary in Edmonton who had tended to Mrs Keats in her dying days.

Little is known of the years he spent in this role, other than that he quarrelled with his master and, according to Charles Cowden Clarke, cultivated his new-found passion for poetry and for nature. Colvin's biography stitched the scant sources together with some liberal imagination to paint a vivid picture of Keats in his teens, wandering in the evenings through 'a country of winding elm-shadowed lanes, of bosky hedge and thicket and undulating pasture-land charmingly diversified with parks and pleasaunces', his mind possessed by the delights of nature blended with 'the beautiful images that already peopled it from his readings in Greek mythology', the charm of his rural surroundings 'enhanced into a strange supernatural thrill by the recurring magic of moonlight'. It is only in adolescence, Colvin observed, that such delights can be drunk in without self-consciousness, 'and no youth ever drank them in more deeply than Keats'. The rich natural imagery of his poems, together with the mythological references gleaned from his well-thumbed copy of John Lemprière's *Bibliotheca Classica; or, A Classical Dictionary*, have their origin in these years of youth in a countryside that was already beginning to vanish under the creeping growth of the London suburbs. When Clarke's Academy closed, the schoolhouse was repurposed as a railway station. There are no meadows and thickets between Enfield and Edmonton now.

*

Near the end of his life, Scott Fitzgerald sought to lead his last lover, Sheilah Graham, through what he called a 'College of One': an ambitious course of reading in literature, history and philosophy. Among the poems on the Keatzian reading list he prepared for her was a short lyric that begins 'In drear-nighted December'. It draws a contrast between nature and humankind. A tree is 'happy' (fortunate) because during December, with the 'sleety whistle' of wind in its boughs, it does not remember the 'green felicity' of spring. A brook is 'Too happy, happy' because when frozen it does not remember bubbling under 'Apollo's summer look'. But it is different for us. We cannot but look back with sorrow on our own 'green felicity', the lost joys of youth:

> Ah! would 'twere so with many
>   A gentle girl and boy!
> But were there ever any
>   Writh'd not at passèd joy?
> The feel of *not* to feel it,
> When there is none to heal it
> Nor numbèd sense to steel it,
>   Was never said in rhyme.

'The feel of *not* to feel it' is an extraordinary line, though one that was considered awkward by Keats's friend Richard Woodhouse, a literary-minded Eton-educated lawyer who created and preserved transcripts of many of the poems: he didn't like 'feel' as a noun, where normal usage would have 'feeling'. When the poem was published posthumously, Woodhouse changed the line to the much weaker 'To know the change and feel it' and in so doing destroyed the originality of the poem. The idea that remembrance of past happiness adds misery when one is in a state of misery: that was an old poetic theme. But Keats set himself the task of doing something new: using poetry to numb the sense of sorrow, to create the feel of not feeling regret for the past. Fitzgerald's tragedy would be that alcohol would increasingly take the place of writing as his way of numbing his senses, making himself not feel the loss of the 'green felicity' of his own youth.

*

Whereas John Keats kept no record of his childhood and rarely made direct allusions to his early years, Francis Scott Key Fitzgerald carefully preserved his early memories. Ernest Hemingway remembered a day in 1925 when Scott and Zelda invited him and his wife to lunch in their dark and airless Paris apartment in the rue de Tilsitt. There was nothing in the room that seemed to belong to the Fitzgeralds except for copies of Scott's books bound in light blue leather with the titles in gold, together with another book that Scott proudly showed his guest. It was his ledger: a thirteen-and-three-quarter-inch tall 'Standard Blank Book' purchased from Brown, Blodgett and Sperry, manufacturing stationers of St Paul, Minnesota, early in his career as an author. Dividing the pages into columns, he kept it as a ledger, meticulously recording the publication details and earnings of all his stories, together with sums received for motion picture sales. Hemingway was bemused that these accounts were 'noted as carefully as the log of a ship' and that 'Scott showed them to both of us as though he were the curator of a museum'. He pointed out his earnings as if he were pointing out a view – in an apartment where 'there was no view'. This hardly seemed consistent with Fitzgerald's apparent life of chaotic spontaneity, as witnessed by his misadventures on an expedition to Lyons that he and Hemingway had just made in order to pick up a car that had had its roof ripped off.

Hemingway made no mention of the last forty pages of the ledger. It was there that Fitzgerald gave his life the same treatment as his earnings. He gradually filled the back end of his precious book with an 'Outline Chart of my Life'. Entries for the earlier years consist of memories of things that the adult Fitzgerald conceived to be formative of his identity. The first page reads:

1896 Sept 24th at 3-30 P.M. a son Francis Scott Key
          Fitzgerald to Edward and Mary Fitzgerald. The
          day was Sunday. The weight was 10 lbs, 6 oz. The
          place was 481 Laurel Ave, St Paul, Minn.
Oct   He was baptized and went out for the first time
          – to Lamberts corner store on Laurel Ave.
Nov   He has the colic.

1897
Feb   The child laughed for the first time.
May   He crawled – and had his first tooth and a cold
          in his head.
July   He said his first word. It was the monosyllable 'up'

These brief entries reveal but also conceal. They do not mention
that he was named after a distant early nineteenth-century
relative of his father. Francis Scott Key was a minor poet best
known for his composition of 'The Defence of Fort M'Henry',
a patriotic lyric inspired by an action in the Anglo-American
war of 1812. It was set to music as 'The Star-Spangled Banner'
and in 1916, at the height of the First World War, President
Woodrow Wilson recognized it for official use on military and
public occasions (it formally became the national anthem by
an Act of Congress fifteen years later). Metaphorically speaking,
'dawn's early light', 'twilight's last gleaming' and 'bright stars
through the perilous fight' were written into Francis Scott Key
Fitzgerald's DNA.

'He was baptized': the concealment here is that he was
baptized a Roman Catholic. This was not a particular imped-
iment in St Paul. The Catholic cathedral where he was baptized
signalled the city's allegiance to old-fashioned values contrasting
with those of neighbouring Minneapolis, the home of nouveau
riche Protestant speculators. But the Catholic background meant

that Scott would never truly belong in the privileged white Anglo-Saxon Protestant circles among which he moved in Princeton and New York. His father, Edward Fitzgerald, was born of Irish stock in the antebellum Confederate South, for which he always harboured a nostalgia. He was always something of an outsider in the business-oriented urban North. He was also a failure, reliant on his wife's inherited income. She was Mollie McQuillan, daughter of a wealthy self-made Minnesota wholesale grocer whose family had emigrated from Ireland.

Soon after his marriage, Edward Fitzgerald launched a business called the American Rattan & Willow Works. It went bankrupt within a few years, perhaps because there was not much of a market for outdoor wicker furniture in one of the coldest states of the Union. He fell back on a job as a salesman with Procter & Gamble, which accounted for Scott's uprooted early years: the ledger records a family move to Buffalo before he was two, to Washington DC in the winter and back to Buffalo in the spring, to Syracuse when he was four and Buffalo again when he was six. Then when he was eleven his father lost his job and the family returned to St Paul. Scott inherited the tendency to drift. As an adult, he never truly settled in one place.

He dramatized himself by writing the outline chart of his life in the third person. In picking out the colic and the cold in his head, then noting that at two years old 'His mother feared consumption for him', he reveals his hypochondriacal tendency. In recording (presumably via his mother) his first laugh, he is flagging the sense of humour that, as with Keats, was one of his mechanisms for survival. And in claiming that his first word was 'up', he launches an image of upward mobility that signals his fascination with social status and with the rich whom he despised but could not resist.

The memories became his own when he was six. As they

flood back, the mask of the third-person voice occasionally slips:

> He began to remember many things, a filthy vacant lot, the haunt of dead cats, a hair-raising buck-board, the little girl whose father was in prison for telling lies, a Rabelaisian incident with Jack Butler, a blow with a baseball bat from the same boy – son of an army officer – which left a scar that will shine always in the middle of ~~my~~ his forehead, a history of the United States which father bought me; he became a child of the American Revolution. Also he boxed with Edgar Miller the grocery man's son, egged on by his father.

It is as if he is writing a template for his future literary themes: the filthy vacant lot with its dead cats foreshadows the ash-strewn dumping ground between East and West Egg in *Gatsby*; the high-speed horse-drawn carriage anticipates the cars that race and crash in his 1920s world; the father in prison for telling lies evokes his fantasists and shady crooks; the indeter-minate Rabelaisian incident suggests the sexual shenanigans that punctuate his stories but about which he is rarely explicit; the fighting and the boxing prepare us for the drunken brawls, but also the sense of his own puniness and his desire to prove himself a man by joining the army. And the 'child of the American Revolution' summons up his loyalty to an older America, pre-war (he is reconstructing his early life, remember, in 1919), even pre-Civil War. Immediately after this first burst of reminiscences, he notes a visit south to the Maryland home of his aunt, where he was a 'ribbon-holder' at the wedding of his cousin Cecilia. 'After the wedding he turned on his two black friends Roscoe and Forrest and with the help of a beggar boy tried to tie them up with ropes': his earliest remembered practical joke, but one with a frisson of the ethnic tensions and the jostling cheek by jowl of wealth and poverty in the old South.

Two months after his ninth birthday, 'I He went to dancing school and fell in love with Nancy Gardner'. At ten, he put on plays in the attic, 'all based on the American Revolution'. At the same age, he developed a tendency to hero-worship: a family friend 'took him to a basketball game and he fell madly into admiration for a dark-haired boy who played with a melancholy defiance'. The following year, he went to confession and lied by saying in a shocked voice to the priest 'Oh <u>no</u>, I <u>never</u> tell a lie.' This would sow the seed of 'Absolution', a short story that would be crucial to his development. By this time, he was in love with another girl, Kitty, whom he kissed a great deal at a 'kissing party'. It was around now that his father lost his job at Procter & Gamble. On hearing the news, Scott returned his swimming money to his mother.

Back in St Paul, they moved in with his grandmother. He was enrolled at St Paul Academy, a private school where most of the boys came from wealthier families. In his first year, he made himself unpopular by showing off, talking too much. 'Will someone poison Scotty or find some means to shut his mouth', said 'The Freshest Boy' in the school (a memory included not only in the ledger but also in a short story with that title). Scotty had plenty to talk about, having inaugurated a lifetime habit of reading in bed, deep into the night.

He had an attack of appendicitis. In basketball, he started in the third team and never got beyond the second; at baseball, he learned to pitch. He wrote plays and stories. A summer holiday tour with his mother gave him a glimpse of the homes of the rich beside the Great Lakes. In the cold winters there were bobsled-rides, skating and skiing. In his early teens he went through a religious phase. In his final year at the academy, he made it to the football team but missed a kick in a crucial game. At fourteen and a half, he was thinking about girls, forming secret clubs and breaking rules: 'Dancing school. Marie. Love. The triangle . . . The founding of The Scandal Detectives. I start to smoke . . . The naughty six . . . The chain of love.' That summer, his last at the St Paul Academy, it was tennis, baseball, no work and ducking school. He stole candy, sailed, played on the railroad and heard the name of a girl called Ginevra King.

In the fall, his parents sent him off to boarding school. The Newman School in New Jersey, just forty minutes out of New York by subway, aimed to prepare the sons of wealthy Roman Catholic families for Yale or Princeton. He went in cocky, convinced that he had 'personality, charm, magnetism, poise, and the ability to dominate others'. His first year did not go well. He struggled academically; he wasn't good enough at sport; his good looks raised suspicion. The second year was better. Lured by the city, he went to shows in New York. He began to work hard, Princeton his ambition. He pitched for the second baseball team. He became adept at debating, wrote more stories and comic operas. And he was taken under the wing of Father Sigourney Fay, a highly cultivated member of the Board who visited the school and nurtured – intimately – boys with good looks and intellectual potential.

Largely by way of a florid correspondence, Fay introduced him to a new cultural sophistication, broadened his learning and his outlook, turned his eyes towards Europe. On a visit to Washington DC, sixteen-year-old Scott took wine with the Monsignor and was introduced to a glamorous visiting English writer, Shane Leslie. Son of a baronet, half Irish and a Catholic convert, educated at Eton and Cambridge, he was a cousin of Winston Churchill and, Fitzgerald later recorded breathlessly, 'he had sat at the feet of Tolstoy, he had gone swimming with Rupert Brooke, he had been a young

Englishman of the governing classes when the sense of being one must have been, as Compton Mackenzie says, like the sense of being a Roman citizen'. Between them, Leslie and Fay made the Catholic Church seem 'a dazzling golden thing', creating by way of elaborate ritual 'the romantic glamour of an adolescent dream'. They cultivated in the impressionable Fitzgerald the dream of becoming America's first great Catholic novelist.

*

He scraped into Princeton. His experience there shaped his first novel, *This Side of Paradise*, but the key to his emotional development was turned during the Christmas break of his sophomore year. The first ledger entry for the calendar year 1915 was 'Met Ginevra'. It was an event that he would never forget, but that at some level he wished to erase.

He had first heard Ginevra King's name from Marie Hersey, she of the fourteen-year-old Scott's ledger entry 'Marie. Love. The triangle'. The two girls were classmates at Westover, a small and exclusive Connecticut finishing school. Ginevra, who was exceptionally pretty, slim, with dark hair and sparkling brown eyes, came to visit her friend in Minnesota. She was sixteen to Scott's eighteen. They met at Marie's house in the well-to-do Summit neighbourhood of St Paul, where the Fitzgeralds lived in a humbler home. Scott was supposed to take the train back east that night, but stayed an extra day so that he could attend a dance being given in Ginevra's honour. In the afternoon, they sat together in the back seat of a friend's car on a drive to Minneapolis; at the party, they danced with each other for most of the evening. But then it was time for him to catch the night train. 'He left for Princeton at 11 – oh! – ', wrote Ginevra in her diary, adding that she was 'absolutely gone' on him. The next day he wrote to her by special delivery and they struck up a sometimes daily correspondence. Neither of them had written such long letters before. They were flirty (why didn't you 'KISS ME', she asked, apropos of their parting at the dance), sometimes jokey, more often romantic, yearning.

They saw each other again in the summer, once in New York and once in Lake Forest, the exclusive community where her family lived in a grand house on Chicago's North Shore. Fitzgerald felt poor and out of place there. They had been together for, by Ginevra's calculation, only fifteen hours, but he convinced himself that he had met the great love of his life. He was distraught the following winter. Because of poor health and equally poor grades, he had been forced to suspend his studies at Princeton. This meant that he was not there when Ginevra sat in the front row, watching the farce that he had co-written with fellow student Edmund 'Bunny' Wilson and that the university's theatrical Triangle Club had

Publicity shot for *The Evil Eye* by Scott Fitzgerald and Edmund Wilson. The image appeared in several newspapers, the caption in the *New York Times* noting that Fitzgerald was considered 'the Most Beautiful "Show Girl" in the Princeton Triangle Club's New Musical Play'.

taken on tour to Chicago. It had been advertised by way of a photograph of Scott looking very fetching in women's clothes.

Scott and Ginevra shared a fantasy of having one 'perfect hour' together. But it was not to be. Visiting her again in Lake Forest the next summer, someone said to him 'Poor boys shouldn't think of marrying rich girls.' In January 1917, two years after the romance had begun, after a wealth of letters and a paucity of kisses, he recorded in his ledger 'Final break with Ginevra.' She destroyed his letters six months later and a year after that, she wrote to tell him that she was engaged to someone else. A few days before receiving the letter, he had met a Southern girl called Zelda Sayre. That was in July 1918. The next page of his ledger begins:

The most important year of
life. Every emotion and
my life work decided.
Miserable and ecstatic
but a great success.
Sept. Fell in love on the 7th

7 September 1918 marked the beginning of the relationship that would shape the rest of his life. Three days earlier, a wedding had taken place. He did not attend, but he pasted the invitation into his scrapbook. Mr and Mrs Charles Garfield King had requested the honour of his presence at the marriage in Chicago of their daughter Ginevra to Mr William Hamilton Mitchell, an ensign in the Flying Corps and the son of the very rich John J. Mitchell, president of the Illinois Trust & Savings Bank.

*

Ginevra King on the cover of *Town and Country Magazine*, July 1918, announcing her forthcoming marriage. Fitzgerald pasted the photograph into his scrapbook.

Figurations of Ginevra appear again and again in Scott Fitzgerald's fictions. She forms a large part of the composite creation that is Daisy Fay – Fitzgerald openly admitted that Daisy's close friend Jordan Baker was drawn from Ginevra's close friend Edith Cummings, who became a champion golfer. Versions of Ginevra are created in stories with such Keatzian titles as 'John Jackson's Arcady' and 'Flight and Pursuit'. She is the remembered love-object in a fine late story called 'Basil and Cleopatra', which ends with the protagonist leaving a dance and walking out onto a veranda alone, where, below a flurry of premature snow, he looks up at the stars which are his 'symbols of ambition, struggle and glory' and he notices that 'one star was no longer there'.

The romance with Ginevra that barely happened is nowhere better conjured back to life than in a story called 'Winter Dreams', published in *Metropolitan* magazine in 1922. The object of desire, Judy Jones, was avowedly based on 'my first girl 18–20 whom I've used over and over and never forgotten'. The story is perhaps Fitzgerald's answer to the challenge laid down in Keats's poem that begins with drear-nighted December.

The first encounter is transposed from a dance to a golf course by a lake. The Fitzgerald figure, Dexter Green, aged fourteen, is a caddy, a role indicative of his social inferiority; Judy Jones is a spoilt little rich girl aged eleven. A decade later, having made his fortune, Dexter returns to the same setting and swims by starlight to a raft on the lake, where he senses a kind of ecstatic belonging: 'for once, he was magnificently attuned to life . . . everything about him was radiating a brightness and a glamor he might never know again'. A speeding motorboat draws up beside the raft and, before he knows it, Judy Jones, now a radiant beauty living in a huge house by the lake, is taking him water-skiing on an uptilted surfboard. She invites him back to her house, where, surrounded by young men of better breeding, he wins her attention with the force of his words ('You sound like a man in a play'). She vouchsafes him the kiss that Fitzgerald did not dare to seek on the night he met Ginevra:

> Suddenly she turned her dark eyes directly upon him and the corners of her mouth drooped until her face seemed to open like a flower. He dared scarcely to breathe, he had the sense that she was exerting some force upon him; making him overwhelmingly conscious of the youth and mystery that wealth imprisons and preserves, the freshness of many clothes, of cool rooms and gleaming things safe and proud above the hot struggles of the poor.
>
> The porch was bright with the bought luxury of starshine. The wicker of the settee squeaked fashionably when he put his arm around her, commanded by her eyes. He kissed her curious and lovely mouth and committed himself to the following of a grail.

This is Dexter Green's moment of 'green felicity'. These two paragraphs offer the most beautiful writing in the story, catching at once the breathlessness of young love, the beauty of the big house, mediated by the narrator's sense of being an outsider, and the delicately incongruous juxtaposition of 'the bought luxury of starshine' with the squeak of a wicker settee (this from the son of the failed wicker-furniture manufacturer). Given the craft of the writing, it at first seems odd that Fitzgerald cut the passage when he reprinted 'Winter Dreams' in his 1926 short-story collection *All the Sad Young Men*. But he had good reason, for by then he had repurposed the paragraphs elsewhere:

> Her porch was bright with the bought luxury of star-shine; the wicker of the settee squeaked fashionably as she turned toward him and he kissed her curious and lovely mouth. She had caught a cold, and it made her voice huskier and more charming than ever, and Gatsby was overwhelmingly aware of the youth and mystery that wealth imprisons and preserves, of the freshness of many clothes, and of Daisy, gleaming like silver, safe and proud above the hot struggles of the poor.

In passages such as this, one may see why Fitzgerald was the polar opposite of the writer with whom he shared a feverish journey from Lyons to Paris in a little Renault with the top ripped off. Hemingway. The master of spare prose. In *A Moveable Feast*, the book that immortalized the drive through France, he described Ezra Pound as 'the man who had taught me to distrust adjectives as I would later learn to distrust certain people in certain situations' (a sentiment slightly undone by the repetition of the lazy adjective 'certain'). Whereas Fitzgerald, Keatzianly, overwhelms the reader with adjectives: not only is the luxury of starshine *bought* and the struggles of the poor *hot*, but Daisy's mouth is curious *and* lovely, her voice huskier *and* more charming, she is safe *and* proud.

After a brief romance, Judy Jones drops Dexter Green and becomes engaged to another man. The engagement is broken and they meet again, by which time he is engaged to someone else. Judy says that she would like to marry him. They spend a night of love together. He breaks his engagement, but she then changes her mind: 'He loved her and he would love her until the day he was too old for loving – but he could not have her.' He never sees her again, but years later, he learns from a friend that her beauty has faded.

> The dream was gone. Something had been taken from him. In a sort of panic he pushed the palms of his hands into his eyes and tried to bring up a picture of the waters lapping at Lake Erminie and the moonlit veranda, and gingham on the golf links and the dry sun and the gold color of her neck's soft down. And her mouth damp to his kisses and her eyes plaintive with melancholy and her freshness like new fine linen in the morning. Why, these things were no longer in the world. They had existed and they existed no more.

But he cannot revivify the feel of those lost moments. The feeling has gone. 'He wanted to care and he could not care': he has erased his green felicity. He has created what Keats called 'The feel of *not* to feel it': 'Even the grief he could have borne was left behind in the country of illusion, of youth, of the richness of life, where his winter dreams had flourished.'

3

'IN THE REALMS OF GOLD'

Shortly after eleven o'clock on the morning of a March day, a man named Samuel Hull entered a drinking establishment. He went up to his wife, who was standing at the bar drinking a glass of cordial. There was a flash and the report of a pistol. Mrs Hull fell to the ground, blood pouring from a large wound in the back of her head. Hull was apprehended by the crowd. A gentleman named Wasfield relieved him of his pistol and marched him into custody. Mrs Hull was rushed to Guy's Hospital.

When the case came to court, Hull admitted that he had fired the shot because his wife had left him and gone to live with another man. Mrs Hull said that she did not wish to prosecute him because she had brought it upon herself by her conduct and she deserved what had happened to her. The fact that she had recovered sufficiently from the head wound to be able to testify in court was testimony to the care she had received in the hospital. The surgeon who had operated on her was also called to testify. His appearance in the witness box was recorded in the newspaper:

Mr Keats, one of the Surgeons belonging to Guy's Hospital, stated, that Mrs Hull was brought into the hospital on the 25th of March. She had received a severe wound in the back part of her head with a pistol ball; the ball had pierced the lobe of her ear, taken a direction along the occiput, and lodged in the neck, from whence the witness extracted it. Mr Keats produced the ball, which fitted the pistol found upon the prisoner.

By a nice coincidence, an adjacent column included a report that the legal instrument of separation ending the marriage of Lord and Lady Byron had been signed and that on this very day, the Noble Lord was leaving for the continent. He would never return to England. The first appearance of the name of Keats in print is to be found here in the London *Morning Chronicle* of 23 April 1816 alongside that of the most famous poet in Europe. Keats, however, appears as a surgeon, not a poet. It was just twelve days later that he had a poem published for the first time, a sonnet addressed 'To Solitude', in which he expresses the wish to be alone in the countryside, not among 'the jumbled heap / Of murky buildings'. As a surgeon, he was 'Mr Keats'; for the poem, the signature was merely 'J. K.'

There is a touch of theatricality about the moment when he produced the pistol ball in the witness box. But he had a right to feel pleased with himself: he had saved Mrs Hull's life even though he was not in fact a qualified surgeon, but rather a 'dresser' – and a newly appointed one at that.

Having quarrelled with his master and left the apprenticeship early, Keats moved into central London. He arrived with a knowledge of how to mix medicines, let blood, extract teeth and set bones. Despite his failure to complete a full term of five years, he passed the examination at the Court of Apothecaries on his first attempt, an achievement not matched by many of his contemporaries. He was helped by his excellent education in the classics at Clarke's Academy: the Latin test was a stumbling block for many, but he had made himself fluent by translating the poetry of Virgil in his spare time. The qualification licensed him to practise as a cross between a pharmacist and what we would call a general (primary care) practitioner. But, either through his own ambition or led by Mr Abbey's eye to the family finances, he enrolled for more advanced study, at Guy's. He began attending medical lectures and witnessing anatomical demonstrations.

GUY'S HOSPITAL.

Guy's Hospital, where Keats did his medical training

Before long, he was given the additional role of dresser to William Lucas, one of the surgeons. According to a fellow pupil, Lucas was 'A tall ungainly awkward man, with stooping shoulders and a shuffling walk, as deaf as a post, not overburdened with brains, but very good-natured and easy, and liked by everyone. His surgical acquirements were very small, his operations generally very badly performed, and accompanied with much bungling, if not worse.' Given this track record, Mrs Hull was perhaps fortunate that the removal of the pistol ball was entrusted to the novice dresser as opposed to the qualified surgeon.

It was not unusual for the assistant to do most of the work. A dresser would undertake all but the major operations and indeed was allowed to perform the smaller and most frequent ones as soon as 'he has been long enough in train to lose the trembling hand'. The dresser was in effect 'an Assistant Surgeon, for all the accidents are submitted to his care and judgement, he takes up the vessels after operations, puts on the bandages, and acts a foremost character in the presence of numberless spectators'. It is striking, though, that Keats performed so skilfully on a head injury so early in his term as a dresser.

His medical knowledge infused its way into his poetry, which is again and again attuned to the beat of the pulse and the heart, to skin that flushes and goes pale, to headaches and orifices and bodily liquids, to fevers and thirst and the exhalation of breath. He was indelibly marked by his walking of the wards among the dying, as may be seen from one of his longer early poems in which he imagines himself in the fresh early morning air, standing tiptoe on a little hill (probably on Hampstead Heath), away from the sights, sounds and smells of the hospital. It is as if he is yearning to throw open the hospital window and let in a healing breeze:

The breezes were ethereal, and pure,
And crept through half-closed lattices to cure
The languid sick; it cool'd their fever'd sleep,
And soothed them into slumbers full and deep.
Soon they awoke clear-eyed: nor burnt with thirsting,
Nor with hot fingers, nor with temples bursting.

Equally, his training in herbal medicine gave a precision to the botanical imagery that he so often deployed in his poetry. The wolf's-bane and nightshade of the 'Ode on Melancholy', the hemlock of the 'Ode to a Nightingale', and the poppy of

'To Autumn' were all in the apothecary's medicine bag: poisons and narcotics that would be fatal in overdose but that, used carefully, served as diuretics, opiates or tranquillizers.

Quick-witted and empathetic, he would have made a very good doctor. However, he told his friend Charles Cowden Clarke that his heart was not in the medical profession. Clarke recalled him saying, 'The other day, during the lecture, there came a sunbeam into the room, and with it a whole troop of creatures floating in the ray; and I was off with them to Oberon and fairy-land.' To another friend, he recollected his last operation: it was the opening of a man's temporal artery, which he performed 'with the utmost nicety'. But, he said, 'reflecting on what passed through my mind at the time, my dexterity seemed a miracle, and I never took up the lancet again'. When his term as Lucas's dresser came to an end in March 1817, he left the hospital.

He had just received finished copies of his first volume of poems. He had decided to take the risk of embarking on a literary career. A fellow apprentice apothecary described him as an 'idle loafing fellow, always writing poetry'. His friend Charles Brown said that his imitation of the style and stanza of Edmund Spenser, written at the age of eighteen, was his first poem. The Spenserian stanza (eight lines of iambic pentameter and a closing alexandrine, with the rhyming scheme *ababbcbcc*) would become one of his favourite forms. Next came a sonnet – another favoured form – in celebration of the fall of Napoleon and the end of the war with France that had endured through his entire life.

Then on a summer's day not long after his move into London, he glimpsed a beautiful woman in the Vauxhall pleasure gardens. He could not get the image of her out of his mind – the soft complexion of her face, the brightness of her eyes, and 'That breast, earth's only Paradise'. The only solution, he suggests, will be to fill a bowl with wine and dissolve into it some drug 'designed / To banish Woman from my mind'. If only she had given him a smile, he would have felt the relief of 'the joy of grief', but as it is she will be 'The halo of my memory' for the rest of his life. Paraphrased thus, the poem sounds like an epitome of the romantic longing that would become the hall-mark of so many of Fitzgerald's stories, but in this case the emotional excess is moderated by the lightness of the versifi-cation. The poem takes the form of a four-stress line, with easy rhyming couplets, in a style that was known as Anacreontic, after the ancient Greek lyric poet Anacreon, who wrote songs in praise of love and wine. Read with hindsight, Keats's couplet 'But I want as deep a draught / As e'er from Lethe's wave was quaffed' sounds like a first draft of a memorable image in the 'Ode to a Nightingale'. Read in the context of the literary tradition inherited by Keats, it is clearly filched (with the key addition of 'Lethe', the river of forgetfulness) from a translation of Anacreon by Byron's friend, the immensely popular Irish poet Tom Moore. Keats's poem begins 'Fill for me a brimming bowl', in imitation of Moore's 'Fill me, boy, as deep a draught / As e'er was fill'd, as e'er was quaff'd'.

Keats, benefiting again from his classical education at Clarke's Academy, headed the manuscript of his poem with a quotation from *The Eunuch*, the most successful play of the Roman comic dramatist Terence: 'What wondrous beauty! From this moment I efface from my mind all women.' This offers a clue as to the occupation of the woman whose face so struck Keats. The lines in Terence are spoken by a character called Chaerea who has glimpsed an extraordinarily beautiful slave-girl and who disguises himself as a eunuch in order to gain access to her. The women he vows to efface from his mind are *mulieres* – respectable women, potential wives. All he wants is to possess the beautiful body of the slave-girl. Eventually, he rapes her and is then forced to marry her. This unsavoury 'marrying the rapist' trope is one that echoes through classical and Renaissance drama – Shakespeare used it in *Measure for Measure*. Chaerea's brother, meanwhile, has fallen in love with the girl's equally beautiful sister, who is a courtesan. The more secluded avenues of the Vauxhall pleasure gardens, known as the Dark Walks, were notorious as a place of amorous assignations. Vauxhall was where sex workers plied their trade. A woman walking alone in the pleasure gardens in the summer of 1814, with her breasts partly exposed, would very probably have been a prostitute. Keats's epigraph in his manuscript is a tacit acknowledgment that the beauty he craves has in all probability been, as he might have put it, soiled by use.

At first sight, one perhaps shouldn't make too much of this little poem. Keats often seems to have dashed off Anacreontics merely as a flexing of his poetic muscles. The fellow student with whom he shared lodgings while a medical student at Guy's recalled that 'in my syllabus of chemical lectures he scribbled many lines on the paper cover'. By the time he recorded this, the cover had long been torn off, but one 'fragment of Doggrel rhyme' remained. It was a mildly blasphemous Anacreontic *jeu d'esprit*:

> Give me women, wine and snuff
> Until I cry out, 'Hold, enough!'
> You may do so sans objection
> Till the day of resurrection;
> For, bless my beard, they ay shall be
> My beloved Trinity.

Keats also liked to write flirtatious poems to respectable girls of his acquaintance, such as Anne and Caroline Mathew. Daughters of a yeast merchant, they had met Keats through his sociable brother George, who was by this time working as a clerk in the counting house of Mr Abbey. When they went to the seaside in the summer of 1815, they sent Keats a curiously shaped shell and a handwritten copy of some verses by Tom Moore. He responded with a pair of poems. The following February, acting on behalf of George, he sent a Valentine poem to another girl, Mary Frogley. It was one of his first attempts to evoke a medieval chivalric world, but also an opportunity to indulge his delight in the beauty of young women's breasts beneath diaphanous clothing. He imagines how she would have looked in the olden days before the age of chivalry was gone:

Ah! I see the silver sheen
Of thy broider'd, floating vest
Cov'ring half thine ivory breast:
Which, O heavens! I should see,
But that cruel destiny
Has plac'd a golden cuirass there;
Keeping secret what is fair.

A boy in his late teens, drawn to the idea of female beauty but too shy and poor to indulge in a real romance, may readily be allowed to vent his half-formed desires in this way. But the feeling evoked by the sight of the woman in Vauxhall seems to have gone much deeper. If we are to believe a later and much greater poem, he could not get her out of his head.

According to Keats's friend Richard Woodhouse, this passing glimpse was the inspiration of a sonnet that Keats wrote three and a half years later – though the poem remembers the gap of time as a full five years. It was published posthumously in Keats's *Life, Letters, and Literary Remains*, with the title 'To – – ' and a footnote identifying the subject as 'A Lady whom he saw for some moments at Vauxhall':

Time's sea hath been five years at its slow ebb,
    Long hours have to and fro let creep the sand,
Since I was tangled in thy beauty's web,
    And snared by the ungloving of thine hand.
And yet I never look on midnight sky,
    But I behold thine eyes' well-memoried light;
I cannot look upon the rose's dye,
    But to thy cheek my soul doth take its flight;
I cannot look on any budding flower,
    But my fond ear, in fancy at thy lips
And hearkening for a love-sound, doth devour
    Its sweets in the wrong sense: – Thou dost eclipse
Every delight with sweet remembering,
And grief unto my darling joys dost bring.

By this time, Keats had been immersing himself in Shakespeare's sonnets, reading them intently and underlining admired phrases in his compact edition. The structure of three quatrains and a couplet, the rendering of passing time through the motions of the tide, the steady iambic beat, the repetition ('I cannot look . . . But') and the resort to the beauties of nature ('the rose's dye' and the 'budding flower') are all learnt from the master. But the image of being snared by the woman's act of ungloving her hand is so specific that it feels like a memory of the encounter in Vauxhall, seared into the memory or, at the very least, invented in the act of 'sweet remembering'. The woman's beauty has so wrought upon Keats that he transforms the bright stars in the midnight sky into the eyes that he met for no more than a moment. Even though they never spoke, and she may not even have noticed him, whatever she was in real life, even a prostitute, she remains for Keats the embodiment of beauty. A beauty that endures precisely because it exists only as a memory, because it has never been touched by use or diminished by the ravage of time. This is an extreme version of Fitzgerald's idealization of Ginevra, Gatsby's of Daisy.

Literary mentor Leigh Hunt

The difference in quality between Keats's early verses and a sonnet such as 'Time's sea', written in February 1818, is startling. Many of the poems in the volume *Poems by John Keats*, which he saw in print just before he left Guy's in March 1817, are overwrought and easily forgotten. He was too much under the influence of Spenser's Elizabethan luxuriance – fresh in its own time, shopworn by Keats's – and the flowery language of the poet and political essayist Leigh Hunt.

Colvin's biography gave Fitzgerald a lively sketch of Hunt: 'He was Keats's senior by eleven years: the son of an eloquent and elegant, self-indulgent and thriftless fashionable preacher, sprung from a family long settled in Barbadoes, who having married a lady from Philadelphia had migrated to England and exercised his vocation in the northern suburbs of London.' For Keats, he became both a literary and a political mentor. Leigh Hunt, together with his brother, edited a liberal magazine called *The Examiner*. Charles Cowden Clarke recalled that he would lend his father's copies of it to Keats, thus laying the foundation for 'his love of civil and religious liberty'. During Keats's time at Guy's, Hunt was in prison for having libelled the Prince Regent. He continued to write poetry and edit the magazine from behind bars, making the best of his confinement by becoming his own interior designer: 'He decorated his apartment in Horsemonger Lane Gaol with a rose-trellis paper and a ceiling to imitate a summer sky, so that it looked, said Charles Lamb, like a room in a fairy tale, and [he] spent money which he had not got in converting its backyard into a garden of shrubs and flowers.' Charles Cowden Clarke went to greet him on the day in February 1815 when he was released; on the way, Keats pressed into his hand a newly minted sonnet celebrating Hunt's productive use of jail time in reading and writing: 'In Spenser's halls he strayed, and bowers fair, / Culling enchanted flowers'.

Hunt settled in a hamlet, consisting of just four houses and ten cottages, on the edge of Hampstead Heath. Once boggy and damp, it had been drained and renamed 'The Vale of Health'. Hunt gathered a literary circle around him and in the autumn of 1816 Keats visited for the first time, in the company of Cowden Clarke. They quickly became friends, Hunt acting as a kind mentor. On one memorable evening, Hunt set a task in which they would each write a sonnet on the theme of 'The Grasshopper and the Cricket', within a set time. Keats finished first. His first line was 'The poetry of earth is never dead'. 'Such a prosperous opening!' said Hunt. There was even higher praise for some lines towards the end – 'On a lone winter morning, when the frost / Hath wrought a silence' – 'Ah that's perfect! Bravo Keats!'

Some evenings, Keats would walk home to the city by moonlight, his head reeling with wine and talk of poetry. On other nights, he stayed over, sleeping on the sofa in the little parlour

that was lined with books, pictures, busts and a portfolio of
engravings, introducing him to such paintings as Poussin's
pastoral *The Realm of Flora* and Titian's erotic *Diana and
Actaeon*. He evoked what Clarke called 'the art garniture' of
Hunt's cottage in his first poetic manifesto, 400 lines of rhyming
couplets under the title 'Sleep and Poetry', which formed the
climax of his first published volume. In announcing his dedication to his own art, he drew upon the language of Hunt and
the imagery of Poussin:

> O for ten years, that I may overwhelm
> Myself in poesy; so I may do the deed
> That my own soul has to itself decreed.
> Then will I pass the countries that I see
> In long perspective, and continually
> Taste their pure fountains. First the realm I'll pass
> Of Flora, and old Pan: sleep in the grass,
> Feed upon apples red, and strawberries,
> And choose each pleasure that my fancy sees;
> Catch the white-handed nymphs in shady places,
> To woo sweet kisses from averted faces, –
> Play with their fingers, touch their shoulders white
> Into a pretty shrinking with a bite
> As hard as lips can make it: till agreed,
> A lovely tale of human life we'll read.

Inspired by the Vale of Health, Keats was developing his
sensuous evocation of nature, as exemplified not only by those
apples and strawberries but also by effects of weather and the
play of light. He was also seeking to make poetry into a form
of seduction, imagining a progress from an averted face to a
hard bite upon a naked shoulder. There may even be a whisper
of the ungloved woman in the Dark Walks of Vauxhall Gardens

in that image of white hands in a shady place. Meanwhile, in channelling the paintings and engravings in Hunt's parlour, he was beginning to think about the power of art to defeat time and mortality. One of the first poems that he had shown to Hunt began with the line 'How many bards gild the lapses of time'. He was now determined to be such a bard himself.

Another, bending o'er her nimble tread,
Will set a green robe floating round her head . . .
              . . . I see afar
O'er-sailing the blue cragginess, a car
And steeds with streamy manes – the charioteer
Looks out upon the winds with glorious fear
(Keats, 'Sleep and Poetry', inspired by Nicolas Poussin, *The Realm of Flora*)

Leigh Hunt's portfolio would have contained an engraving hand-coloured after the original, in which the nimbly treading figure's robe is green and the sky around the charioteer is blue.

The title page of Keats's debut volume, published in March 1817, bore a quotation from Edmund Spenser and an engraving of a poet wearing a laurel wreath, based on the bust of Shakespeare on the monument near his grave in Holy Trinity Church, Stratford-upon-Avon. A few months later, Keats made a pilgrimage there with his Oxford friend Benjamin Bailey, writing their names on the wall of the house where Shakespeare was born, along with those of hundreds of other tourists. The Elizabethans, Shakespeare supremely, would always be his chief poetic model.

The 1817 volume begins with a sonnet of grateful dedication to Leigh Hunt, its opening line establishing the Keatzian trademark that would also be Fitzgerald's: 'Glory and loveliness have passed away'. Bookended by the long poems 'I stood tiptoe on a little hill' and 'Sleep and Poetry', the collection brings together quasi-Elizabethan romance, lyrics addressed to young ladies, literary epistles in rhyming couplets, and a selection of sonnets. Keats never lost a tendency to objectify the female body that has not dated well:

> Light feet, dark violet eyes, and parted hair;
>> Soft dimpled hands, white neck, and creamy breast,
>> Are things on which the dazzled senses rest
> Till the fond, fixed eyes, forget they stare.

In his defence, he does end this sonnet by saying that what really attracts him is the combination of such physical charms with intelligence, beautifully expressed. It is, however, uncomfortable that he talks about moistening his palate on beauty and then compares himself to a shark devouring the woman's words.

In technical accomplishment, the sonnets are much the best thing in the book. There is a freshness and wistfulness in their atmosphere. Sometimes Keats sounds as if he is anticipating the voice of Robert Frost by a hundred years:

> Keen fitful gusts are whispering here and there
>   Among the bushes, half leafless and dry;
>   The stars look very cold about the sky,
>   And I have many miles on foot to fare.

*

One sonnet in particular stood out.

Cowden Clarke often shared books with Keats. Not all of them were his own. A journalist on *The Times* newspaper, who was also a supporter of Hunt, had lent Clarke a beautiful copy in large-scale folio format of George Chapman's Elizabethan translation of Homer. He pored over it with Keats and they began comparing passages with the versions in the polished Augustan couplets of Alexander Pope. When Ulysses weeps upon the loss of his men in a shipwreck, Pope had 'From mouth and nose the briny torrent ran, / And lost in lassitude lay all the man'. Clarke and Keats found this anaemic, whereas they were delighted and amazed by Chapman's expansion of the passage. Keats's eyes lit up as he read

> Then forth he came, his both knees falt'ring, both
> His strong hands hanging down, and all with froth
> His cheeks and nostrils flowing, voice and breath
> Spent to all use, and down he sank to death.
> The sea had soak'd his heart through.

It came as an epiphany. 'Lost in lassitude lay all the man' was Latinate, vague and abstract. But 'The sea had soak'd his heart through' is Anglo-Saxon, immediate and sensuous. The image is attuned to the body, in harmony with the tears and the loss of breath. This was the true voice of feeling, poetry felt upon the pulses.

The next morning, Cowden Clarke came down to breakfast. On his table there was a letter with no other enclosure than a sonnet:

> Much have I travell'd in the realms of gold,
>   And many goodly states and kingdoms seen;
>   Round many western islands have I been
> Which bards in fealty to Apollo hold.
> Oft of one wide expanse had I been told
>   That deep-brow'd Homer ruled as his demesne:
>   Yet did I never breathe its pure serene
> Till I heard Chapman speak out loud and bold:
> Then felt I like some watcher of the skies
>   When a new planet swims into his ken;
> Or like stout Cortez when with eagle eyes
>   He star'd at the Pacific – and all his men
> Look'd at each other with a wild surmise –
>   Silent, upon a peak in Darien.

Keats had won an *Introduction to Astronomy* as a school prize. One chapter was called 'Of the new planet': it described Sir William Herschel's discovery in 1781 of a hitherto unknown planet, which he called Georgium Sidus, King George's Star (the name did not gain international acceptance, and Uranus was eventually settled upon instead). The simile of the 'watcher of the skies' turns the discovery of a beautiful book of poetry into a bright star in the reader's mental firmament.

Clarke's Academy had also introduced him to William Robertson's *History of America*, the first detailed English-language account of the Spanish empire in central America.

Robertson pulled no punches with regard to the atrocities of the conquistadors and the disease-borne genocide of indigenous peoples, but he did proffer his readers a memorable description of Vasco Núñez de Balboa climbing a mountain in Darien (present-day Panama) and becoming the first European to see the Pacific. Balboa fell on his knees to thank God for leading him to a new horizon (and promptly vowed to take possession of the ocean in the name of Spain). 'His followers,' wrote Robertson, 'observing his transports of joy, rushed forward to join in his wonder, exultation and gratitude.' Keats brilliantly freezes the action the moment before the men rush forward, linking their 'wild surmise' in a moment of stunned silence to the sense of wonder that he shared with his friend as they pored over Chapman's renderings of Homer into the Elizabethan language that was also Shakespeare's.

Having not read his American history for some years, and dashing off the sonnet straight after returning home having stayed up until dawn discussing poetry with Clarke, Keats may be forgiven for mixing up Balboa with another conquistador, Hernán Cortés (who was indeed 'stout' in a portrait that Leigh Hunt attributed to Titian). Fitzgerald certainly forgave him: when he read the sonnet with Sheilah Graham, together with an extract from Chapman's *Iliad* as reinforcement, 'Scott pointed out the mistake of Cortez for Balboa – "Silent upon a peak in Darien." "When an immortal like Keats makes a mistake," he said, "that too is immortal."'

This sonnet was quickly recognized as Keats's first mature poem. Hunt showed it to the acknowledged intellects of the day such as the philosopher William Godwin and the critic William Hazlitt, who expressed their admiration. In December 1816 Hunt published it in his *Examiner* magazine in an article called 'Young Poets', written with the purpose of introducing to the public three writers who, he said, constituted a 'new school' that would revive the poetry of Nature. The first two were Percy Bysshe Shelley and John Hamilton Reynolds, a witty but second-rate poet who would become a close friend of Keats. The third, 'the youngest of them all, and just of age', was John Keats. According to Hunt, the sonnet on Chapman's Homer, especially its latter six lines, was 'powerful and quiet' in its excellence, exemplified by the felicitous choice of the verb 'swims'.

A few weeks after his twenty-first birthday, Keats could say that he was publicly acknowledged as a poet – though the association of his name with Leigh Hunt would have mortal consequences.

4

'SOME STIR OF HEART'

They could not in the self-same mansion dwell
    Without some stir of heart, some malady;
They could not sit at meals but feel how well
    It soothed each to be the other by;
They could not, sure, beneath the same roof sleep
But to each other dream, and nightly weep.

With every morn their love grew tenderer,
    With every eve deeper and tenderer still;
He might not in house, field, or garden stir,
    But her full shape would all his seeing fill . . .
            (Keats, 'Isabella; or, The Pot of Basil')

S ketching his backstory to the public in a feature in the *Saturday Evening Post* during the first year of his celebrity, Scott Fitzgerald gave a crisply self-deprecating account of his undergraduate career at Princeton. He explained that, having seen a musical comedy called *The Quaker Girl* while at high school, he started filling his notebooks with ideas for musical comedies of his own. Near the end of his last year at school, he noticed that one of the scores on his piano was for a show that had been staged by the Triangle Club of Princeton University.

That, he said, decided him on Princeton, where he spent his entire freshman year writing an operetta: 'To do this I failed in algebra, trigonometry, coordinate geometry and hygiene.' But the Triangle Club accepted his show and a tutor helped him through the summer, allowing him to retake his exams and return as a sophomore, with the intention of playing the part of a chorus girl in his musical. But then his health collapsed and he dropped out for the rest of the year: 'Almost my final memory before I left was of writing a last lyric on that year's Triangle production while in bed in the infirmary with a high fever.'

This account is a little economical with the truth: in reality, he only failed geometry in his freshman year and he also failed the retake despite the tutoring; this meant that as a sophomore he was banned from extracurricular activities, though that did not stop him from writing for the Triangle Club and being elected its secretary. It was from junior year that he dropped out, meaning that he had to retake the year in 1916–17.

This was when, by his own account, he turned his energies from the stage to the page: 'I had decided that poetry was the only thing worth while, so with my head ringing with the meters of Swinburne and the matters of Rupert Brooke I spent the spring doing sonnets, ballads and rondels into the small hours.' He had got the idea that 'every great poet had written great poetry before he was twenty-one', so he had only a year in which to produce 'a book of startling verse'. And then the war came. Most of the poems that he published in the Princeton student literary magazine can only be described as sub-Rupert Brooke:

I lie upon my heart. My eyes like hands
Grip at the soggy pillow. *Now the dawn*
Tears from her wetted breast the splattered blouse
Of night; lead-eyed and moist she straggles o'er the
    lawn . . .

As for Keats, he knew he was not good enough to imitate him, so he parodied him instead, rewriting the 'Ode on a Grecian Urn' as a student's address to an unopened work of Greek literature. Whereas Keats compensated for his lack of Greek by relishing Chapman's English translation of Homer, Fitzgerald in 'To my Unused Greek Book (*Acknowledgments to Keats*)' jokingly excuses himself from classwork by arguing that it is better for an ancient classic to remain unread than for it to be murdered ('raped', indeed) by a clumsy student translation:

> Thou still unravished bride of quietness,
>   Thou joyless harbinger of future fear,
> Garrulous alien, what thou mightst express
>   Will never fall, please God, upon my ear.
> What rhyme or reason can invest thy shape
>   That is not found in countless syllabi?
> What trots and cribs there are, what ponies rich,
>   With all thou sing'st and in a clearer key.
> Expose thee to a classroom's savage rape?
>   Nay! Better far remain within thy niche.

'Trots' and 'ponies' were alternative slang terms for 'cribs', that is to say literal translations used by students, often illicitly, in preparation for classes or exams.

His love of poetry had in fact been fostered since his freshman year, mainly due to the influence of an older student who became a close friend. He was called John Peale Bishop and he was the model for the character of Thomas Parke D'Invilliers in Fitzgerald's autobiographical debut novel. Amory Blaine, the author's alter ego, is beginning to become disillusioned with Princeton, finding his fellow students 'one part deadly Philistines and one part deadly grinds', when in D'Invilliers he finds a kindred spirit 'who could mention Keats without stammering'.

D'Invilliers introduces him to the works of Oscar Wilde and Keats's 'La Belle Dame sans Merci', with the result that 'The world became pale and interesting'. Late in life, advising his daughter on her literary education, Fitzgerald acknowledged his debt to Bishop. He explained that it is not easy to get into poetry without guidance: 'You need, at the beginning, some enthusiast who also knows his way around – John Peale Bishop performed that office for me at Princeton. I had always dabbled in "verse" but he made me see, in the course of a couple of months, the difference between poetry and non-poetry.' This led him to the conclusion that some of the professors who were teaching poetry 'really hated it and didn't know what it was about'.

Fitzgerald really loved poetry and did know what it was about, but he was acutely conscious of the inferiority of his own efforts to those of the accomplished Bishop. His other close Princeton friend, Edmund 'Bunny' Wilson, an exceptionally acute critic, found 'a depth and dignity', of which he had not thought Fitzgerald was capable, in a poem called 'Princeton – the Last Day'. Upon reading it, the poised and sophisticated Wilson – son of a prosperous lawyer, the same age as Fitzgerald but having sailed through his studies and already graduated – told his friend that he was 'becoming a genuine poet'. But this was 1917, the year that T. S. Eliot published *Prufrock and other Observations*. In Chicago, Harriet Monroe's *Poetry* magazine was giving a platform to innovative writers such as Hilda Doolittle and Ezra Pound. Fitzgerald, by contrast, could not shake off the influence of the English poets of the Romantic tradition – Keats, Matthew Arnold, Algernon Charles Swinburne, Rupert Brooke. His farewell to Princeton begins by sounding like a pastiche of Arnold writing about Oxford or Brooke about Cambridge: 'The last light wanes and drifts across the land, / The low, long land, the sunny land of spires.' The poem is peopled with 'the ghosts of evening' tuning their lyres, with dreams and lotus flowers; it ends with the cliché of glowing embers summoning up 'the splendor and the sadness of the world'.

In *This Side of Paradise* Fitzgerald put his recognition of his own limitations into the mouth of his protagonist. Amory declaims the 'Ode to a Nightingale' to the bushes. 'I'll never be a poet', he says as he finishes:

> I'm not enough of a sensualist really; there are only a few obvious things that I notice as primarily beautiful: women, spring evenings, music at night, the sea; I don't catch the subtle things like 'silver-snarling trumpets.' I may turn out an intellectual, but I'll never write anything but mediocre poetry.

The silver-snarling trumpets are remembered from 'The Eve of St Agnes', another Keats poem that Fitzgerald revered. Together with Bishop and Wilson, Fitzgerald had spent 'ecstatic hours pursuing the Beautiful', primarily by means of immersion in the European Romantic tradition. As he neared the end of his time at Princeton, he was coming to realize that his vocation was to create beauty in prose as opposed to poetry.

The May 1917 issue of the university literary magazine that included 'Princeton – The Last Day' opened with 'Babes in the Wood', the most accomplished of Fitzgerald's early stories. It is as fresh and real as the poem is stale and derivative because it was written from the heart: the story is a barely fictionalized account of the evening when he stayed on in St Paul so that he could attend the dance for Ginevra King. It beautifully captures the frisson of youthful desire. 'Flirt smiled from her large black-brown eyes and shone through her intense physical magnetism', Fitzgerald writes of the Ginevra character: that magnetism extends to the reader, who is drawn towards the expectation of a climactic kiss, only to have it suspended in the manner of Keats's 'Grecian Urn', where the lovers are frozen at the moment before their embrace. Instead of trying to imitate Keats's language and verse-form, Fitzgerald mapped the feeling of the poem onto his personal experience, recollected in limpid prose:

> Everything was wonderful to-night, most of all this romantic scene in the den with their hands clinging and the inevitable looming charmingly close. The future vista of her life seemed an unended succession of scenes like this, under moonlight and pale starlight, and in the backs of warm limousines and in low cosy roadsters stopped under sheltering trees – only the boy might change, and this one was so nice. 'Isabelle!' His whisper blended in the music and they seemed to float nearer together. Her breath came faster. 'Can't I kiss you Isabelle – Isabelle?' Lips half parted, she turned her head to him in the dark. Suddenly the ring of voices, the sound of running footsteps surged toward them. Like a flash Kenneth reached up and turned on the light and when the door opened and three boys, the wrathy and dance-craving Peter among them, rushed in, he was turning over the magazines on the table, while she sat, without moving, serene and unembarrassed, and even greeted them with a welcoming smile. But her heart was beating wildly and she felt somehow as if she had been deprived.

The pleasurably painful yearning endures because there has been no consummation; that, perhaps, is the essence of romance.

He knew that the story was well written. Later, he would submit it to *The Smart Set*, earning him $30, which he spent on a magenta feather fan for a girl he had met in Alabama. Then, having polished the prose and changed the name of his alter ego from Kenneth to Amory, he incorporated it in *This Side of Paradise*, divided into two sections called 'Isabelle' and 'Babes in the Wood'. He probably chose Isabelle as the name for Ginevra's avatar because another of his favourite Keats poems was 'Isabella; or, The Pot of Basil', a tale of love and jealousy developed from a story in the *Decameron* of Boccaccio. Like Scott and Ginevra at the grand house in St Paul, Lorenzo and Isabella in the opening stanza of the poem 'could not in the self-same mansion dwell / Without some stir of heart'.

Fitzgerald hated to waste anything he had written. Acknowledging that he was no poet, he recast 'Princeton – The Last Day' as prose and incorporated it as the coda to book one of *This Side of Paradise*. This was a clever trick.

No more to wait the twilight of the moon
In this sequestered vale of star and spire;
For one, eternal morning of desire
Passes to time and earthy afternoon.

These lines read as predictable late Romantic poetry. But recast as prose – 'No more to wait the twilight of the moon in this sequestered vale of star and spire, for one eternal morning of desire passes to time and earthy afternoon' – they become a sentence with underlying iambic rhythm that reads as a young romantic narrator's self-conscious heightening of his memory of student days into an outburst of unusually lyrical prose. As Fitzgerald later explained to his daughter, the attempt to write poetry had helped him to refine his art of prose: 'I don't think anyone can write succinct prose unless they have at least tried and failed to write a good iambic pentameter sonnet, and read Browning's short dramatic poems, etc. – but that was my personal approach to prose.'

*

July 1918. Alabama heat. A dance at the Montgomery Country Club. The two-storey clubhouse stood beneath a row of oak trees. Beside it, a water tower and a tennis court surrounded by sagging wire. Bright banners were suspended between the twinned pillars of the dusty veranda, where hammocks would be slung on sleepy afternoons. Beneath the low-hung rafters of the clubhouse there was an atmosphere of emotional saturation.

Zelda Sayre, in the month of her eighteenth birthday, had a reputation as a girl who thought she could do anything and get away with it. She had just graduated from high school, where she was voted 'Most Attractive' girl in her class. She provided the mouth for the composite picture of the Ideal Graduating Senior. According to the society page of the local newspaper, where her name frequently appeared, 'She has the straightest nose, the most determined little chin and the bluest eyes in Montgomery.' She was also the best dancer in town. During a ball at the City Auditorium the following spring she would don a yellow and black jester's costume to represent 'Folly', winning tumultuous applause for her rendition of 'The Folly Dance' with the assistance of miniature balloons. At the Country Club, she was persuaded to perform 'The Dance of the Hours'.

Zelda Sayre, 1917

Half the world away in the mud of Flanders, thousands of young men were being gunned down in a war that had gone on for so long that scarcely anyone could remember how or why it had begun. But an end was at last in sight. The United States had entered the war and Montgomery was alive to voices from the north and west: soldiers and airmen, in training, awaiting the call to Europe. Many of them were certain that they would soon be dead. Lieutenant F. Scott Fitzgerald of the 67th Infantry imagined himself as the American Rupert Brooke, destined for immortality in the role of the writer cut off before his prime.

With his Country Club membership card in his pocket, he was in the company of a group of officers from nearby Camp Sheridan, where he had been stationed for the past few weeks. He noticed the girl who danced with her long golden hair flying free. She wore it unpinned, unlike the older girls. Her frilled dress was a child's, not a woman's. She reeled with the intoxication of the dance – or of punch sneaked from the bar.

Later, he would say that when he looked at her for the first time everything inside him melted. Abandoning the superior officers he was supposed to be attending, he went straight to the girl and introduced himself. They danced together. Recreating the moment in her novel *Save Me the Waltz*, written many years after the event, Zelda wrote that her perception of him was as a smell that was as fresh as his twenty-one-year-old face. To her, he was like new goods in a fine fabric store, his starched collar 'exuding the delicacy of cambrics and linen and luxury bound in bales'. His uniform had been tailored by Brooks Brothers of New York City. In his retrospective account, she was somehow different from the other pretty Southern girls he had danced with through the summer. 'If ever there was a pair whose fantasies matched', Edmund

Wilson would write, 'it was Zelda Sayre and Scott Fitzgerald'. The fantasy was of instant magnetic attraction; in reality, they both continued dating other people for several weeks, Scott sometimes taking perverse pleasure in seeing Zelda kiss rival suitors.

When they started dating in earnest, he took her back to the Country Club and carved their names in the doorpost to commemorate the place where they met. His name was in bigger letters than hers because, he said, he would one day be very famous and she was Miss Zelda Nobody. For now, though, he was a nobody and she was the daughter of a Justice of the Supreme Court of Alabama. Fitzgerald was as precise in the notation of his feelings as in the alignment of his brass-buttoned tunic: according to his ledger, it was on 7 September 1918 that he fell unequivocally in love. That winter, now discharged from the army without having seen active service, he wired Zelda Sayre from New York:

DARLING HEART AMBITION ENTHUSIASM AND CONFIDENCE I DECLARE EVERYTHING GLORIOUS THIS WORLD IS A GAME AND WHI[L]E I FEEL SURE OF YOU[R] LOVE EVERYTHING IS POSSIBLE I AM IN THE LAND OF AMBITION AND SUCCESS AND MY ONLY HOPE AND FAITH IS THAT MY DARLING HEART WILL BE WITH ME SOON.

*

Concealing his writing pad behind a manual entitled *Small Problems for Infantry*, Second Lieutenant Fitzgerald had enlivened the dull months of his training for the war by writing 'a somewhat edited history of me and my imagination' in the form of an autobiographical novel entitled *The Romantic*

Egotist. He took his hero from boyhood to prep school to Princeton, with various romantic encounters along the way. Dramatizing himself for the 'Who's Who' article in the *Saturday Evening Post*, he recalled the writing process:

> Every Saturday at one o'clock when the week's work was over I hurried to the Officers' Club, and there, in a corner of a roomful of smoke, conversation and rattling newspapers, I wrote a one-hundred-and-twenty-thousand-word novel on the consecutive week-ends of three months. There was no revising; there was no time for it. As I finished each chapter I sent it to a typist in Princeton. Meanwhile I lived in its smeary pencil pages. The drills, marches and Small Problems for Infantry were a shadowy dream. My whole heart was concentrated upon my book.

Shane Leslie sent the manuscript to the distinguished publishing house of Charles Scribner's Sons. In August 1918, Scott was rewarded with a rejection letter that was, to say the least, not unencouraging: 'We have been reading "The Romantic Egoist" with a very unusual degree of interest; – in fact no ms. novel has come to us for a long time that seemed to display so much originality, and it is therefore hard for us to conclude that we cannot offer to publish it as it stands at present.' The main reservations of Scribner's editor Maxwell Perkins were that the story failed to work towards a strong conclusion and that not enough significance had been given to some of the key incidents, 'such as the affairs with girls'. Perkins positively relished the book's unconventionality of form – its fragmented structure, the fact that some sections were written in verse – but his commercial instincts warned him against a story in which the hero failed to discover either himself or his ideal mate. A rapid and superficial revision, including an attempt to provide a more dramatic conclusion, failed to satisfy Perkins, and he wired a second rejection just over two weeks before the war came to an end.

The self-portrait for the *Saturday Evening Post* offers a snapshot of Fitzgerald's life in the year 1919. He arrived in New York in the early spring, aged twenty-two and still smarting with the disappointment of not having been deployed to Europe in the last days of the war. Imagining that he could 'trail murderers by day and do short stories by night', he presented his card 'to the office boys of seven city editors, asking to be taken on as a reporter'. The newspapers sent their office boys out to tell him that they didn't need him, so instead he became 'an advertising man at ninety dollars a month, writing the slogans that while away the weary hours in rural trolley cars'. After hours, through the early summer, he wrote stories, 'the quickest written in an hour and a half, the slowest in three days'.

Initially, no one bought them: he had (he was exaggerating) 'one hundred and twenty-two rejection slips pinned in a frieze about my room'. He wrote movie scripts and song lyrics, poems and sketches, jokes and 'complicated advertising schemes'. Near the end of June he made his first commercial sale: his revised version of 'Babes in the Wood', which was published in *The Smart Set* that autumn. Then on the Fourth of July, 'utterly disgusted' with himself and all the editors, he went home to St Paul. 'I informed family and friends that I had given up my position and had come home to write a novel. They nodded politely, changed the subject and spoke of me very gently. But this time I knew what I was doing. I had a novel to write at last, and all through two hot months I wrote and revised and compiled and boiled down.'

What he omitted from the newspaper piece was the story of his emotional life at this time. The end of the war did not mean the end of sudden death. Far from it: this was the period of the Spanish flu. During his training in Montgomery, he had dated not only Zelda but also a Southern belle called May Steiner. When he was in New York the following year, she fell seriously ill with the virus and, according to Zelda, all her beautiful hair had fallen out. She planned to come north for treatment and meet up with Scott. But he had lost interest in her. Guiltily, he would write into his second novel, *The Beautiful and Damned*, a subplot in which the autobiographical protagonist Anthony Patch dumps a girl called Dorothy Raycroft, based on May, when – or even because – she becomes seriously ill.

He was affected more deeply by the death of another victim of the Spanish flu. Early in the New Year, before his discharge from Camp Sheridan, he received a telegram telling him that his beloved mentor Monsignor Fay had succumbed to pneumonia. The ledger records the news alongside quarrels and disastrous drinking. Having caught the flu himself, Fitzgerald was confined to the base hospital, meaning that he could not get leave to attend the funeral. His sadness only intensified the depth and volatility of his passion for Zelda. When he went north to New York, they exchanged 'wild letters' and telegrams. He sent her an engagement ring that had belonged to his mother. She 'relegated it to her trophy box' and wrote to him about flirtations with other men, even as she professed her love for him. On one occasion, she returned from a dance at Georgia Tech wearing the fraternity pin of an Atlanta golfer, who had been her date. She sent the pin back to him with a warmly worded note. Erroneously (or deliberately?), she posted the note to Scott and a letter meant for Scott to the golfer. Scott told her to stop writing to him, but before long he was taking the train south and telling Zelda that they must marry immediately. He dramatized the scene in his story 'The Sensible Thing':

He seized her in his arms and tried literally to kiss her into marrying him at once. When this failed, he broke into a long monologue of self-pity, and ceased only when he saw that he was making himself despicable in her sight. He threatened to leave when he had no intention of leaving, and refused to go when she told him that, after all, it was best that he should.

She returned his ring.

This rejection gave him the incentive to leave his job in New York and spend the summer completing his novel in the quiet of St Paul. 'Since I last saw you,' he wrote to Edmund Wilson, 'I've tried to get married + then tried to drink myself to death but foiled, as have been so many good men, by the sex and the state I have returned to literature.' He was only half-joking in this implication that the rewriting of *The Romantic Egotist* was a reaction against both Prohibition and Zelda's breaking off of their informal engagement on the grounds of his poor financial prospects. The new novel, he was hinting, would be both the first blast of the trumpet against the repressive ways of the older generation and the means of regaining Zelda. Returning to New York from Montgomery after the break-up, he was by his own account drunk for three weeks. The only thing that made him stop drinking was the introduction of Prohibition.

He had learned a few tricks during his brief stint as an advertising man. Where Keats needed Leigh Hunt to promote him to the public, Fitzgerald was a supreme self-promoter. Invited to speak at the convention of the American Booksellers Association following the huge success of his novel on its publication the following year, he declined on the grounds that he did not want to talk about himself because that is what he had done in the book. He explained that it had taken him three minutes to conceive it, three months to write it and his whole life to collect the data for it. The three minutes, he claimed, had come to him on the very day when America went dry, the so-called 'thirsty first'. The novel was 'a sort of substitute form of dissipation'. Given the amount of work he had already done towards the book, this remark was disingenuous: it was intended both to suggest that he could write with the speed of genius, and to further his image as spokesman of the young generation who despised the prohibitions of their elders. This 'Author's Apology' was tipped into the third printing of the novel. It was here that he adapted the French Romantic novelist Stendhal's claim that classicism meant the literature of our grandfathers, while Romanticism was the literature of the present: 'My whole theory of writing I can sum up in one sentence: An author ought to write for the youth of his own generation, the critics of the next, and the schoolmasters of ever afterward.'

The day after telling Wilson about his new novel, Fitzgerald provided Max Perkins at Scribner's with a detailed account of its structure. Then early in September 1919, he sent the book itself. Its new title, a quotation from Rupert Brooke, was *This Side of Paradise*. Scribner's acceptance of it, just before Scott's twenty-third birthday, was, he claimed in his memoir 'Early Success', the proudest moment of his life.

Then the postman rang, and that day I quit work and ran along the streets, stopping automobiles to tell friends and acquaintances about it – my novel *This Side of Paradise* was accepted for publication. That week the postman rang and rang, and I paid off my terrible small debts, bought a suit, and woke up every morning with a world of ineffable toploftiness and promise.

The author in his prime

5

'DOUBLE-LIVED IN REGIONS NEW'

Bards of Passion and of Mirth,
Ye have left your souls on earth!
Have ye souls in heaven too,
Double-lived in regions new? . . .
    Thus ye live on high, and then
On the earth ye live again;
And the souls ye left behind you
Teach us, here, the way to find you . . .
Here, your earth-born souls still speak
To mortals, of their little week;
Of their sorrows and delights;
Of their passions and their spites;
Of their glory and their shame;
What doth strengthen and what maim.
Thus ye teach us, every day,
Wisdom, though fled far away.
   ('Ode' by Keats on the subject of poetic influence,
     on the syllabus of Fitzgerald's 'College of One')

The work that he quit was in the car barn of the Northern Pacific Railroad. An old friend was a supervisor there and Scott fancied the idea of some manual labour at the end of a summer's writing. Told to report in old clothes, he arrived in dirty white flannels, a polo shirt and sweatshirt, together with a blue cap. A few days later he rectified this sartorial faux pas by purchasing some overalls, which were promptly stolen. If we are to believe a story written some years later, he was also reprimanded by the foreman for sitting down while he was hammering.

As always with Fitzgerald, even the smallest incident was raw material for myth-making. In reality, he quit the job after just a few days, *before* the arrival of the letter from Max Perkins accepting his novel. The idea of quitting work *because* he could now call himself a professional novelist was a mere flourish of self-dramatization. The process of myth-making continued after his death. The dirty white flannels were noted by his first biographer in 1951, but by the time we reach a biography of 1994 they had become 'elegant white flannels', thus creating an image of the dandyish Jazz Age man about town wandering insouciantly into a world of horny-handed toil.

Only a few manuscript chapters of *The Romantic Egotist* survive, but they are enough to reveal that the original novel was close to the first half of *This Side of Paradise* in both manner and matter. The rewriting consisted for the most part of substantial cutting and a shift from first-person to third-person narrative. This more detached authorial voice allowed Fitzgerald to be inside and outside his hero, to participate in the youthful romanticism while simultaneously ironizing the egotism. He was taking a leaf out of the book of Keats, who sought to distinguish his own kind of poetry from what he called 'the wordsworthian or egotistical sublime'. The romantic in Fitzgerald said that the hallmark of all his work was 'taking things hard' – whether professional failure, the rebuff of a girl, or the inevitable disappearance of youth and innocence. The artist in him knew that his special stylistic gift was to make his readers share the sense of taking it hard while also realizing that the characters who do so are in the grip of a Peter Pan syndrome, a refusal to grow up.

The principal love interest in *The Romantic Egotist* was Isabelle, the self-confident girl from 'Babes in the Wood' who was based on Ginevra. She retains her place in part one of *This Side of Paradise*. Fitzgerald told his publisher that part two of the revised novel was entirely new, save for a single chapter. The starting point for the fresh material is an intense but short-lived affair between the hero, now renamed Amory Blaine, and a debutante called Rosalind. There had been a Rosalind in *The Romantic Egotist*, but, according to Scott's explanatory letter to Max Perkins, 'Isabelle and Rosalind of the RE have become just Isabelle while the new Rosalind is a different person.'

It is the latter's rejection of Amory that precipitates him into the downward spiral of the novel: a drunken spree ended only by Prohibition, an encounter with a wild suicidal girl named Eleanor Savage, seedy business in a hotel room in Atlantic City where he takes the rap when Rosalind's brother is caught with a prostitute (adapted from a real-life incident when the detective of the Hotel Astor in New York found a naked girl in Scott's bedroom), and then a walk back to Princeton punctuated by bouts of verbose theorizing on the merits of socialism. The interior journey is summed up on the final page, where Amory's spiritual development is explicitly attributed to the loss of Rosalind:

> There was no God in his heart, he knew; his ideas were still in riot; there was ever the pain of memory; the regret for his lost youth – yet the waters of disillusion had left a deposit on his

soul, responsibility and a love of life, the faint stirring of old ambitions and unrealized dreams. But – oh, Rosalind! Rosalind! . . .

'It's all a poor substitute at best,' he said sadly.

The inspiration for this 'new Rosalind' was Zelda. Years later, Scott remarked in a letter that *This Side of Paradise* was written 'about a love affair that was still bleeding as fresh as the skin wound on a haemophile'.

Born in 1896, flunked out of Princeton due to excessive time spent on extracurricular activities, literary aspirations, poor financial prospects, a job in New York advertising: in all these respects Amory Blaine is Scott Fitzgerald. Amory is in certain respects an idealized self-image – he is very nearly six feet tall, whereas, like Keats, Scott was self-conscious about being below average height – but the literary tastes and social attitudes of character and author are as one. The resemblance extends to a penchant for list-making and a rich fantasy life. Amory dreams of becoming the youngest general in the world; Scott achieved his dream of becoming the youngest author on Scribner's list (with the symbolic exception of Keats, who was there by virtue of their publication of Colvin's biography). For both hero and author, 'It was always the becoming he dreamed of, never the being.'

In snatches of dialogue, Fitzgerald was clearly imagining the discussions about him that went on between Zelda and her mother:

MRS CONNAGE: Oh, *I* won't interfere. You've already wasted over two months on a theoretical genius who hasn't a penny to his name, but *go* ahead, waste your life on him. *I* won't interfere.

ROSALIND (*As if repeating a tiresome lesson*): You know he has a little income – and you know he's earning thirty-five dollars a week in advertising—

MRS CONNAGE: And it wouldn't buy your clothes. (*She pauses but* ROSALIND *makes no reply.*) I have your best interests at heart when I tell you not to take a step you'll spend your days regretting.

Scott seems genuinely to have believed that when Zelda read the novel she would see how truly he loved her and that once it was in print her concerns about his inability to keep her wardrobe up to date would be swept away by the glamorous prospect of being married to a famous author. That was why on receiving news of the book's acceptance his first concern was not the prospective royalty but the speed of publication. 'Terms ect I leave to you,' he wrote hastily to Perkins (with his habitual misspelling of 'etc'), 'but one thing I can't relinquish without at least a slight struggle':

Would it be utterly impossible for you to publish the book Xmas – or say by February? I have so many things dependent on its success – including of course a girl – not that I expect it to make me a fortune but it will have a psychological effect on me and all my surroundings and besides open up new fields. I'm in that stage where every month counts frantically and seems a cudgel in a fight for happiness against time.

He cannot wait for the moment when a clean printed copy is pressed into Zelda's hands. That hand, he imagines, will then be his.

Zelda would have had good reason to recognize herself in Rosalind. The first thing we are told about the heroine is that

'She is one of those girls who need never make the slightest effort to have men fall in love with them.' That was certainly true of Zelda. Only two types of men can resist Rosalind's allure: 'dull men are usually afraid of her cleverness and intellectual men are usually afraid of her beauty'. This was also true of Zelda: she told Scott as much in a letter. The reader also swiftly learns that Rosalind 'once told a roomful of her mother's friends that the only excuse for women was the necessity for a disturbing element among men'. Shortly before Scott wrote this in *This Side of Paradise*, Zelda remarked to him in another letter that women really should 'just awake to the fact that their excuse and explanation is the necessity for a disturbing element among men'.

We do not know Zelda's reaction to Scott's incorporation of phrases from her letters into his novel. But there can be no doubt that she would have been flattered by Rosalind's most attractive features: 'her fresh enthusiasm, her will to grow and learn, her endless faith in the inexhaustibility of romance, her courage and fundamental honesty'. And then there was her beauty, in which 'all criticism of Rosalind ends': the glorious yellow hair ('the desire to imitate which supports the dye industry'), the 'eternally kissable' mouth, the 'gray eyes and an unimpeachable skin with two spots of vanishing color'.

Rosalind is slender and athletic, delicious and inexpressible. She says things like 'I have to be won all over again every time you see me.' Her defining action is a gracefully executed dive from a great height. Her pose is that of a carefree child: 'I'm just a little girl. I like sunshine and pretty things and cheerfulness – and I dread responsibility. I don't want to think about pots and kitchens and brooms. I want to worry about whether my legs will get slick and brown when I swim in the summer.' She shares Amory's (and Scott's) Keatzian romanticism: the belief that beauty is defined by its transience, that all great happiness is a little sad because the scent of roses means the death of roses, that violent delights have violent ends, and that 'selfish people are in a way terribly capable of great loves'. In all this, and a great deal more, Rosalind is Amory/Scott's ideal woman.

What Zelda did not know was that Rosalind, the 'once-in-a-century blend' apparently based on herself, was recycled goods. In January 1917, a year and a half before the first encounter with Zelda, the Princeton student literary magazine published a one-act playlet by Scott called 'The Débutante'. It was reprinted in the magazine *The Smart Set* in November 1919, one of the first of his pieces to find a commercial home. The heroine – beautiful, witty, selfish, manipulative – was based on Ginevra King. Far from being the 'entirely new' piece of writing that Scott told Max Perkins it was, the 'Débutante' chapter of *This Side of Paradise* was a revised version of the playlet. Cecelia says of Rosalind: 'she treats men terribly. She abuses them and cuts them and breaks dates with them and yawns in their faces – and they come back for more.' This sounds like an account of the flirtatious Zelda but it is actually taken over verbatim from 'The Débutante'. It originally served as an account of the flirtatious Ginevra.

This is not to say that Scott committed some sort of literary crime. All writers recycle their materials. All good writers create characters who are amalgamations of experience and imagination, not quasi-photographic portraits of real people. The real Ginevra provided Scott with the impulse to create the fictional Helen Halcyon in 'The Débutante' and then the real Zelda provided him with the impulse to turn Helen into the more fully realized but still fictional Rosalind of *This Side of Paradise*. At the same time, Rosalind was shaped by other fictional sources including the crisp-talking heroines of Oscar Wilde's comedies and a range of female characters in the novels that Fitzgerald was imitating. Ultimately – as with so many literary characters – she has a precedent in Shakespeare: 'Rosalind' is a marriage of Ginevra and Zelda, but she is also a daughter of her namesake, the witty and independent heroine of *As You Like It*.

Shane Leslie recommended Fitzgerald to Scribner's on the basis that he was an American Rupert Brooke. Fitzgerald endorsed the identification by weaving some of his own Brookean poetry into the novel and naming it after a phrase in Brooke which is duly quoted as an epigraph on the title page: 'Well this side of Paradise! . . . There's little comfort in the wise.' Like his creator, Amory Blaine is said to look like the exquisitely beautiful Rupert Brooke.

Rupert Brooke: a photograph from the cover of *The Bookman*, Christmas 1917, which Fitzgerald pasted into his scrapbook

It is the wild girl Eleanor Savage who makes this comparison. Throughout his relationship with her, Amory self-consciously plays the part of Brooke: 'What he said, his attitude toward life, toward her, toward himself, were all reflexes of the dead Englishman's literary moods.' As her surname suggests, Eleanor is a character who represents raw sexuality as opposed to ideal-ized beauty. Unlike the other women in the book, she was not based on someone Fitzgerald knew, but rather on a woman described to him by his spiritual mentor Monsignor Fay. She is a projection of a Catholic tendency, ultimately going back to the biblical story of Eve and the serpent, to associate evil with sex and temptation with women. Fitzgerald channels into her his anxieties about sex, but he does so via the medium of Brooke:

> The problem of evil had solidified for Amory into the problem of sex. He was beginning to identify evil with the strong phallic worship in Brooke and the early [H. G.] Wells. Inseparably linked with evil was beauty – beauty, still a constant rising tumult; soft in Eleanor's voice, in an old song at night, rioting deliriously through life like superimposed waterfalls, half rhythm, half darkness. Amory knew that every time he had reached toward it longingly it had leered out at him with the grotesque face of evil. Beauty of great art, beauty of all joy, most of all the beauty of women.

Passages such as this reveal a sexual (and sexist) pathology that is one of the aspects of Fitzgerald that has dated least well. It is the same pathology that reveals the sometime cult figure of Rupert Brooke as a man of his era and class, not a poet for all time.

Like Amory Blaine in the novel, Fitzgerald owned a copy of Brooke's collected poems. It included an introduction that singled out for particular praise a poem called 'Blue Evening', in which Brooke, while an undergraduate at King's College, Cambridge, linked hope and anguish in the heart to the play of April twilight upon the river, with ghostly figures flitting under the trees and light burning in the 'fiery windows' of the ancient college buildings. Its language was imitated by

Fitzgerald in 'Princeton – The Last Day', with its waning light over the 'land of spires' and its evocation of the end of college days through 'Pale fires' that 'echo the night from tower top to tower'. 'Blue Evening' is laden with glimmers, dreams and 'still ecstatic fading skies' of the kind that Fitzgerald would reach for again and again at the most romantic moments in his stories and novels. 'In its whispering embraces of sense,' he would have read in the introduction to his copy of Brooke's collected poems, 'in the tranquil euthanasia of the end by the touch of speechless beauty, it seems to me a true symbol of life whole and entire.' For the critic George Edward Woodberry, who wrote this introduction, Brooke was explicitly the inheritor of the Keats who wrote of 'Beauty that must die, / And Joy whose hand is ever at his lips / Bidding adieu'.

Another early edition of Brooke's collected poems, first published in 1918, began with a long hagiographic memoir by his literary patron Edward Marsh, in which the poet was represented as a latter-day Keats destined for sickness and early death in Mediterranean heat. Marsh carefully constructed parallels between the two poets. Brooke spent his summer vacations during his Cambridge university years at Lulworth on the coast of Dorset. Reading poetry as he sat on the rocks, his copy of Keats slipped out of his pocket and was swept away to sea. Some time later, he made a discovery about his idol:

Oh, I've read Keats and found the most AMAZING thing. The last place he was in was Lulworth. His ship was becalmed outside. He and Severn [his friend] went ashore and clambered about the rocks all day – his last fairly happy day. He went aboard and wrote, that evening, his last poem – that sonnet. The ship took him to Italy, coughing blood and suffering Hell because he wouldn't see Fanny [his beloved] any more.

'That sonnet' is 'Bright Star', a poem that would also possess Fitzgerald's imagination.

Keats was also a formative influence upon the book that was the model for *This Side of Paradise*. Amory Blaine's journey through the loss of innocence, of religious faith and of a girl rhymes with that of Michael Fane in Compton Mackenzie's long, overwrought, but still very readable novel *Sinister Street*, which was published to huge acclaim just before the First World War. Henry James was typical in considering it one of the best novels of the age. Written in highly lyrical prose, it tells the story of the autobiographical protagonist's school and university days, his immersion in and loss of religious faith, and his youthful love life, in particular his passion for a girl who falls into prostitution. Compton Mackenzie claimed, anticipating Fitzgerald, that 'the modern novel will achieve universality through poetry, for poetry is immortality in a radiance of words'. He specifically said that it was reading the poetry of Keats that taught him to write prose. The epigraph to the second part of the novel is a quotation from Keats's preface to his long poem *Endymion*: 'The imagination of a boy is healthy, and the mature imagination of a man is healthy; but there is a space of life between, in which the soul is in a ferment, the character undecided, the way of life uncertain, the ambition thick-sighted.'

It is this intermediate space of a young man's emotional and intellectual growth through his teens and early twenties which Mackenzie explores in *Sinister Street* and Fitzgerald in *This Side of Paradise*, as Keats did in *Endymion*. As a sixth-former in school the novel's hero Michael Fane learns for repetition the odes of Keats and finds 'the expression of his mood' in the lines from the 'Ode on a Grecian Urn' that would so haunt Fitzgerald. 'Fair youth, beneath the trees, thou canst not leave / Thy song . . . She cannot fade, though thou

hast not thy bliss, / For ever wilt thou love, and she be fair!':
'These lines were learnt in June, and for Michael they enshrined
immortally his yearning. Never had the fugitive summer glided
so fast, since never before had he sat in contemplation of its
flight . . . Thus for him would the trancèd scene for ever
survive.'

For Edmund Wilson, who never allowed his friendship to
dull his critical intelligence, the twin influence of Keats and
Sinister Street was the cause of the weakness of *This Side of
Paradise*. He argued that the novel upon which Fitzgerald's
reputation was founded had 'almost every fault and deficiency
that a novel can possibly have'. Above all, it was 'highly imitative': 'Fitzgerald, when he wrote the book, was drunk with
Compton Mackenzie, and it sounds like an American attempt
to rewrite *Sinister Street.*' According to Wilson, Mackenzie had
a 'capacity for pretty writing that he says he learned from
Keats', but lacked 'both the intellectual force and the emotional
imagination to give body and outline to the material which he
secretes in such enormous abundance':

With the seeds he took from Keats's garden, one of the best-
arranged gardens in England, he exfloreated so profusely that
he blotted out the path of his own. Michael Fane, the hero
of *Sinister Street*, was swamped in the forest of description; he
was smothered by creepers and columbine. From the time he
went up to Oxford, his personality began to grow dimmer . . .
As a consequence, Amory Blaine, the hero of *This Side of
Paradise*, had a very poor chance of coherence: Fitzgerald did
endow him, to be sure, with a certain emotional life which the
phantom Michael Fane lacks; but he was quite as much a
wavering quantity in a phantasmagoria of incident that had no
dominating intention to endow it with unity and force. In short,
one of the chief weaknesses of *This Side of Paradise* is that it

is really not *about* anything: its intellectual and moral content amounts to little more than a gesture – a gesture of indefinite revolt.

*

Beneath the title-page epigraph from Rupert Brooke, *This Side of Paradise* has a quotation from Oscar Wilde: 'Experience is the name so many people give to their mistakes'. Wilde was another key influence on the young Fitzgerald. Amory Blaine is a child of Dorian Gray. The essential Wildean insight was that life imitates art as frequently as – more frequently than? – art imitates life. Impressionist painting, for example, altered the way in which people perceived the world around them: only after Monet, Wilde remarked, did sunsets become hazy. 'Where, if not from the Impressionists, do we get those wonderful brown fogs creeping down our streets, blurring the gaslamps and changing the houses into monstrous shadows? . . . The extraordinary change that has taken place in the climate of London during the last ten years is entirely due to this particular school of Art.'

A Wildean reading of Fitzgerald would reverse the claim that Rosalind was inspired by Zelda and Ginevra. It would say instead that Zelda and Ginevra were inspired by Rosalind. That is to say, Fitzgerald dreamed a kind of girl – making his dream, as all readers do, out of both his reading and his fantasies – and then projected that dream on to the girls he dated. While he was merely an undergraduate dreamer, the strategy was a recipe for heartache; once he was a published author, it worked like a dream. Miss Zelda Nobody from Alabama was happy to become a somebody by way of Rosalind.

The novel thus became an essential part of the courtship whereby, like a knight in an ancient romance, Scott won back

the mistress he had lost. Two months after receiving the acceptance letter from Scribner's, he returned to Alabama in quest of
a renewed acceptance from Zelda. Like the knight laying sword
and helmet at his lady's feet, he gave her a typescript copy of
the novel. In return, she agreed that she would marry him as
soon as the book was published. He took the train back to
New York and she wrote with her reaction to what she had
read: 'Why can't I write? I'd like to tell you how fine I think
the book is and how miserably and completely and – a little
unexpectedly – I am thine.'

'Why can't I write?' But Zelda could write. She had won a
prize for an accomplished short story called 'The Iceberg',
published in her high-school literary magazine. Furthermore,
her letters to Scott during their courtship are more vividly
written than his to her. She had many other gifts, too. The
portrait of Rosalind is nowhere closer to a portrait of Zelda
than when Scott compliments his heroine thus: 'She danced
exceptionally well, drew cleverly but hastily, and had a startling
facility with words, which she used only in love-letters.' Zelda
could have become a dancer. She could have become a painter.
And her love letters are crafted with the art of a writer. Late
in life, she lamented to her daughter 'I wish that I had been
able to do better one thing and not so given to running into
cul-de-sacs with so many.' She brimmed over with talents but
lacked application.

Inspired by the example of her husband-to-be, she half-
heartedly began a story of her own soon after reading the
typescript of *This Side of Paradise*: 'but after two pages on my
heroine I discovered that I hadn't even started her, and, since
I couldn't just write forever about a charmingly impossible
creature, I began to despair. "Vamping Romeo" was the name,
and I guess a man would have had to appear somewhere before
the end.' The effort dissolved into nothing more than banter

in a love letter: 'there wasn't any plot, so I thought I'd ask you how to decide what they're going to do'.

> And so you see, Scott, I'll never be able to do anything because I'm much too lazy to care whether it's done or not – And I don't want to be famous and fêted – all I want is to be very young always and very irresponsible and to feel that my life is my own – to live and be happy and die in my own way to please myself.

But could her life be entirely her own when Scott was busy making it into the stuff of his novels, using her letters and even a passage from her diary to spice the character of Rosalind?

At some level the cry 'Why can't I write?' should be read as meaning 'Why can't I have credit for my writing?' Reading the typescript of *This Side of Paradise*, she would have found a sequence of its most lyrical prose when Amory walks into a graveyard just a couple of pages from the end of the book:

> There was a dusky, dreamy smell of flowers and the ghost of a new moon in the sky and shadows everywhere. On an impulse he considered trying to open the door of a rusty iron vault built into the side of a hill; a vault washed clean and covered with late-blooming, weepy watery-blue flowers that might have grown from dead eyes, sticky to the touch with a sickening odor.
>
> Amory wanted to *feel* 'William Dayfield, 1864.'
>
> He wondered that graves ever made people consider life in vain. Somehow he could find nothing hopeless in having lived. All the broken columns and clasped hands and doves and angels meant romances. He fancied that in a hundred years he would like having young people speculate as to whether his eyes were brown or blue, and he hoped quite passionately that his grave would have an air about it of many, many years ago. It seemed

strange that out of a row of Union soldiers two or three made him think of dead loves and dead lovers, when they were exactly like the rest, even to the yellowish moss.

These are the words of someone who can write with considerable fluency. To Zelda they must have sounded familiar. In early summer, some weeks before Scott resumed work on the novel of which this passage was the culmination, she had told him in a letter of her love of twilight, of the smell that brings together beauty and decay:

Something in me vibrates to a dusky, dreamy smell – a smell of dying moons and shadows –

I've spent today in the grave-yard – It really isn't a cemetery, you know, trying to unlock a rusty iron vault built in the side of the hill. It's all washed and covered with weepy, watery blue flowers that might have grown from dead eyes – sticky to touch with a sickening odor – The boys wanted to get in touch to test my nerve to-night – I wanted to *feel* 'William Wreford, 1864.' Why should graves make people feel in vain? I've heard that *so* much, and Grey is *so* convincing, but somehow I can't find anything hopeless in having lived – All the broken columns and clasped hands and doves and angels mean romances – and in an hundred years I think I shall like having young people speculate on whether my eyes were brown or blue – of course, they are neither – I hope my grave has an air of many, many years ago about it – Isn't it funny how out of a row of Confederate soldiers, two or three will make you think of dead lovers and dead loves – when they're exactly like the others, even to the yellowish moss? Old death is so beautiful – so very beautiful – We will die together – I know –

Sweetheart –

124 out of the 186 words – precisely two-thirds – of Scott's graveyard sequence are lifted directly from Zelda's letter, with many more only slightly altered, as when the pronouns are changed from first person to third. If Zelda's letter had been a published source, Scott could easily have found himself being accused of plagiarism. It was perhaps as some small recompense for his borrowings that he gave the character of Rosalind credit for being able to write – in her love letters.

The most striking shift in the graveyard scene is that from the real inscription observed by Zelda ('William Wreford, 1864') to the imagined one noted by Amory ('William Dayfield, 1864'), together with the alteration of 'Confederate soldiers' to 'Union soldiers'. The tone of nostalgia combined with the heaviness of the weather gives the passage a distinctively Southern sensibility. In this sense, the sequence reads somewhat incongruously in the New England climate, both intellectual and physical, that Amory inhabits.

A feel for the old South was one of Zelda's great gifts to Scott. It enabled him to become an all-American novelist. He came from the Midwest, while Princeton and New York offered him the north. Zelda's South and then his own experience of Hollywood – not to mention a brief stint as a cowboy on a Montana ranch in the summer of 1915 – completed the picture. Or was the gift a curse, making him an *all-white* American novelist? There can be no denying that he imbibed the worst of the South's craving for the antebellum era: its racial prejudice.

Zelda's generosity of spirit was such that she expressed no resentment at Scott's use of her words. She seems to have been genuinely touched that he had included her in his novel not only as the beautiful Rosalind but also as a source of beautiful prose. That his writing was coming to rely so deeply on her seemed all the more reason to join her life to his. *This*

Side of Paradise was published on 26 March 1920 and a week later Zelda and Scott were married in a low-key ceremony in the rectory of St Patrick's Roman Catholic Cathedral in Manhattan. She wore 'a blue-grey spring suit adorned by the single corsage of white orchids Scott had sent her'. In the summer, Scott wrote a thank you letter to Shane Leslie, through whose good offices he had established the publishing relationship with Scribner's: 'I married the Rosalind of the novel, the Southern girl I was so attached to, after a grand reconciliation.'

Between the 'grand reconciliation' and the marriage, Fitzgerald had a brief but intensely sexual affair in New York with an English actress whose face he had first seen in the pages of *Vanity Fair*. In accordance with the Wildean principle of life imitating art, her name was Rosalinde – though her role was that of Eleanor Savage in the novel. She was four years older than Scott, uninhibited and emancipated. They met in the Plaza Hotel and almost immediately jumped into a closed hansom cab, which drove them round Central Park as they discovered each other's bodies, every bit in the manner of Flaubert's Madame Bovary and her lover. Rosalinde Fuller's diary gives the lie to Fitzgerald's later claim that Zelda was the first person he slept with: there was, she wrote, 'no end to our delight and discovery of one another. We made love everywhere, in theatre boxes, country fields, under the sun, moon and stars. We seemed to be riding on some unreal circus railway, clinging together.' Zelda did not find out. Perhaps Scott was trying out the role of artist as playboy. It did not suit him. He needed Zelda as his centre of levity for the life of fame that, he was convinced, now awaited him. But he did not yet want her baby: several weeks before they married, he sent her pills for an abortion. She refused to take them and the pregnancy scare turned out to be a false alarm.

For Scott, the promotion of his novel was as essential as its writing and publication. In his first letter to Perkins after hearing of the book's acceptance, he eagerly enquired about the jacket design and offered to 'fix up data for advertising and have a photo taken next week with the most gigantic enjoyment'. His experience with the Barron Collier advertising agency made him appreciate the proposed sales slogan, 'A Novel about Flappers written for Philosophers'. The type of liberated young woman known as a 'flapper' can be dated back to the middle of the war, but so successful was the Scribner's–Fitzgerald publicity machine that *This Side of Paradise* soon became not only a number one nationwide bestseller but also the book credited with the creation of the whole Jazz Age world of sexually liberated flappers, fast cars and bootleg partying.

'At certain moments,' Scott wrote much later, 'one man appropriates to himself the total significance of a time and place.' By saturating his first novel with an aura of the young and the new, he became such a man himself. *This Side of Paradise* conjures up undergraduate life with great assurance; it is disturbingly well informed on drinking sprees and prescient on motoring as embodiment of the speed of the new – the sharpest writing in the book comes in a scene describing a car crash. But, to the surprise of readers coming to the book with a prior knowledge of the image that it created, neither the word 'flapper' nor the phrase 'Jazz Age' appears anywhere in it.

The publicity campaign rather than the novel itself was what led to the publication in January 1921 of an interview under the headline 'Fitzgerald, Flappers and Fame'. Here Scott acknowledged that Rosalind – and, by an alarming implication, Zelda – was more type than individual: 'I'm sick of the sexless animals writers have been giving us . . . Personally, I prefer this sort of girl. Indeed, I married the heroine of my stories. I would not be interested in any other sort of woman.' Publicity quotes of this kind established an image of both the Fitzgerald heroine and Zelda herself as the kind of girl who is summed up in an exchange in the 'Débutante' chapter just moments before Rosalind's first entrance:

ALEC: Does Rosalind behave herself?

CECELIA: Not particularly well. Oh, she's average – smokes sometimes, drinks punch, frequently kissed – Oh, yes – common knowledge – one of the effects of the war, you know.

Flapperdom was thus tied to sexual liberation and anti-Prohibitionism.

On the first page of *This Side of Paradise* Amory Blaine's mother is said to have moved in the circles of the 'subtle celebrities' of old money and old Europe. One of the purposes of the novel was to establish Amory Blaine's alter ego Scott Fitzgerald – son of a Midwestern soap salesman far removed from both old money and old Europe – as a new kind of celebrity. It therefore made good promotional copy for the young author who had shot to fame as spokesman of his generation and inventor of the 'Flapper' to say in the interview that he had married the heroine of his stories. He was living the dream and in so doing becoming the modern celebrity who brazenly embraces the public eye as opposed to the older kind whose status had been defined by privacy, exclusivity and an array of highly 'subtle' social and cultural codes. Zelda colluded in the role of trophy wife that was essential to this new image, but a terrible price would be paid for the process that was so seemingly casually – but perhaps calculatingly – alluded to in Scott's conversion of her from woman into type.

What a "Flapper Novelist" Thinks of His Wife

Scott Fitzgerald, Creator of Modern Girl Types in Current Fiction, Interviews His Own Bride in the Intimacy of Their Happy Long Island Home

Is She His Model?

IS Zelda Sayre Fitzgerald, wife of Scott Fitzgerald, author of flapper fiction stories, the heroine of her husband's books? That's what a lot of "best seller" patrons have been wondering.

If so, is she the living prototype of that species of femininity known as the American flapper? If so, what is a flapper like in real life? Here is a tabloid picture of Zelda Fitzgerald:

Flappers. She likes them reckless and unconventional, because of their quest in search of self-expression.

Sports. Golf and swimming.

Jazz music, "because it is artistic," and dancing for its sheer abandon. Not ambitious to be a "joiner"—just enjoy life to the full. Large families "so children have a chance to be what they want to be." Wants her own daughter to be "rich, happy and artistic."

If she had to earn her own living would go in for the ballet or the movies. Failing in that, she would try writing.

Home is the place to do what you like to do—not to live by the clock in a conventional way.

Newspaper clipping speculating that Rosalind is Zelda

6

'CERTAIN ETHEREAL CHEMICALS'

In the 1930s, Scott Fitzgerald arranged his notes and jottings in categories running from A to Z. He began with 'Anecdotes', followed by 'Bright Clippings', 'Conversations and Things Overheard', 'Description of Things and Atmosphere', 'Epigrams, Wise Cracks and Jokes', 'Feelings & Emotions (without girls)'. Typed up by a secretary, the notebooks are now preserved in two spring binders in the Fitzgerald collection at Princeton University Library, complete with their alphabetized separator cards. This was where he recorded ideas, observations, quotations, and passages from his short stories that he wished to preserve for possibly recycling in future novels.

In the section called 'Bright Clippings', there is a note claiming that *Blossom Time*, a show based on the life of Franz Schubert which played to capacity houses on Broadway from 1921 to 1923, was 'the greatest musical romance ever written' and another entry copying down an Egyptian proverb to the effect that the worst things in life are being in bed unable to sleep, longing for someone who does not come, and trying but failing to please. Between these two notes is a carefully transcribed quotation: 'Men of Genius are great as certain ethereal Chemicals operating on the Mass of neutral intellect – but they have not any individuality, and determined Character – – – – – Keats.'

This is from a letter of November 1817, in which Keats laid out for the first time his equation of beauty and truth via the medium of the imagination. Colvin's biography included a long discussion of the letter supported by an ample extract, but without quotation of this particular sentence. Fitzgerald had clearly read the letter itself and been impressed by the thought. The quotation follows exactly the punctuation and capitalization of the text in which he read it, though 'and determined Character' is a slip (either his or his typist's) for 'any determined Character'.

He owned the 1899 'Cambridge Edition' of John Keats, bound in red cloth with the poet's name in a realm of gold on the front, encircled by a laurel wreath. Published by Houghton Mifflin of Boston and New York, and printed on the Riverside Press in Cambridge, Massachusetts, this was the standard American one-volume edition. It was edited by Horace Elisha Scudder, an all-round man of letters and frequent contributor to *The Atlantic*, who in his preface acknowledged his debts to the pioneering Keats scholars H. Buxton Forman and Sidney Colvin. Distinctively, this book included not only the complete poems, but also all the letters that had hitherto been gathered and edited. This was *The Complete Poetical Works and Letters of John Keats*. The title page reproduced Joseph Severn's posthumous-painted imaginary portrait of Keats sitting in his room in Hampstead, deep in a book. Above him on the wall, there is a portrait of Shakespeare, his literary 'presider', though this is too dark to be visible in the reproduction. The door to the garden is open, as if to let in the song of the nightingale.

There are 212 letters in this edition. In the course of the following sixty years, about forty more were discovered and collected, but those available to Fitzgerald were sufficient to give him an intimate sense of Keats's life, work, loves and literary theories. For their insight into the development of a young writer's mind, they are among the most remarkable ever written.

They are also revelations of Keats's kindness and empathy. The earliest to survive (not known to Fitzgerald) was written during his time at Guy's Hospital. Keats sent it to his eleven-year-old sister Fanny along with a piece of silk and pasteboard for her to make him an eyeshade, presumably for the purpose of helping him to focus in the operating theatre. He also enclosed a skipping rope that he had purchased in order to encourage her 'to jump and skipp about, to avoid those nasty Chilblanes that so troubled you last Winter'. This kind of thoughtfulness and indeed his medical mind for bodily pains are apparent from this first letter to his very last (which was known to Fitzgerald); there, he asked his friend Charles Brown to pass on news of his health to his sister Fanny, 'who walks about my imagination like a ghost'.

The letters are the place where Fitzgerald, like so many other readers and critics before and after him, tracked the development of John Keats into poetic maturity in the span of just two years, between late 1817 and the autumn of 1819. The seeds for that extraordinary growth were sown around the time of his twenty-first birthday. He told the young artist Joseph Severn, who would eventually accompany him to Italy and be at his bedside when he died, that he was looking forward with high anticipation to two things: the chance to see 'some beautiful Scenery – for poetical purposes', and the opportunity to take breakfast with the artist Benjamin Robert Haydon. A decade older than Keats, Haydon was an energetic force in London cultural life, bringing together in his studio fellow artists, writers and the well-to-do. His speciality was large-scale 'history' painting, both classical and biblical: he was working on *Christ's Entry into Jerusalem*, in which he peopled the crowd with the heads of figures ranging from Newton and Voltaire to William Wordsworth and his own mother. Keats met him at Leigh Hunt's cottage one evening in November 1816. He was so excited that in the morning he sent Haydon a sonnet describing him as one of three 'Great spirits' sojourning on earth. The other two were Leigh Hunt and William Wordsworth.

Friendship with Leigh Hunt and Haydon also brought Keats into the circle of William Hazlitt – pugnacious journalist, critic, political commentator and essayist – and the kind, witty, quirky Charles Lamb, who worked as a clerk in the East India House while also caring for his sister Mary, who in a fit of madness had killed their mother and injured their father with a carving knife. Hazlitt, whose public lectures Keats attended, would be a major influence on the development of his ideas about poetry.

Benjamin Robert Haydon: according to Keats he was one of the 'Great Spirits now on earth sojourning' and was a worthy successor to Raphael

Keats and Haydon met frequently in the following months, sometimes at Haydon's studio, at other times in the homes of their shared literary acquaintances, and occasionally in the rooms in Poultry, the short street in the City of London that Keats was now sharing with his brothers. They talked of poetry, painting, passion, philosophy and immortality. Haydon declared that he had enjoyed reading and discussing Shakespeare with the young poet 'more than with any other human being'. The mind of Keats was full of Shakespeare at this time. In one of the first letters in Fitzgerald's edition, he adapted to his own situation a much-loved speech of Sir John Falstaff in *Henry IV Part 1*: 'Banish money – Banish sofas – Banish Wine – Banish Music; but right Jack Health, honest Jack Health, true Jack Health – Banish health and banish all the world.' 'Banish plump Jack' becomes 'Banish health'. There was hardly ever a time when Keats was not anxious about his health. The same is true of Fitzgerald. The world evoked in his novels – with its money, sofas (such as the one upon which Daisy and Jordan are reclining when Nick first sees them), music and wine (and stronger liquor) – was one that would eventually lead to the banishment of Jack Health from the life of its author.

It was principally for the sake of his health that, in a nervous state, Keats went to the Isle of Wight in the spring of 1817. This was a time when the benefits of salty air and sea-bathing were being vigorously promoted by doctors and early tourism entrepreneurs. Travelling to Southampton to catch the ferry boat across to the island, Keats would have passed close to the cottage in Hampshire where, just a few days before, Jane Austen had abandoned *Sanditon*, the novel on exactly this theme that she had been working on until she fell into the illness that would take her life that summer.

'But the sea, Jack, the sea – the little waterfall – then the white cliff', Keats wrote to his friend Reynolds. Once ensconced in his lodgings, he unboxed an edition of Shakespeare and plunged into the plays. He was delighted to find a portrait of Shakespeare in the corridor, doubly so when his landlady allowed him to hang it in his room. Haunted by the description of the sea in *King Lear*, he wrote a sonnet, which he included in his letter to Reynolds:

> It keeps eternal whisperings around
>   Desolate shores, and with its mighty swell
>   Gluts twice ten thousand caverns . . .

The sea, like Shakespeare, was a source of comfort: 'O ye! Who have your eyeballs vex'd and tir'd, / Feast them upon the wideness of the Sea.' He thought about poetry so much that he could not get to sleep at night. Reading the essays of his friend Hazlitt, he also relished the power of sentences of good prose.

This was a time of total immersion in literature. 'I find that I cannot exist without poetry – without eternal poetry – half the day will not do – the whole of it.'

'It keeps eternal whisperings': the sea at Margate

From the Isle of Wight, he moved to another seaside resort, Margate on the east coast of Kent. Back in London, and wandering in its rural outskirts, he imagined windswept fields as an inland sea. His artist friend Joseph Severn left the most lyrical of all descriptions of Keats's response to nature, which Fitzgerald was able to read in Colvin's biography:

Nothing seemed to escape him, the song of a bird and the under-note of response from covert or hedge, the rustle of some animal, the changing of the green and brown lights and furtive shadows, the motions of the wind . . . and the wayfaring of the clouds: even the features and gestures of passing tramps, the colour of one woman's hair, the smile on one child's face, the furtive animalism below the deceptive humanity in many of the vagrants, even the hats, clothes, shoes, wherever these conveyed the remotest hint as to the real self of the wearer.

With his painter's eye, Severn watched Keats closely, noting the way that he seemed taller than his five feet and three-quarters of an inch, 'partly from the perfect symmetry of his frame, partly from his erect attitude and a characteristic backward poise (sometimes a toss) of the head, and, perhaps more than anything else, from a peculiarly dauntless expression, such as may be seen on the face of some seamen'. The only time he seemed small was when he was reading or when walking 'rapt in some deep reverie; when the chest fell in, the head bent forward as though weightily overburdened, and the eyes seemed almost to throw a light before his face'. Severn gives us the most vivid description we have of Keats in the open air, so it deserves to be quoted at length:

> Certain things affected him extremely, particularly when 'a wave was billowing through a tree', as he described the uplifting surge of air among swaying masses of chestnut or oak foliage, or when, afar off, he heard the wind coming across woodlands. 'The tide! The tide!' he would cry delightedly, and spring on to some stile, or upon the low bough of a wayside tree, and watch the passage of the wind upon the meadow grasses or young corn, not stirring till the flow of air was all around him, while an expression of rapture made his eyes gleam and his face glow . . . The only thing that would bring Keats out of one of his fits of seeming gloomful reverie – the only thing, during those country-rambles, that would bring the poet 'to himself again' was the motion 'of the inland sea' he loved so well, particularly the violent passage of wind across a great field of barley. From fields of oats or barley it was almost impossible to allure him; he would stand, leaning forward, listening intently, watching with a bright serene look in his eyes and sometimes with a slight smile, the tumultuous passage of the wind above the grain. The sea, or thought-compelling images of the sea, always seemed to restore him to a happy calm.

*

Though he found inspiration by the sea and in the country, Keats also loved cities that glowed with a sense of history. Like the fictional Gatsby a century later, he was drawn to the romance of Oxford. In the late summer of 1817, visiting Benjamin Bailey, a theology student whom he had met through the Reynolds family, he wrote to his little sister that 'This Oxford I have no doubt is the finest City in the world – it is full of old Gothic buildings – Spires – towers – Quadrangles – Cloisters Groves & is surrounded with more Clear streams than ever I saw together.' In wandering through the city and boating on its surrounding waterways – the rivers Isis and Cherwell, the streams Seacourt, Botley, Bulstake and Castle Mill – he thought about the long poem he was writing. 'Do not the Lovers of Poetry like to have a little Region to wander in where they may pick and choose, and in which the images are so numerous that many are forgotten and found new in a second Reading: which may be food for a Week's stroll in the Summer?' His first book of poetry had garnered a handful of respectful reviews, written mostly by his friends, but it had failed to achieve significant sales or to establish him as a major new voice on the London literary scene. He wanted to stretch his poetic sinews and to create something with more impact. In an age when the market for verse was being increasingly challenged by the popularity of the novel, the best hope for sales and profile was the long poetical 'romance' – this was the form in which Sir Walter Scott and Lord Byron had achieved their fame.

Begun in April on the Isle of Wight and completed in November during a short stay in rural Surrey, *Endymion: A Poetic Romance*, is divided into four books, each of about a thousand lines, written at a rate of about fifty lines a day. Keats would work from breakfast until early afternoon, then take some exercise. Inspired by his love of classical mythology and influenced by the sensuous verse of Thomas Chatterton (to whose memory it is dedicated), as well as by Shelley's coming-of-age poem *Alastor* and a variety of other sources such as a long poem called *The Man in the Moon* by Shakespeare's contemporary Michael Drayton, *Endymion* tells the story of a shepherd-prince in ancient Greece who falls in love with an idealized goddess, personified by the moon.

The poem begins by evoking a pastoral landscape and gathering a group of children, maidens and shepherds, who sing a hymn to the nature-god Pan. Their leader, Endymion, falls asleep and dreams. The main narrative is his account of his visions, told sometimes in real time and sometimes in retrospect to his sister Peona. In book two, he descends into the underworld, where he meets Venus and Adonis, exemplars of love between a goddess and a mortal; in three, he emerges on the ocean floor and encounters Glaucus, another figure from classical mythology, who represents a mortal entrapped by a suprahuman figure, the enchantress Circe; and in the final book Endymion falls in love with a beautiful Indian girl, for whom he forsakes his moon-ideal, only to discover, very abruptly at the end of the poem, and to his great relief, that the girl is in fact the earthly embodiment of the goddess. Through this trick, earthly love is 'spiritualized' and the idealized conception of beauty is made earthly.

The poem's most memorable line is its opening. Keats's fellow medical student Henry Stephens claimed some responsibility for its creation. He said that one evening at twilight he was working at his medical studies while Keats was dreaming. Keats suddenly announced that he had composed a line of poetry: 'A thing of beauty is a constant joy'. 'What think you of that, Stephens?' he asked. 'It has the true ring, but is wanting in some way,' Stephens replied. After an interval of silence, Keats came back with 'A thing of beauty is a joy for ever'.

'What think you of that, Stephens?'
'That it will live for ever.'

Colvin quoted the alleged exchange in his biography, arguing
that although the reminiscence was probably dressed up for
effect, it is likely that Keats wrote the opening lines of the poem
before he abandoned his medical studies in March 1817 and
then used them the following year as the gateway to *Endymion*.

In both style and theme, the opening meditation on the power
of beauty resembles the mood of the two long poems that
bookended his first volume, 'I stood tiptoe upon a little hill'
and 'Sleep and Poetry'. The argument is that natural beauty
brings health to human beings, relieves us from the pains of
life, calms our breath and is the equivalent of restorative sleep
filled with good dreams. For this reason, we wreathe

A flowery band to bind us to the earth,
Spite of despondence, of the inhuman dearth
Of noble natures, of the gloomy days,
Of all the unhealthy and o'er-darkened ways
Made for our searching: yes, in spite of all,
Some shape of beauty moves away the pall
From our dark spirits.

Beauty is embodied in the sun, the moon, trees that give shade,
'daffodils / With the green world they live in', cooling streams
and forest glades 'Rich with a sprinkling of fair musk-rose
blooms'. Crucially for Keats, it is also to be found in the
example of 'the mighty dead': 'All lovely tales that we have
heard or read' are 'An endless fountain of immortal drink, /
Pouring unto us from the heaven's brink.' He regards literature
as well as nature as a source of enduring beauty.

The daffodils in this passage might be a hint that Keats has been reading Wordsworth. He told Haydon that he was convinced that the three things to rejoice at in the age were Haydon's paintings, Hazlitt's 'depth of taste' and Wordsworth's long poem *The Excursion*. Haydon generously added a fourth: '*John Keats' genius!*' Wordsworth was the era's leading worshipper of the beauties of nature, so the opening of *Endymion* may be a nod to the 'Prospectus' that prefaces *The Excursion*:

> Beauty – a living Presence of the earth,
> Surpassing the most fair ideal Forms
> Which craft of delicate Spirits hath composed
> From earth's materials – waits upon my steps;
> Pitches her tent before me as I move.

Wordsworth's phrase 'ideal Forms' has a history going back to Plato's notion that there is a perfect idea of Beauty – as of Truth and the Good – in a realm beyond the physical world. The beautiful things that we see are but shadows of this ideal. This theory led to Plato's attack on artistic creation in *The Republic*: if the things of this world are shadows, then the artist's imitation of things offers only a shadow of a shadow, twice removed from the ideal of Beauty and Truth. The counter to this argument came in the so-called Neoplatonic philosophical tradition, associated especially with Plotinus in the third century CE and Marsilio Ficino in Renaissance Italy. The Neoplatonic revision of the theory turned on the proposition that through the power of imagination, inspired artists have a quasi-mystical capacity to bypass the shadows of the material world and create in their work earthly manifestations of the 'ideal Forms'. The narrative of *Endymion* might accordingly be described as a progression from Platonism to Neoplatonism. In the first book, Beauty, personified as a goddess, is unobtainable, out of this world, as far away as the moon. At the climax of the fourth book, when the goddess is revealed in the living, breathing earthly form of the Indian girl, Beauty pitches her tent before Endymion. The meaning of love, said Ficino, is 'the desire to enjoy beauty' and that is what Endymion does at the climax of the poem, when he is united with the Indian girl and in mutual ecstasy they vanish together.

While he was finishing *Endymion*, Keats was in correspondence with Benjamin Bailey, the most academic of his friends. From Bailey's bookshelves in Oxford he had taken down such volumes as *The Works of Plato Abridged*; together, they had conversed by day and night about philosophy, religion and poetry. Now in his letters Keats was working out his own thoughts about beauty. Bailey's studies were preparing him for Christian ministry, but Keats lacked faith in what he called 'the great Consolations of Religion'. He found comfort instead in 'the Beautiful', which he defined as 'the poetical in all things'. The poetical was, he believed, an earthly remedy against 'wrongs within the pale of the World', by which he meant the hierarchies and tyrannies of church and state. In one letter to Bailey, he attacked a bishop who was apparently blocking his friend's ordination, while at the beginning of the third book of *Endymion*, written in Oxford when he was staying with Bailey and under the influence of Hazlitt's radical politics, he had launched into an assault on those who 'lord it o'er their fellow-men' – the reactionary regimes of Britain and Europe in the aftermath of the end of the Napoleonic Wars. Beauty was a bulwark against the malign influence of power on society.

Writing again to Bailey on 22 November 1817, just a few days before he finished *Endymion*, Keats contrasted the arrogance and egotism of 'Men of Power' with the capacity of 'Men of Genius' to dissolve themselves into their creations. The true artist does not have 'any individuality, any determined Character'.

This is the passage that Fitzgerald copied into his notebook: 'Men of Genius are great as certain ethereal Chemicals operating on the Mass of neutral intellect'. Keats derived his metaphor from the lectures he heard and read while training at Guy's Hospital: 'If spirit of wine be distilled with almost any of the acids, the produce is a liquor which has obtained the name of *Aether*, from its extreme lightness and volatility.' The *Pharmacopoeia* of Keats the apothecary described the process whereby a mixture of sulphuric acid and alcohol could be distilled into an 'ethereal liquor' of exceptional clarity. By analogy, poets distil their earthly materials into a pure form.

The clear liquor was called 'ethereal' because it was believed that above the earthly atmosphere there existed a pure, invisible element called 'ether', filling all of what we now call 'space'. Keats was also aware of this meaning of the word. Back in May, early in the composition of *Endymion*, he had written to Haydon about how being a poet involved 'looking upon the Sun, the Moon, the Stars, the Earth and its contents, as materials to form greater things – that is to say ethereal things'. Ethereal poetry would have, as one commentator on Keats has put it, 'the same relation to ordinary reality that ether had to air: it would be purer, higher, and free from mutability'. In another letter to Bailey, Keats divided 'Ethereal things' into several categories, including 'Things real, such as existences of Sun moon and Stars – and passages of Shakespeare', and 'Things semireal, such as love, the clouds etc. which require a greeting of the spirit to make them wholly exist.' Here Shakespeare, the epitome of genius, has ascended to the empyrean and joined the heavenly bodies in the ether. Keats's hope is that in 'greeting' (a lovely choice of verb) earthly beauties in the distillery of his poetic imagination, he too will create something that is timeless, beautiful and true.

The idea is developed in the next paragraph of the letter in which Fitzgerald found the 'ethereal Chemicals' quotation: 'I am certain of nothing but of the holiness of the Heart's affections, and the truth of Imagination. What the Imagination seizes as Beauty must be truth – whether it existed before or not, – for I have the same idea of all our passions as of Love: they are all, in their sublime, creative of essential Beauty.' This is Keats's first articulation of the aphorism that will be voiced by his Grecian urn: 'Beauty is truth, truth beauty'.

The letter goes on to compare the artistic imagination to the dream of Adam in John Milton's *Paradise Lost*: 'he awoke and found it truth'. Alone in Eden, Adam dreams that God has fashioned a beautiful woman to be his partner; when he wakes up, Eve is there. For Keats, the imagination also has the power to conjure a memory of beauty back to life and, by what we might call the etherealizing process, make it more beautiful than it was in reality:

have you never by being surprised with an old Melody, in a delicious place by a delicious voice, *felt* over again your very speculations and surmises at the time it first operated on your soul? – do you not remember forming to yourself the Singer's face – more beautiful than it was possible, and yet with the elevation of the Moment you did not think so? Even then you were mounted on the Wings of Imagination, so high that the prototype must be hereafter – that delicious face you will see.

Writing to his publisher some months later, as *Endymion* was being prepared for the press, Keats articulated his axioms for poetry. First, 'It should strike the reader as a wording of his own highest thoughts, and appear almost a remembrance', and secondly, 'Its touches of beauty should never be half-way, thereby making the reader breathless, instead of content. The rise, the progress, the setting of Imagery should, like the sun, come natural to him, shine over him, and set soberly, although in magnificence, leaving him in the luxury of twilight.' Reading the 'ethereal Chemicals' letter and coming across the passage about the old melody, the singer's face, and the recreation of that face through flight on the wings of imagination, making it more beautiful than it could really have been, Fitzgerald found in Keats a wording of his own highest thoughts. The idea answered to his remembrance of Ginevra and laid the ground for the most characteristic yearnings of his mature fiction. In 'the luxury of twilight', Gatsby is haunted by the face of the Daisy he had once kissed.

The idea that the perfect embodiment of beauty is to be found in a woman has a history as long as that of Western art. Apelles was said to be the greatest artist of ancient Greece; his representation of Venus, goddess of love, was considered to be his most beautiful work. From Renaissance sonnets to nineteenth-century bohemian muse-worship, the celebration of – and desire to possess – female beauty was the hallmark of the heterosexual male artist. In a counter-tradition, of which Michelangelo and Shakespeare were a part, but our poet and novelist were not, the idealized object of desire is a beautiful young man. Keats and Fitzgerald were men of their times, ardent in their passion for beauty and acutely sensitive to the cultural traditions they inherited. So it is hardly surprising that they both objectified women in ways that to the twenty-first century seem atavistic.

'O for a life of sensations rather than of Thoughts!' cried Keats in the 'ethereal Chemicals' letter. Too often in *Endymion*, he indulges sensation at the expense of thought. 'His every sense had grown / Ethereal for pleasure', he writes of Endymion. Typical phrases are 'all this gush of feeling', 'to dream deliciously', 'soft ravishment', and 'Dost kiss? O bliss! O pain!' The urbane and very adult Lord Byron was not impressed. He took the view that the sensibility of Keats never grew beyond adolescence: 'such writing is a sort of mental masturbation – Keats is always frigging his *Imagination*'. There is, most readers would agree, a juvenile excitement in the way in which he writes about the idealized love-object and Endymion's various attempts at union with her: lips are 'slippery blisses', while breasts are 'tenderest, milky sovereignties'. The body of the Indian girl, with her 'curls of glossy jet', is displayed as a fragrant delight:

> There she lay,
> Sweet as a muskrose upon new-made hay,
> With all her limbs on tremble.

To a modern sensibility, this is doubly offensive in both its objectification and its 'Orientalist' exoticizing of the imagined sexual allure of a young woman from the East.

Endymion longs to lie for ever in the arms of his ideal love. 'Fondling and kissing every doubt away', he whispers the hyperboles of first love in an overflow of sibilance:

> O known Unknown! From whom my being sips
> Such darling essence, wherefore may I not
> Be ever in these arms? In this sweet spot
> Pillow my chin for ever? Ever press
> These toying hands and kiss their smooth excess?
> Why not for ever and for ever feel
> That breath about my eyes? Ah, thou wilt steal
> Away from me again, indeed, indeed –
> Thou wilt be gone away, and wilt not heed
> My lonely madness.

And yet, as in Fitzgerald's love stories, the writing is driven less by the rapture of consummation than by the longing and then the loss. Without the 'lonely madness', there would be no poetry. Grief, Endymion discovers, is contained 'In the very deeps of pleasure'. The Indian girl is first heard chanting a song to 'Sorrow' – Keats copied it into one of his letters to Bailey – and Endymion grows to maturity only after he has retreated to a 'Cave of Quietude'. Keats was beginning to see that beauty and desire were not enough to make true poetry: he would also have to embrace solitude and suffering.

*

Endymion is by far Keats's longest poetic work. There are forceful lines, as when the narrator writes of the protagonist that 'The very music of the name has gone / Into my being'. The rhyming couplet is handled with more flexibility than in the poems published in the 1817 volume. And one can see Keats beginning, as he would later advise Shelley, to 'load every rift with ore' by compounding his adjectives and evoking scent, taste, temperature and the beat of the pulse:

> rain-scented eglantine
> Gave temperate sweets to that well-wooing sun;
> The lark was lost in him; cold springs had run
> To warm their chilliest bubbles in the grass;
> Man's voice was on the mountains; and the mass
> Of nature's lives and wonders puls'd tenfold,
> To feel this sun-rise and its glories old.

For all these qualities, only the most ardent Keatzians consider *Endymion* a complete success. Matthew Arnold, whose essay on Keats was a great influence on Fitzgerald, resented the fact that it occupied such a large proportion of the poetic *oeuvre*. The young poet regarded it as a test of his powers of imagination.

He tried too hard to pass the test, creating an overload of luxuriance that would make him vulnerable to harsh criticism, even ridicule. In the first of his November 1817 letters to Bailey, he sensed that trouble was on the way, reporting that *Blackwood's Edinburgh Magazine* had launched an attack on Leigh Hunt: 'I never read any thing so virulent – accusing him of the greatest Crimes – dep[r]eciating his Wife his Poetry – his Habits – his company, his Conversation.' The literary assault was branded as the first in a series on what the *Blackwood's* reviewer, looking loftily down on these lower-middle-class Londoners, christened 'The Cockney School of Poetry'. In the motto at the head of the essay, a second name appeared in large capital letters alongside that of HUNT. It was KEATS. He had no doubt that the knives were being sharpened for the next attack and that he would be its victim.

He was both ashamed and proud of his romance. He wanted to do his best for his new publisher, John Taylor, who with his business partner James Augustus Hessey was willing to take the risk of publishing unknown young poetic talents alongside the usual, more profitable fare of sermons and moral tracts. Keats suggested that criticism might be forestalled by an apologetic preface: 'I fought under disadvantages. Before I began I had no inward feel of being able to finish; and as I proceeded my steps were all uncertain. So this Poem must rather be considered as an endeavour than a thing accomplish'd: a poor prologue to what, if I live, I humbly hope to do.' Neither Taylor nor Reynolds, on whose judgment Keats always relied, thought that it was a good idea to include this, so Keats wrote a less defensive preface, attributing any mawkishness that might be perceived in the poem not to himself but to the adolescent state of his protagonist.

As Taylor prepared *Endymion* for the press, Keats suggested improvements. Towards the end of book one, Endymion outlines a theory of happiness to his sister Peona. Dissatisfied with his draft, Keats sent Taylor a 'mending' of the passage's opening:

> Wherein lies Happiness? In that which becks
> Our ready Minds to fellowship divine;
> A fellowship with essence, till we shine
> Full alchymized and free of space.

This is a versifying of his theory of 'ethereal Chemicals'. For Keats, the whole sequence was the key argument of the poem, the element of which he was proudest. It offered what he called 'a kind of Pleasure Thermometer': happiness is to be found in an ascent from the beauties of nature (such as the smooth touch of a rose petal) to the harmonies of music to the steadiness of friendship to the passion of erotic fulfilment.

The argument is an inversion of the Platonic ascent from the body to the soul. Pride of place in the copy of the *Works of Plato Abridged* on Benjamin Bailey's bookshelf in Oxford was given to the dialogue on the last days of Socrates, *Phaedo*, with the translator's explanatory subtitle 'Of the Immortality of the Soul'. Socrates prepares himself for death by arguing that the philosopher must reject the pleasures of sex, accept the mortality of the body, and relish instead the immortal soul that has a share in eternal truth, beauty and goodness. Keats, by contrast, makes a kiss the thing that offers 'fellowship divine': in *Endymion*, it is 'earthly love' that 'has power to make / Men's being mortal, immortal'. Endymion tells his sister that even a modest press of his lips upon the moon-goddess's cheek creates the sensation of his body being dipped 'Into a warmer air'. Indeed, the poem argues, flowers would not bloom, fruit swell and seed harvest 'If human souls did never kiss and greet'.

Bailey, the Christian Platonist, hated this idea, regarding it as a 'false, delusive, and dangerous conclusion', all too close to 'that abominable principle of *Shelley's* – that *Sensual Love* is the principle of *things*'. Byron thought that it was simply ridiculous: 'I remember Keats somewhere says that "flowers would not blow, leaves bud," etc. if man and woman did not kiss. How sentimental.' Clearly Byron, who complained of the expense of sleeping with 200 women during his exile in Venice, was unsentimental about kisses. Keats's poem, by contrast, is flush with kisses because they were new to him.

*

When he moved to Margate, after the brief stay on the Isle of Wight during which he began the poem, he met up with his brother Tom. After three weeks of intense reading and writing by the sea, they went inland to Canterbury, the destination of Chaucer's pilgrims, where they revelled in the atmosphere of old streets and medieval cathedral. Tom returned to London, leaving John to take a break at another seaside resort, Hastings. He stayed in an outlying village, recommended to him by Haydon. Now part of St Leonards-on-Sea, then it was called Bo Peep. And it was here that Keats glimpsed the possibility of kisses.

She was a young woman of about his age, but she is tantalizingly elusive. Her name was Isabella Jones – though Keats never mentioned it in any of his extant letters or poems. He encountered her again in London the following year, when a sense of her very stylish character would emerge. All he said about their meeting in Hastings was that he 'warmed with her' and 'kissed her'. At some point, he gave her the manuscript of a love poem, which after his death she passed over to his publisher:

Oh, breathe a word or two of fire!
  Smile as if those words should burn me,
Squeeze as lovers should – oh, kiss
  And in thy heart inurn me!
    Oh, love me truly!

However, since he sent a copy of the same poem to Jane Reynolds, we cannot assume that the relationship was more than a flirtation of the kind in which he habitually indulged with the sisters of his friends. Though he would become intrigued by this young woman, it is unlikely that his 'warming' with her went beyond a kiss.

Her surviving letters reveal that she had a witty and highly literary sensibility, so it is hardly surprising that, whatever she was doing in Hastings, she enjoyed the company of a rising poetic star who had just reached his age of majority. Self-conscious as he always remained about his diminutive stature, he had grown handsome. Bailey remembered his appearance at the time: a wide smile with a slightly thick upper lip, his eyes 'full and fine, and softened into tenderness' or beaming 'with a fiery brightness', his hair 'beautiful – a fine brown, rather than auburn, I think; and if you placed your hand upon his head, the silken curls felt like the rich plumage of a bird'.

With the enigmatic lady in Hastings, there was the beginning of a meeting of minds. Keats seems to have undergone a darker initiation when staying with Bailey in Oxford that autumn. He was ill on returning to London. In his first letter from there to his Oxford host, he mentioned that he had taken a dose of mercury, which had 'corrected the Poison'. A few weeks later, he complained of 'suffering for vicious beastliness'.

Though mercury was sometimes prescribed for conditions such as rheumatism, its primary use was as the standard treatment for gonorrhea and syphilis, infections known as 'venereal poison'. Being a town filled with young gentlemen of means, Oxford was very well supplied with prostitutes. 'Vicious beast-liness' can hardly suggest anything other than that Keats took advantage of the available service. The Victorian doctor who years later befriended Keats's fellow medical student Henry Stephens was coy but unequivocal: 'In the autumn of the same year, 1817, he visits a friend, Bailey by name, at Oxford, and in that visit runs loose, and pays a forfeit for his indiscretion, which ever afterwards physically and morally embarrasses him.'

THE BEAUTIFUL WOMAN
WITHOUT MERCY

S idney Colvin's life of Keats was published by Charles
Scribner's Sons in November 1917, the month that Scott
Fitzgerald began *The Romantic Egotist*, which editor
Maxwell Perkins would reject, then accept in heavily revised
form as *This Side of Paradise*. One of the ways in which Colvin
brings Keats back to life is through a sequence of lengthy
quotations of anecdotes written by people who knew and loved
him. They are like short stories inserted into a longer narrative,
rather as Fitzgerald recycled material from his short stories into
his novels. Among the most memorable is Benjamin Robert
Haydon's account of what he called 'the immortal dinner' that
took place in his studio just after Christmas 1817, in the shadow
of his huge painting of *Christ's Entry into Jerusalem*. The guests
included the supreme romantic egotist William Wordsworth,
the mischievous Charles Lamb, and Keats, just twenty-two,
nervous and a little wounded because he had recently met
Wordsworth for the first time and read a passage from
Endymion, only for the revered poet to dismiss it as 'a very
pretty piece of Paganism'.

The heads in the crowd in Haydon's painting included not
only Keats, Wordsworth and Hazlitt but also Sir Isaac Newton.

Lamb provoked the dinner guests by mocking Haydon for putting in his picture a man 'who believed nothing unless it was as clear as the three sides of a triangle'. Haydon's diary account of the evening continues: 'And then he and Keats agreed he [Newton] had destroyed all the poetry of the rainbow by reducing it to its prismatic colours. It was impossible to resist [Lamb], and we all drank "Newton's health, and confusion to mathematics."' In his poem 'Lamia', Keats would return to the opposition between romance and science, known at the time as 'natural philosophy':

> Do not all charms fly
> At the mere touch of cold philosophy?
> There was an awful rainbow once in heaven:
> We know her woof, her texture; she is given
> In the dull catalogue of common things.
> Philosophy will clip an Angel's wings,
> Conquer all mysteries by rule and line,
> Empty the haunted air, and gnomed mine –
> Unweave a rainbow.

Endymion, too, may be read as a critique of philosophy. Platonic 'ideal Forms' exist only in an abstract realm, in the mind of man. The poem, by contrast, strives towards the realization of beauty upon the earth. It imagines that beauty may be possessed physically as opposed to mentally by means of a kiss, an act of love. As Keats put it in the 'ethereal Chemicals' letter, a life of sensations proceeding directly from the body to the imagination is preferable to the philosopher's life of abstract thought, locked within the head.

*

The young Scott Fitzgerald was equally interested in the opposing claims of philosophy and romance.

His main source of income was the writing of stories for popular magazines such as *The Smart Set*, *Metropolitan* and the *Saturday Evening Post*. His marriage to Zelda took place a week after the publication of *This Side of Paradise*, before they could have known it was to be a roaring success. The stories and their potential spin-offs, not the novel, were the thing that gave Zelda confidence in Scott's financial prospects. A month earlier, he had wired with the news that 'I HAVE SOLD THE MOVIE RIGHTS OF HEAD AND SHOULDERS TO THE METRO COMPANY FOR TWENTY FIVE HUNDRED DOLLARS I LOVE YOU DEAREST GIRL'. The movie did not take long to make: it was released a few months later, while the Fitzgeralds were spending the first summer of their married life in a rented house in Westport, Connecticut.

The original story, 'Head and Shoulders', was Scott's first appearance in the mass-circulation *Saturday Evening Post*. Its protagonist is a teenage prodigy called Horace Tarbox. Having graduated precociously from Princeton, at the age of seventeen he is at Yale writing a master's dissertation on modern philosophy: 'I am a realist of the School of Anton Laurier – with Bergsonian trimmings' (Henri Bergson was regarded as the quintessential philosopher of modernity, whereas Anton Laurier is a fiction). At the behest of his cousin Charlie Moon, Horace is seduced from his studies by Marcia Meadow, a beautiful blonde chorus girl with a voice like a harp. She comes into his room, floating in the diaphanous gauzy dress of a flapper. She does not have wings, remarks Fitzgerald, 'but audiences agreed generally that she didn't need them'. She looks like an angel and she has arrived to clip the cold philosophy of Horace Tarbox.

They sit by his fireplace in the easy chairs that he has named after the philosophical sceptics Berkeley and Hume. He wonders for a moment if she is a phantom of his imagination. She begins by addressing him with the name of an ancient Persian philosopher who was also a poet synonymous with romance: 'Well, Omar Khayyam, here I am beside you singing in the wilderness.' Scott Fitzgerald was happy to share a name with Edward FitzGerald, the orientalist whose English translation of the *Rubáiyát of Omar Khayyám* had become the cult poem of the *fin de siècle* era, just as Bergson was its cult philosopher. Edward FitzGerald's aestheticism marked him as an influential Victorian Keatzian. He swooned with delight on hearing of the publication of the love letters from this 'fiery Soul' to Fanny Brawne.

Marcia counters Horace's dreary philosophical realism with the argument that life should be about fun and kisses, lamenting his refusal to give her one with 'Brazilian' (her misapprehension of 'Bergsonian') trimmings. She does, however, persuade him to go to see her on stage and take her out to dinner afterwards. He is in several respects disturbed by her performance of an acrobatic dance that exposes her breasts. She tells him that she deals with its ardours by rubbing liniment into her shoulders every night. Her show transfers to New York, he stalks her to her apartment, they kiss and, to the chagrin of the academic community, they agree to marry, calling themselves Head (him) and Shoulders (her).

For a few months, she is 'a continual source of astonishment to him – the freshness and originality of her mind, her dynamic, clear-headed energy, and her unfailing good humor'. When the marriage begins to falter, they agree an arrangement whereby she will start reading books (beginning with the diaries of Samuel Pepys) in return for him working out at Skipper's Gymnasium three times a week. He turns out to be as gifted on the gymnastic rings as he is at mathematics and philosophy.

He invents a particularly impressive contortion modelled on 'the fourth proposition of Euclid'. A fat man who is watching wonders with which circus Euclid performed. When Marcia becomes pregnant and is forced to leave the stage, the fat man gives Horace an introduction that allows him to take up a new career as a professional trapeze artist, performing at the Hippodrome. By a twist that perhaps answers to the Bergsonian philosophical principle of 'multiplicity', Marcia, confined to the apartment with their baby, writes a bestselling Jazz Age romantic novel called *Sandra Pepys, Syncopated*. The couple become famous as Head and Shoulders – she the Head, he the Shoulders.

The screen adaptation released by Metro Pictures was called *The Chorus Girl's Romance*, a title neatly suggestive of Marcia as author of a romance as well as the romance itself. It is lost, save for a few stills, but the structural elegance of Fitzgerald's plot must have made for a wonderfully silly silent movie. Light-hearted as the story is, the underlying dialectic is serious and indeed Keatzian: the life of thought versus that of sensations, the head against the body, romance as the opposite of philosophy. There is also an underlying anxiety on Fitzgerald's part: by marrying a flapper, was he risking his own future as a serious, quasi-philosophical novelist? Might he find himself becoming nothing more than the literary circus performer of the roaring twenties? Perhaps the solution to this dilemma was to embrace both identities, to be an ethereal chemical magically synthesizing flapperdom and philosophy. The clever thing about 'Head and Shoulders' is that it reveals Fitzgerald's acquaintance with Hume and Schopenhauer, William James and Bergson, even as it rejects them in the name of Omar Khayyam and popular romantic fiction. In the autumn of 1920, cashing in on the success of *This Side of Paradise*, Scribner's published a debut collection of Scott's short stories under a title inspired by this story: *Flappers and Philosophers*.

Advertisement for *The Chorus Girl's Romance* with Viola Dana's hairstyle resembling that of the flapper on the dust jacket of Fitzgerald's first short-story collection

Gareth Hughes as 'philosopher' Horace Tarbox (resembling Scott) and Viola Dana as 'flapper' Marcia Meadow (resembling Zelda)

*

At Westport, Scott had begun work on his second novel. Its theme was 'the life of one Anthony Patch between his 25th and 33d years (1913–1921)'. He is 'one of those many with the tastes and weaknesses of an artist but with no actual creative inspiration'. The story was to tell of 'How he and his beautiful young wife are wrecked on the shoals of dissipation'. Scott was writing from experience: he and Zelda were beginning to wreck themselves by entering upon a life of dissipation. In genteel Westport, they skinny-dipped, they got into fights, they threw wild weekend parties, on one occasion sending a false alarm to the fire brigade; the story goes that when the first responders asked for the location of the fire, Zelda pointed to her breast and said 'Here.' And when Scott took his new wife to show her off at Princeton, pretending she was his mistress, he got drunk and was defenestrated from a members' club.

In the autumn, they moved to an apartment on 59th Street in New York City, one block to the west of 5th Avenue. It was sufficiently close to the Plaza Hotel for them to call in their meals. They entered further into a haze of drunken parties and altercations in nightclubs, but this did not stop Scott from finishing a draft of his novel. He sent it to his agent, Harold Ober, asking him to get it serialized in three or four parts. The Paul R. Reynolds Literary Agency, in which Ober was a partner, was by this time advancing their precocious and profligate new star author loan after loan on the promise of stories, books and movie scripts.

As always, Fitzgerald struggled to find the right title for his novel. An aborted early version took its name from Samuel Taylor Coleridge's poem 'Kubla Khan': *The Demon Lover*. In the letter telling Scribner's the outline of the plot, the book was called *The Flight of the Rocket*, suggestive of a blaze of glory followed by a precipitous descent and perhaps also subliminally remembering Endymion's aim for the moon. As the manuscript neared completion, the working title became *The Beautiful Woman without Mercy*. This was a translation of the title of Keats's ballad 'La Belle Dame sans Merci', in which a knight is found 'Alone and palely loitering' in a desolate landscape where 'The sedge is withered from the lake / And no birds sing'. The narrator asks what is wrong with him. He has met a beautiful lady with long hair and wild eyes, who looks at him as if in love, making 'sweet moan'. She takes him to her grotto, where he shuts 'her wild wild eyes / With kisses four', at which she lulls him to sleep and to a dream in which

> I saw pale kings, and princes too,
>   Pale warriors, death-pale were they all;
> They cried – 'la belle Dame sans merci
>   Thee hath in thrall!'

Keats wrote this most mysterious of his poems when he was in thrall to Fanny Brawne and haunted by the thought that he might, like his brother Tom, become 'death-pale' with tuberculosis. Steeped in the tradition of medieval ballads and romances, as well as a love of Spenser's *Faerie Queene*, an epic romance replete with beguiling enchantresses, the poem was a particular influence on the Victorian Pre-Raphaelite artists who were inspired by Keats's medievalism. For Fitzgerald, it exemplified the idea of romantic love as a destructive force.

Anthony Patch wastes much of his life between his twenty-fifth and thirty-third year waiting for, and risking the loss of, an inheritance from his puritanical millionaire grandfather. Lacking the talent to create and the discipline to work, he devotes himself to the pursuit of pleasure and of beauty. He discovers, however, that women are not beautiful things to be possessed. He runs mad for Gloria Gilbert, a party-loving Southern belle who owes a great deal to Zelda. He finds magic in her kiss, which transports him to the 'remote harmonies' of 'far guitars and waters lapping on a warm Mediterranean shore'. But there is a sting: 'She was beautiful – but especially she was without mercy.' Like the enchantress in Keats, she can transform the world of the man-at-arms into a place that is 'cold and full of bleak wind'. She is *la belle dame sans merci* who lived in his heart'. She has the power to kill anything in him that menaces her 'absolute sway'.

Fitzgerald thought better than to retain a title that implicitly laid the blame for the descent into dissipation squarely on the shoulders of the woman, so he abandoned *The Beautiful Woman without Mercy* and plumped instead for *The Beautiful and Damned*. Not 'the beautiful and *the* damned' because that would have suggested two different kinds of people. The beautiful *are* damned.

Having submitted his typescript, he and Zelda sailed to Europe for the first time. On the whole, they were not impressed. The only place that Fitzgerald liked was Oxford, where he went on a pilgrimage through the city of gables and cupolas that was the setting of *Sinister Street*, the novel that had shaped *This Side of Paradise*. In London, they met up with Shane Leslie, who escorted them into the slums of the East End, where Jack the Ripper had committed his crimes. In Paris, they hung around hoping without success for a sight of the grand old man of French letters, poet and novelist Anatole France, who had just won the Nobel Prize in Literature. They were asked to leave their hotel, allegedly because of Zelda's habit of tying her belt to the elevator bell so that it remained on their floor while she was dressing.

The grubby streets and general sense of decay in Italy provoked a letter to 'Bunny' Wilson that anticipates the views of the vile Tom Buchanan in *The Great Gatsby*. Fitzgerald damned Europe as being of 'merely antiquarian interest', with a 'negroid streak' creeping northwards 'to defile the Nordic race'. The Italians had 'the souls of blackamoors', while France made him 'sick'. As for the English, they should have let Germany win the war so that Europe could have been cleansed by Teutonic racial purity – a chilling sentiment to hear four years before the publication of *Mein Kampf*. Europe was through. The future was (white) America: 'We will be the Romans in the next generation as the English are now.' The only redeeming feature of this tirade of racist abuse is Fitzgerald's acknowledgment that his sentiments were 'all philistine, anti-socialistic, provincial + racially snobbish'. It would be good, but probably wishful thinking, to believe that he was only engaging in banter intended to provoke his cultured and increasingly left-wing friend.

With Zelda pregnant, they felt ripe for some provinciality of their own. They returned to Minnesota for a year, during which their only daughter was born. Scott made a note in his ledger of the first words that Zelda said as she came round from the anaesthetic with which she had been sedated after her long and difficult labour: 'Oh god, goofo' (her nickname for him), 'I'm drunk. Mark Twain' (an allusion to his famous remark 'the report of my death was an exaggeration'?). And then: 'Isn't she sweet – she has the hiccups. I hope its beautiful and a fool – a beautiful little fool.' Even this most intimate moment was ripe for recycling. Daisy recalls giving birth to her daughter Pammy in *The Great Gatsby*:

> I woke up out of the ether with an utterly abandoned feeling, and asked the nurse right away if it was a boy or a girl. She told me it was a girl, and so I turned my head away and wept. 'All right,' I said, 'I'm glad it's a girl. And I hope she'll be a fool – that's the best thing a girl can be in this world, a beautiful little fool.'

Zelda wanted their daughter to be called Patricia, but Scott insisted that she should be Frances Scott Key Fitzgerald. He always called her Scottie; for a while, Zelda called her Pat.

Scott continued to write short stories as his novel was prepared for publication. Again and again, beauty was his theme. In 'May Day', a story salvaged from *The Demon Lover*, the abandoned first attempt at a second novel: 'She was a complete, infinitely delicate, quite perfect thing of beauty, flowing in an even line from a complex coiffure to two small slim feet.' Here a woman is a thing of beauty, whereas in 'The Diamond as Big as the Ritz', the finest of the stories written at this period, Fitzgerald romanced the beauty of things: 'Afterward John remembered that first night as a daze of many colors, of quick sensory impressions, of music soft as a voice in love, and of the beauty of things, lights and shadows, and motions and faces.' This is an anatomy of beauty into the elements that a century earlier had given Keats a repertoire of sense impressions for his poetry.

*

As in his first novel, though to a lesser degree, Fitzgerald experimented in *The Beautiful and Damned* with different styles – a transition into playscript formula, jump cuts between fragments of narrative and of philosophizing, a series of diary entries (filched from Zelda, as she noted in her review of the novel entitled 'Friend Husband's Latest'). Among the more revealing of these interjections is a 'Flash-Back in Paradise' in which Beauty is personified, very much in the Keatzian manner. Fitzgerald italicized the sequence, perhaps in recognition of the stylistic incongruity of introducing an allegorical figure into an ostensibly realistic story of contemporary New York high life:

Beauty, who was born anew every hundred years, sat in a sort of outdoor waiting room through which blew gusts of white wind and occasionally a breathless hurried star. The stars winked at her intimately as they went by and the winds made a soft incessant flurry in her hair. She was incomprehensible, for, in her, soul and spirit were one – the beauty of her body was the essence of her soul. She was that unity sought for by philosophers through many centuries.

Ever since the *Symposium* of Plato, philosophers had reflected on the progression from physical to spiritual beauty and the notion that the Beautiful was defined by perfect formal unity. Fitzgerald knew this from both his undergraduate classes at Princeton and his immersion in the Romantic literary tradition. Coleridge, from whom he took that other rejected title *The Demon Lover*, argued that the essence of poetry – by which he meant all the creative arts, including music's poetry of the ear and painting's of the eye – is 'the excitement of emotion for the immediate purpose of pleasure through the medium of beauty' and that 'the BEAUTIFUL, contemplated in its essentials' is 'that in which the *many*, still seen as many, becomes one . . . Multëity in Unity'.

Though there are multiple sources for Fitzgerald's ideas about Beauty, the imagery with which he represents it (or 'her', as in his usual personification) is again and again Keatzian. The flurry of the wind in Beauty's hair in the 'Flash-back in Paradise' brings a whispered memory of Keats's figure of beauty in autumn, sitting on the floor of a granary, her 'hair soft-lifted by the winnowing wind'. And for both writers, the key metaphor for the conjoining of self and beauty is a kiss. In Keats's second book, words 'Written in starlight on the dark above' speak to Endymion's 'inward senses': '*I'll kissing snatch / Thee into endless heaven. Awake! Awake!*' On hearing – or rather imagining – these words,

The youth at once arose: a placid lake
Came quiet to his eyes; and forest green
Cooler than all the wonders he had seen.

Kiss after kiss in Fitzgerald's second book is evoked with similar effects of nightlight and shadow, liquidity and cool:

She turned her face up to him, pale under the wisps and patches of light that trailed in like moonshine through a foliage. Her eyes were gleaming ripples in the white lake of her face; the shadows of her hair bordered the brow with a persuasive unintimate dusk . . . Her beauty was cool as this damp breeze, as the moist softness of her own lips.

As in Keats, beauty and the kiss are always evanescent: 'Such a kiss – it was a flower held against the face, never to be described, scarcely to be remembered; as though her beauty were giving off emanations of itself which settled transiently and already dissolving upon his heart.' Because it is fleeting, the sensation may appear unreal. Gloria appeals to the part of Anthony 'that cherished all beauty and all illusion'. The same part of him, that is, which has as one of its prized possessions an original letter in the hand of John Keats, purchased at a vastly inflated price. So it is that 'There was the union of his soul with Gloria's, whose radiant fire and freshness was the living material of which the dead beauty of books was made.'

The paradox for Fitzgerald is that the only way of immortalizing the freshness of youth and the radiant moment of a kiss is in the 'dead' form of ink on the page. 'There's no beauty without poignancy and there's no poignancy without the feeling that it's going, men, names, books, houses – bound for dust – mortal.' This is Gloria (standing in for Zelda), explaining her love for the old South on the grounds that it has gone, and comparing that love to Anthony's for his Keats letter, yellowed with age.

In the chapter of quasi-platonic dialogue called 'Symposium', Anthony's friend, cynical Maury Noble, discourses on the idea that even books, written in the hope of preserving beauty, are bound for dust:

> And so I turned, canny for my years, from the professors to the poets, listening – to the lyric tenor of Swinburne and the tenor robusto of Shelley, to Shakespeare with his first bass and his fine range, to Tennyson with his second bass and his occasional falsetto, to Milton and Marlow, bassos profundo. I gave ear to Browning chatting, Byron declaiming, and Wordsworth droning. This, at least, did me no harm. I learned a little of beauty – enough to know that it had nothing to do with truth – and I found, moreover, that there was no great literary tradition; there was only the tradition of the eventful death of every literary tradition . . . Then I grew up, and the beauty of succulent illusions fell away from me.

('Eventful' is a misprint for 'eventual'.) What, then, will take the place of the great poetic tradition that ran from Marlowe and Shakespeare through Shelley and Byron to the zenith of late Romanticism in the flowing verse of Algernon Charles Swinburne?

Later in the novel, Fitzgerald comes up with an archly self-referential answer. Anthony announces that 'The arts are very old.' A few glasses relax 'the tension of his nerves' and he is able to respond to the question 'Which art?'

> All of them. Poetry is dying first. It'll be absorbed into prose sooner or later. For instance, the beautiful word, the colored and glittering word, and the beautiful simile belong in prose

now. To get attention poetry has got to strain for the unusual word, the harsh, earthy word that's never been beautiful before. Beauty, as the sum of several beautiful parts, reached its apotheosis in Swinburne. It can't go any further – except in the novel, perhaps.

His friend then interrupts him impatiently:

You know these new novels make me tired. My God! Everywhere I go some silly girl asks me if I've read *This Side of Paradise*. Are our girls really like that? If it's true to life, which I don't believe, the next generation is going to the dogs. I'm sick of all this shoddy realism. I think there's a place for the romanticist in literature.

Fitzgerald was, a little too self-consciously, trying to have it both ways, to be a realist and a romanticist. On the one hand, he acknowledges the death of the Romantic tradition: while Gloria shops for dresses, Anthony reclines on his couch and laments that 'cloth of Samarcand was remembered only by the romantic poets' – a nod to the 'spiced dainties, every one / From silken Samarcand' in Keats's 'The Eve of St Agnes'. When Anthony hits rock bottom, he tries to sell his Keats letter. His very craving for romance is punished. Romantic love is revealed to be a will-o'-the-wisp: 'The breathless idyl left them, fled on to other lovers.' Realism demands that for a couple to survive they must mature from dreams of romance into 'the stuff of all life, by way of deep and intimate kindnesses they develop toward each other, by way of their laughing at the same absurdities and thinking the same things noble and the same things sad'. That would be a grown-up kind of loving.

And yet, even in Anthony's decline into alcoholism he is given little epiphanies. The language of Romantic lyricism is revived in prose that transforms a city of traders and money men into a place of beauty that is a joy for a moment:

> There was a kindliness about intoxication – there was that indescribable gloss and glamour it gave, like the memories of ephemeral and faded evenings. After a few high-balls there was magic in the tall glowing Arabian night of the Bush Terminal Building – its summit a peak of sheer grandeur, gold and dreaming against the inaccessible sky. And Wall Street, the crass, the banal – again it was the triumph of gold, a gorgeous sentient spectacle.

In the symposium, Maury undid Keats's equation of beauty and truth; in the giddiness of cocktail hour, Anthony revives 'The fruit of youth or of the grape, the transitory magic of the brief passage from darkness to darkness – the old illusion that truth and beauty were in some way entwined.' It was ominous, though, that Fitzgerald could imagine the sustaining of the Keatzian truth-beauty equation only by putting his protagonist in a state of intoxication.

Anthony is damned by his indolence, his romanticism and his drinking; Gloria by her reliance on her looks. Fitzgerald is cruel in giving her a high opinion of her own physical beauty: 'In the end then, her beauty was all that never failed her. She had never seen beauty like her own. What it meant ethically or aesthetically faded before the gorgeous concreteness of her pink-and-white feet, the clean perfectness of her body, and the baby mouth that was like the material symbol of a kiss.' Even a perfect body is, however, subject to age. When she is struck down with the Spanish flu, she begins to worry about losing her looks. Lured to the promise of the screen, she auditions for the part of a beautiful young woman in a movie: 'It cheered her that in some manner the illusion of beauty could be sustained, or preserved perhaps in celluloid after the reality had vanished.' But the producer decides they need a younger woman. He does, nevertheless, offer Gloria the small character part of a very haughty rich widow.

Even as Fitzgerald made the claim that the novel, his form, would take up the mantle of poetry that had reached its apotheosis in the Romantic tradition, he also recognized that a new art form might be able to do something that literature could not. Neither a poem nor a painting, nor for that matter the 'brede' on a Grecian urn, can immortalize the living movement of youth. The figures on Keats's urn are frozen in time, even as the object itself endures through time. That is why it is a 'Cold Pastoral'. Now, though, there was such a thing as a moving picture. The future belonged to Hollywood.

Within months of its publication, *The Beautiful and Damned* was turned into a movie. The casting choices repeated the trick of *The Chorus Girl's Romance*, which had been marketed with a publicity shot that could have passed for an image of Scott and Zelda. This time, Marie Prevost as Gloria and Kenneth Harlan as Anthony bore an uncanny resemblance to the figures on the cover of the book, who in turn bore an uncanny resemblance to Zelda and Scott. Harlan and Prevost, a celebrated starlet who had begun her career as an onscreen 'Bathing Beauty', were having a high-profile affair. As a publicity stunt to promote the film, Warner Brothers announced that they would marry on set. Gifts and fan mail poured in. There was only one problem: they were both already married (Harlan to his second wife). Jack Warner was not happy with newspaper headlines such as 'Marie Prevost will be a Bigamist if She Marries Kenneth Harlan'.

The film was still a success – though it did not have the effect of immortalizing Marie Prevost in the way that Gloria hopes to be immortalized on film. In contrast to those Grecian urns that have survived for over 2,000 years, the print was lost within decades. Harlan and Prevost went on to secure divorces and marry quietly. In 1929, the year of the Crash, their marriage broke up (Harlan went on to marry six more times). Warner Brothers had released Prevost, who could not handle the transition to talkies, so her career was already in a tailspin. Born the same year as Fitzgerald, she drank herself to death three years before him. Two days passed before she was found alone in her apartment with a pile of empty liquor bottles, a promissory note made out to Joan Crawford, and her pet dachshund Maxie, whose barking and whining over her corpse was beginning to trouble the neighbours.

The Fitzgeralds, too, were becoming celebrities. Which is another way of saying that, like Marie Prevost, they were beautiful and damned.

The Beautiful and Damned: Marie Prevost as Gloria Gilbert . . . with a remarkable resemblance to Zelda

The book and the movie

... and Zelda's original suggestion for a cover image: herself,
with flapper bob, naked in a champagne glass

'NEGATIVE CAPABILITY'

On his return to London from seaside and countryside, Keats immersed himself in the cultural life of the city. His friend Reynolds was on holiday, and this gave him the opportunity to act as stand-in theatre reviewer for the liberal *Champion* magazine. Writing under the influence of Hazlitt's unprecedentedly astute dramatic criticism, he raved about the dynamic star Edmund Kean's 'intense power of anatomizing the passions of every syllable' of Shakespeare. 'Other actors are continually thinking of their sum total effect throughout a play', he suggested, whereas Kean 'delivers himself up to the instant feeling, without a shadow of a thought about anything else'.

He was less impressed with the venerable American artist Benjamin West's *Death on the Pale Horse*, which was on exhibition in Pall Mall. A twenty-five-feet wide and fifteen-feet tall representation of the four horsemen of the apocalypse, it now hangs in the Pennsylvania Academy of the Fine Arts. It was in Keats's opinion a remarkable achievement for a man who was, like Shakespeare's King Lear, in his eightieth year. And yet he told his brothers that the painting left him cold; it had 'nothing to be intense upon; no women one feels mad to kiss; no face swelling into reality'. He had been reading Hazlitt's collection of essays *The Round Table,* in which he found the term 'gusto', meaning the artist's power of strong projection into the object of creation. Gusto creates intensity, which gives 'reality' to the great work of art. West's painting lacked the gusto of Kean's acting and Shakespeare's writing.

Keats's thinking was maturing at an astonishing pace, partly thanks to the fructifying influence of Hazlitt, the sharpest critical mind in his circle of acquaintance. Another essay in *The Round Table* argued that the ambition of actors should be 'to be *beside themselves*', to negate the self in the act of becoming a character. This was the key to Kean's intensity. Keats also annotated his copy of Hazlitt's book *Characters of Shakespear's Plays*, reading the chapter on *King Lear* with particular care, underlining such phrases as 'we see not Lear, but we are Lear' – again, the idea of empathetic projection. Thinking hard about *King Lear*, Keats adduced the principle that 'the excellence of every Art is its intensity, capable of making all disagreeables evaporate, from their being in close relationship with Beauty & Truth'. A month later, he sat down to reread the play, preparing himself for the intensity of the experience by writing a sonnet arguing that by making himself 'burn through' the tragedy, he would be purified and given 'new phoenix wings to fly at my desire'.

Walking home with friends after seeing the Christmas pantomime, Keats reflected on Kean's ability to become a Shakespearean villain or hero on stage and on Shakespeare's gift of dissolving himself into all his characters. It struck him that the quality that led to greatness in literature, and 'which Shakespeare possessed so enormously', was '*Negative Capability*, that is, when man is capable of being in uncertainties, Mysteries, doubts, without any irritable reaching after fact & reason'. Coleridge, in contrast to Shakespeare, was too restless in his search for philosophical truth: he 'would let go by a fine isolated verisimilitude caught from the Penetralium of mystery, from being incapable of remaining content with half-knowledge . . . with a great poet the sense of Beauty overcomes every other consideration, or rather obliterates all consideration'. Keats's mind is working at high speed here. In its first use, 'consideration' means 'every other aspect of the process of creation', but on its second it means 'thought' or 'rationalization'. By this account, Coleridge is like those actors who can't stop thinking about 'their sum total effect' throughout the play, whereas Shakespeare is like Kean, totally absorbed in the moment, concerned only with the Beauty – the rightness – of the phrase and the line.

As in Immanuel Kant's theory that the Beautiful, in contrast to the Agreeable and the Good, is *disinterested*, a creation born of negative capability is its own self, free from the imposition of the artist's own identity. The greatest artists are content with half-knowledge; they are willing to leave some of the mystery of life uncaught, to open a space that is then filled by their appreciative readers. Keats elaborated the thought in a letter written a few weeks later: 'We hate poetry that has a palpable design upon us – and if we do not agree, seems to put its hand into its breeches pocket.' As if to reach for a pistol, that is. 'Poetry should be great & unobtrusive, a thing which enters into one's soul, and does not startle it or amaze it with itself – but with its subject.'

In the new year, he made a weekly excursion across London to hear Hazlitt's public lectures on the English poets at the Surrey Institution, a venue on the busy lower-middle-class south bank of the river Thames. In his lecture on Shakespeare and Milton, Hazlitt played off the tendency of contemporary poets – Wordsworth above all – 'to surround the meanest objects with the morbid feelings and devouring egotism of the writers' own minds' against the art of Shakespeare, who was 'the least of an egotist that it was possible to be' and whose 'genius shone equally on the evil and on the good, on the wise and foolish, the monarch and the beggar'. Keats ran with the idea later in the year, suggesting that the true poetical character to which he aspired stood apart from 'the wordsworthian or egotistical sublime':

> it is not itself – it has no self – it is every thing and nothing – It has no character – it enjoys light and shade; it lives in gusto, be it foul or fair, high or low, rich or poor, mean or elevated – It has as much delight in conceiving an Iago as an Imogen. What shocks the virtuous philosopher delights the cameleon Poet.

His dilemma was that he wanted to be a Shakespearean chameleon and yet he also wanted to write about his own feelings, in the manner of Wordsworth. This led him to turn to the sonnets, where Shakespeare gave the appearance of writing about his own feelings, while meditating more generally on great themes of love, time and mortality.

Keats's earlier sonnets had been in the Italianate form (one set of rhymes running through an octave, another in a sestet), but now he began imitating the form of the Shakespearean (three quatrains and a couplet). A few days after hearing Hazlitt lecture on Shakespeare, he sent his latest effort to Reynolds:

> When I have fears that I may cease to be
>   Before my pen has glean'd my teeming brain,
> Before high-piled books, in charactry,
>   Hold like rich garners the full ripen'd grain;
> When I behold, upon the night's starr'd face,
>   Huge cloudy symbols of a high romance,
> And think that I may never live to trace
>   Their shadows, with the magic hand of chance;

And when I feel, fair creature of an hour!
   That I shall never look upon thee more,
Never have relish in the faery power
    Of unreflecting love; – then on the shore
Of the wide world I stand alone, and think
Till Love and Fame to nothingness do sink.

The first line is a fusion of the beginning of one of Shakespeare's sonnets – 'When I have seen by time's fell hand defaced' – and the end of one of Shelley's: 'that thou shouldst cease to be'. The decay of all things leads Shakespeare to lament his love because it, too, must one day decline. Shelley's 'thou' was Wordsworth: the 'cease to be' line was the close of a sonnet lamenting the Lake Poet's decline from radical apostle of nature to reactionary slave of government. Wordsworth has, Shelley proposes, ceased to be as an independent imagination. Keats's sonnet laments the possibility that he might die before he has experienced love, as in the Shakespeare, or even *begun to be* as a poet of the kind that Wordsworth has ceased to be. He yearns for both romantic love and poetic fame, but fears that the only thing which lies before him is a sea of loneliness and then mortality.

His friend Woodhouse speculated that, as in the Shakespearean sonnet that Keats wrote a few days later ('Time's sea'), the 'fair creature of an hour' in this poem was the beautiful woman glimpsed for a moment several years before in Vauxhall Gardens. She could, however, equally well have been Isabella Jones, with whom he had shared those few precious hours in Hastings. Around this time, Keats also wrote a group of mildly erotic fleet-footed lyrics about blushing and kissing, which seem more apt for her than the unknown woman of Vauxhall.

Scott Fitzgerald reckoned that 'When I have fears' and 'On first looking into Chapman's Homer' were among Keats's 'three or four great sonnets'. A prose-poet of high romance, he filled his own fictions with symbols such as 'the night's starr'd face' and the shadows of evening. The wild surmise of Cortez and his men merged with Keats standing alone on the shore of the wide world into Gatsby's gaze towards the green light of Daisy's dock.

*

Fear of mortality was weighing on Keats because his brother Tom had begun spitting blood, suggesting the onset of tuberculosis. In early March 1818, Keats joined him at another seaside health resort, Teignmouth in Devon. Tom seemed to get worse and then rather better, at which point Keats wrote to Haydon with new plans. They would return to town, and Keats would put a knapsack on his back and embark on a tour on foot through northern England and Scotland. He even wondered about walking through Europe, as Wordsworth had done as a young man. He needed travel and natural sublimity to help him work through 'The innumerable compositions and decompositions which take place between the intellect and its thousand materials before it arrives at that trembling delicate and snail-horn perception of beauty.'

The composition on which he was working in Teignmouth was sparked by a remark in one of Hazlitt's lectures. Discussing John Dryden's English adaptations from *The Decameron*, Hazlitt suggested that 'a translation of some of the other serious tales in Boccaccio', for example 'that of Isabella', 'if executed with taste and spirit, could not fail to succeed in the present day'. Perhaps pricking up his ears at the echo of the Hastings lady's name, Keats read the story in a seventeenth-century English translation that began with a summary of the plot:

The three Brethren of Isabella, slew a Gentleman that secretly loved her. His Ghost appeared to her in her Sleep, and shewed her in what place they had buried his Body. She (in silent manner) brought away his Head, and putting it into a Pot of Earth, such as Flowers, Basile, or other sweet Hearbes are usually set in, she watered it (a long while) with her Tears. Whereof her Brethren having intelligence, soon after she dyed, with mere conceit of Sorrow.

Fitzgerald's glimpse of Keats in the act of creation: a page from Keats's holograph of 'Isabella', reproduced in Colvin's biography

Keats turned Boccaccio's prose novella into sixty-three stanzas of *ottava rima* (two triple rhymes followed by a couplet), a form pioneered by Boccaccio himself and still considered in Keats's time to be suitably Italianate. He and Reynolds hatched a plan to put together a series of narrative poems based on Boccaccio's collection of tales, some of which were raucous and sexy, others romantic and tragic. This was the only one that Keats accomplished. His fair copy, completed by the end of April 1818, was headed 'The Pot of Basil', but when it was published in his 1820 collection it was called 'Isabella; or, The Pot of Basil'.

Keats grew dissatisfied with it, considering that it risked smoking him out as someone with 'too much inexperience of life'. It is at its best in minute details, for example when Isabella frantically digs up her lover's body, stopping only 'to throw back at times her veiling hair'. Literally, her hair is getting in the way of her eyes; metaphorically, it is a veil because she is mourning.

He struggled to find the right words to give the young lovers when they flush with desire and voice their love to each other. In the end, he opted for silence on the woman's part:

'Lorenzo!' – here she ceased her timid quest,
But in her tone and look he read the rest.

Worried that his writing would appear 'mawkish', he omitted a draft passage of charming dialogue in which Isabella offers to clip a ringlet of her hair as a love-token.

'Then should I be,' said he, 'full deified;
And yet I would not have it, clip it not;
For Lady I do love it where 'tis tied
About the Neck I dote on; and that spot
That anxious dimple it doth take a pride
To play about.'

The dimple is a lovely detail that should not have been relegated to the cutting-room floor.

The Pre-Raphaelite painters such as William Holman Hunt and John Everett Millais revelled in the medievalism of 'Isabella', but Keats was shrewd in coming to realize that the problem with the poem was its melodrama. Burying your lover's head in a pot of basil and watering it with your tears is an extreme externalization of grief. In order to mature as a poet, Keats would have to explore suffering *inside* the head.

From the Painting by Holman Hunt.

Isabella or the Pot of Basil.
"Sweet Basil, which her tears kept ever wet."
—KEATS.

In early May, he wrote to Reynolds after Tom had endured a sleepless night of fever. He said that he was glad that he had kept his medical books, then suggested that suffering is a route to knowledge: 'Until we are sick, we understand not.' He compared human life to a 'large Mansion of Many Apartments'. We begin in 'the infant or thoughtless Chamber'. Then the 'thinking principle' awakens and we are drawn into 'the Chamber of Maiden-Thought', where we are intoxicated by the beauties of the world – the light, the atmosphere – until, like Wordsworth in 'Tintern Abbey', outgrowing his youthful joy as he hears 'The still sad music of humanity', our vision is sharpened and our nerves are convinced 'that the World is full of Misery and Heartbreak, Pain, Sickness and oppression'. The chamber darkens and we are lost in a mist, feeling what

Wordsworth called the 'burden of the Mystery'. It is almost as if Keats is growing up in the very course of writing this long letter. As he approaches its sign-off, he writes one of his most moving sentences:

> Tom has spit a leetle blood this afternoon, and that is rather a damper – but I know – the truth is there is something real in the World: Your Chamber of Life shall be a lucky and a gentle one – stored with the wine of love – and the Bread of Friendship.

The mood is sacramental: religious communion with the body and blood of Christ is replaced by earthly love and friendship.

*

Their brother George had news. Having reached the age of twenty-one, he had received a portion of the family inheritance, quit his position in Mr Abbey's counting-house, and become engaged to be married to Georgiana Wylie, a girl he had known for some years. He had, furthermore, taken the bold decision – which seventeen-year-old Georgiana had the pluck to support – to emigrate to America. The government out there was selling hundreds of acres of land in the Midwest at a cheap price, so George was going to set himself up as a farmer in Kentucky. Tom and John would have to return for the wedding and to share their brother's last weeks before leaving England. Tom bore the first part of the journey 'remarkably well', but then he haemorrhaged, so they had to proceed slowly, taking overnight stops along the way, meaning that they did not arrive in London for a week.

The idea of walking to the north had been proposed by a new friend, Charles Brown, who lived in the other half of

Wentworth Place, a house in Hampstead where the Keats boys had frequently been received with great kindness by a family called Dilke. Brown had begun his working life in business but had been able to devote himself to literary pursuits on receipt of an inheritance from his brother. He had achieved some success with a 'serio-comic opera' at Drury Lane entitled *Narensky; or, The Road to Yaroslaf*, a preposterous love story involving banditti in a forest near a Russian village.

Now the road trip would have an additional purpose: to see off George and Georgiana. Though he had been unwell and warned by his doctor that he shouldn't go out, two weeks later Keats set off with his brother George, new sister-in-law, and Brown. They headed for the busy coach terminal at the Swan with Two Necks in Lad Lane, central London, where they boarded for Liverpool.

The first staging post was near St Albans, where Keats's medical friend Stephens was practising. He joined them for a brief reunion at the inn and was impressed by Keats's affection towards Georgiana, who, he said, was 'somewhat singular and girlish in her attire' but with an 'imaginative poetical cast' that made her a being whom 'any man of moderate sensibility might easily love'. Just over twenty-four hours later, they arrived in Liverpool. They stayed at the Crown Inn and shared a last dinner. The next day, George and Georgiana joined other emigrants aboard an American ship called the *Telegraph*, bound for Philadelphia. They would wait aboard for several days before the cargo was loaded and the wind changed to set them on their way.

Keats was never good at partings. He didn't go down to the dock with his brother and sister-in-law, even though he must have known that he might never see them again. He didn't even know the name of the ship. Together with Brown, he had slipped away at dawn. At 4 a.m., they had walked out of the seaport through the morning mist, heading towards the Lake District. He sought to cheer Tom with a lively journal-letter, describing his pleasure in the beauties of Windermere and Rydal Water, along with his disappointment at the news, which he heard from a waiter at the inn where they stayed in Ambleside, that William Wordsworth the sometime radical was out and about campaigning for the Tory party in the upcoming by-election. Shelley's sonnet was all too true: the 'Poet of Nature' whose voice in 'honoured poverty' had woven 'Songs consecrate to truth and liberty' had 'ceased to be' as a spokesman for beauty and fraternity.

Nevertheless, Keats and Brown called at Rydal Mount, Wordsworth's home. He was out – campaigning, no doubt – so Keats left a note on the mantelpiece, propped against a portrait of Dorothy Wordsworth. Perhaps more than her brother, she would have appreciated the eye for nature that Keats was developing. Early in the morning, before breakfast, he and Brown had gone in search of the Ambleside waterfalls. Keats scrambled nimbly into a wooded valley, following the sound of the cataract. His account of what he saw is comparable in precise observation to the glorious language of Dorothy's diaries:

> The different falls have as different characters; the first darting down the slate-rock like an arrow; the second spreading out like a fan – the third dashed into a mist – and the one on the other side of the rock a sort of mixture of all these. We afterwards moved away a space, and saw nearly the whole more mild, streaming silverly through the trees.

'Silverly' is an especially felicitous choice of adverb, perhaps remembered from Shakespeare's use of it in *King John* to describe tears flowing down a grieving man's cheek. The entire scene was inspirational to Keats. 'What astonishes me more than any thing', he continues his letter to Tom,

> is the tone, the coloring, the slate, the stone, the moss, the rock-weed; or, if I may so say, the intellect, the countenance of such places. The space, the magnitude of mountains and waterfalls are well imagined before one sees them; but this countenance or intellectual tone must surpass every imagination and defy any remembrance. I shall learn poetry here and shall henceforth write more than ever, for the abstract endeavor of being able to add a mite to that mass of beauty which is harvested from these grand materials, by the finest spirits, and put into etherial existence for the relish of one's fellows.

The theory of 'ethereal Chemicals' is at work again here. Keats envisions the poet as a pharmacist harvesting natural elements and creating what could almost be imagined as a pill that enables the reader to feel and taste – to 'relish' – beauty. The brilliance of the metaphor is in the pun whereby 'finest spirits' refers both to great poets and to the rectified alcohol in the distillation process that created ether.

At the foot of Helvellyn, Wordsworth's favourite mountain, Keats composed a *bon voyage* letter to George and Georgiana, dispatching it to the Crown Inn and hoping it would reach them before they sailed. He found it easier to say goodbye in writing than in person. But the *Telegraph* had left Liverpool by the time the letter arrived at the port, so it was returned to him at a London address. He realized that there would be little point in sending frequent letters, since they would take weeks to arrive on the other side of the Atlantic, so he got into the habit of writing journal-like epistles, up to sixty pages long, and dispatching them every few months.

Throughout the walking tour, he kept up his correspondence

with all three of his siblings, recording his impressions of the Highlands of Scotland, the grave of Robert Burns, the top of Ben Nevis (Britain's highest mountain), Fingal's Cave in the Hebrides (a 'hollowing out of Basalt Pillars' associated with the legendary Gaelic poet Ossian), and, having crossed the Irish Sea, the Giant's Causeway. Following the principles of his 'Mansion of Many Apartments' letter, he allowed his imagination to dwell not only on the natural beauty of the landscape, but also on human suffering, notably 'the worse than nakedness, the rags, the dirt and misery of the poor common Irish'. He despaired of the possibility of the condition of the colonized Irish people being improved by philanthropy. Near Belfast, they passed the strangest sedan chair he had ever seen, bearing a woman whom he called the Duchess of Dunghill, before correcting himself with the acknowledgment that her poverty was no laughing matter:

> Imagine the worst dog kennel you ever saw, placed upon two poles from a mouldy fencing – In such a wretched thing sat a squalid old Woman squat like an ape half starved from a scarcity of Buiscuit in its passage from Madagascar to the cape, – with a pipe in her mouth and looking out with a round-eyed skinny lidded, inanity – with a sort of horizontal idiotic movement of her head – squab and lean she sat and puff'd out the smoke while two ragged tattered Girls carried her along – What a thing would be a history of her Life and sensations.

His prose captured his empathy for her, but it was beyond his reach to write a poem about her.

Keats and Brown walked for 600 miles and rode a further 400. They planned to keep going for several months. Adventures on the road and the beauties of nature had matured Keats's mind and given him raw material for his work: 'I should not have consented to myself these four Months tramping in the highlands but that I thought it would give me more experience, rub off more Prejudice, use [me] to more hardship, identify finer scenes[,] load me with grander Mountains, and strengthen more my reach in Poetry, than would stopping at home among Books.' At the same time, the tour was a distraction from his grief at losing one brother to America and fearing the loss of the other to tuberculosis. In late August he altered his plans on hearing that Tom's condition was worsening. Leaving Brown to finish the tour alone, he headed back to Hampstead.

He returned not only to a declining brother, but also to a savaging of *Endymion* in *Blackwood's Edinburgh Magazine*. Reviewer J. G. Lockhart, signing himself 'Z', loftily diagnosed 'The case of Mr John Keats' as a prime example of the 'malady' whereby, thanks to the success of the peasant poet Robert Burns, the lower orders had presumed to believe that they could write poetry:

> This young man appears to have received from nature talents of an excellent, perhaps even of a superior order – talents which, devoted to the purposes of any useful profession, must have rendered him a respectable, if not an eminent citizen. His friends, we understand, destined him to the career of medicine and he was bound apprentice some years ago to a worthy apothecary in town. But all has been undone by a sudden attack of the malady to which we have alluded. Whether Mr John had been sent home with a diuretic or composing draught to some patient far gone in the poetical mania, we have not heard. This much is certain, that he has caught the infection, and that thoroughly. For some time we were in hopes, that he might get off with a violent fit or two; but of late the symptoms are terrible. The phrenzy of the 'Poems' [his first book] was bad enough in its way, but it did not alarm us half so seriously as the calm, settled, imperturbable drivelling idiocy of 'Endymion'.

The review continued with lengthy quotations and much sneering aimed at Keats's luxuriant language, erotic self indulgence and digressions into radical politics. He was branded, with Leigh Hunt, as the epitome of the vulgar 'Cockney' poet. The conclusion to the article told him to get back in his proper place: 'It is a better and a wiser thing to be a starved apothecary than a starved poet; so back to the shop Mr John, back to "plasters, pills, and ointment boxes," &c. But, for Heaven's sake, young Sangrado, be a little more sparing of extenuatives and soporifics in your practice than you have been in your poetry.' The Tory *Quarterly Review* followed suit, with a review that began by attacking Leigh Hunt and the Cockney School in general, then turned to the language of *Endymion*:

> our author, as we have already hinted, has no meaning. He seems to write a line at random, and then he follows not the thought excited by this line, but that suggested by the rhyme with which it concludes. There is hardly a complete couplet inclosing a complete idea in the whole book. He wanders from one subject to another, from the association, not of ideas but of sounds.

Keats brushed off these assaults, and his other bad reviews, with extraordinary fortitude. He told George and Georgiana in America that the attacks on him were 'a mere matter of the moment – I think I shall be among the English Poets after my death'. And to his publisher Hessey he acknowledged his own failings as a necessary part of his growth as a writer:

> Had I been nervous about its being a perfect piece, & with that view asked advice, & trembled over every page, it would not have been written; for it is not in my nature to fumble – I will write independantly. – I have written independently *without*

Judgment – I may write independently, and *with judgment,* hereafter. – The Genius of Poetry must work out its own salvation in a man: It cannot be matured by law & precept, but by sensation & watchfulness in itself – That which is creative must create itself – In Endymion, I leaped headlong into the Sea, and thereby have become better acquainted with the Soundings, the quicksands, & the rocks, than if I had stayed upon the green shore, and piped a silly pipe, and took tea & comfortable advice. I was never afraid of failure; for I would sooner fail than not be among the greatest.

'VISIONS OF DELIGHT'

'I never was in love', he wrote to Reynolds in September 1818,

> Yet the voice and shape of a woman has haunted me these two days – at such a time, when the relief, the feverous relief of Poetry seems a much less crime – This morning Poetry has conquered – I have relapsed into those abstractions which are my only life – I feel escaped from a new strange and threatening sorrow. – And I am thankful for it – There is an awful warmth about my heart like a load of Immortality.

All of a sudden he was confronted with a welter of conflicting feelings: 'Poor Tom – that woman – and Poetry were ringing changes in my senses.'

Her name was Jane Cox. A cousin of Reynolds and his sisters, she had taken refuge in their house, having fallen out with her wealthy grandfather. Keats was mesmerized by her eyes and her walk. 'When she comes into the room she makes an impression the same as the Beauty of a Leopardess.' She emitted a 'magnetic Power' that gave him 'life and animation'. She made him negatively capable: he forgot himself for the moment because he was living in her. But it was no more than the feeling of an instant: 'You will by this time think I am in love with her; so before I go any further I will tell you I am not – she kept me awake one Night as a tune of Mozart's might do.'

He compared her to Charmian, the attendant of Cleopatra in Shakespeare's greatest play about erotic passion. That was partly because she was dark-skinned. Keats's description of her 'rich eastern look' suggests that she was very probably biracial. Jane Cox was born in India, where it was not uncommon for military personnel to have children by indigenous women.

Nothing happened between them, beyond some mild flirtation watched over by the jealous Reynolds sisters, but to Keats it was as if the Indian maid of his *Endymion* had been incarnated in the Reynolds family drawing room, life imitating art. 'I should like her to ruin me', he wrote to Georgiana, only half-jokingly, 'and I should like you to save me.' Then he pulled back by means of a quotation:

I am free from Men of Pleasure's cares
By dint of feelings far more deep than theirs.

'This is Lord Byron, and is one of the finest things he has said.' Given Byron's reputation as a libertine, Europe's most famous Man of Pleasure (beside Casanova), this sounds like one of the least characteristic things for him to say. That is because Keats was misremembering. The couplet is to be found nowhere in His Lordship's collected poems. Byron slipped into his mind because, for all his protestations to the contrary, the irresistible Jane Cox had got him thinking about the pleasures of the flesh. Keats was actually slightly garbling a quotation from *The Story of Rimini* by his first poetic mentor, Leigh Hunt. Its context was canto three, 'The Fatal Passion', in which Paolo and Francesca dissolve into blisses and kisses.

Picking up his journal-letter two weeks later, Keats described another encounter with a woman at greater length. The scene is set evocatively enough to suggest that, had he lived, he could have become a fine novelist. 'Since I wrote thus far I have met with that same Lady again, whom I saw at Hastings and whom I met when we were going to the English Opera. It was in a street which goes from Bedford Row to Lamb's Conduit Street.' He passed her, then turned back. She seemed glad to see him and not offended that he had walked by and only then stopped. They walked on together towards Islington, where they called on a friend of hers who kept a boarding school there. 'She has always been an enigma to me,' Keats then wrote, 'she has been in a Room with you and with Reynolds and wishes we should be acquainted without any of our common acquaintance knowing it.'

On leaving Islington, he offered to accompany her home. They walked 'some times through shabby, sometimes through decent' streets, leaving him guessing as to the nature of her home. The implication is that she could have been anything from a fine lady to a prostitute, though the conversation at the friend's in Islington had suggested a degree of gentility. They arrived at 34 Gloucester Street, Queen Square, in the district of central London that is now Bloomsbury. She took him upstairs into her sitting room, 'a very tasty sort of place with Books, Pictures, a bronze Statue of Buonaparte, Music, æolian Harp; a Parrot, a Linnet – a Case of choice Liqueurs &c. &c.' She behaved, Keats reported to George and Georgiana, in the kindest manner, making him 'take home a Grouse for Tom's dinner' and asking for his address so that she could send more game. Then he made a pass at her:

As I had warmed with her before and kissed her – I though[t]
it would be living backwards not to do so again – she had a

better taste: she perceived how much a thing of course it was and shrunk from it – not in a prudish way but in as I say a good taste – She cont[r]ived to disappoint me in a way which made me feel more pleasure than a simple kiss could do – she said I should please her much more if I would only press her hand and go away. Whether she was in a different disposition when I saw her before – or whether I have in fancy wrong'd her I cannot tell – I expect to pass some pleasant hours with her now and then: in which I feel I shall be of service to her in matters of knowledge and taste: if I can I will – I have no libidinous thought about her – she and your George [i.e. Georgiana] are the only women à peu près de mon age whom I would be content to know for their mind and friendship alone.

This is a woman of considerable charisma and poise, as well as a tremendous sense of style in the decor of her apartment. She is in full command of her sexuality, willing to kiss and 'warm' with the young poet while taking the sea air in Hastings, yet with the self possession back in London to invite him upstairs but proceed no further.

Keats referred to her only one more time, in his next letter to America: 'Talking of game (I wish I could make it) the Lady whom I met at Hastings and of whom I said something in my last I think, has lately made me many presents of game, and enabled me to make as many – She made me take home a Pheasant the other day which I gave to Mrs Dilke.' This letter was written the following February, suggesting that some sort of relationship endured for several months.

Sidney Colvin was unable to identify this mysterious woman of refined taste, with her caged birds, Aeolian harp and choice liqueurs. But in the 1930s, the poet Edmund Blunden wrote a biography of John Taylor, Keats's publisher. In the course of his research, he discovered a batch of affectionate, witty and mildly flirtatious letters to Taylor from a Mrs Isabella Jones. There were party invitations ('I now claim your promise of assisting at my House Warming which takes place on Wednesday next – you shall have pretty women to look at') and, most tellingly, a long letter which revealed that Taylor had shared with her Joseph Severn's account of Keats's death in Rome. She did not like it, in particular because Severn seemed to focus so much on himself ('I light the fire, make his breakfast & sometimes am obliged to cook – make his bed and even sweep the room . . . Keats calling me to be with him'):

> What will you say when I confess that I am greatly disappointed – that I *could* not shed a single tear – and that I do not like Mr S – . I never saw so much egotism and selfishness displayed under the mask of feeling and friendship . . . I sat down to the task, with a mind prepared to sympathise with all poor K[eats's] sufferings – and ones best feelings are checked by an elaborate account of sweeping rooms – making beds and blowing fires! I feel a relapse taking placing [*sic*] – my ears tingle – my pen shakes – I shall be a *stiffened corpse* if I do not conclude.

Another letter, to Taylor from his business partner Hessey, makes clear that they knew Mrs Jones very well and admired her greatly. It also mentioned that she was in the habit of going to the seaside resort of Hastings. In addition to this, Keats's friend Richard Woodhouse had in his possession various transcripts of Keats poems marked as 'from Mrs Jones'. His copy of 'The Eve of St Agnes' was annotated 'The Poem was written on the suggestion of Mrs Jones'.

There can, therefore, be no doubt that Isabella Jones was the lady first met in Hastings, then seen at the English Opera, then visited in her tasty upstairs sitting room in Queen Square. Her reaction to Severn's account reveals that she was very fond of Keats. And another letter, this one by Reynolds, proves that she was a lively presence among the group of writers who in the late Regency and early 1820s contributed to the *Champion* and its successor, the *London Magazine*: 'What days – were *the* days of the London! – I "try back" as the Huntsman says – over the hours of early Hood – Earnest-Hessey – bleak Dr Darling – twinkling Clare, – "tipsy-joy and jollity" Lamb – Drear-Carey, – Long-*taled* Cunningham – and beautiful Mrs Jones! – Where are all? – or most of them?' She must have had great charm to shine in the brilliant company of such writers as Thomas Hood, John Clare, Charles Lamb, Henry Cary (translator of Dante), and author of tales Thomas Mounsey Cunningham. As for her beauty, it caught the eye of society artist A. E. Chalon: she was the sitter for catalogue number 895, *Portrait of a Lady*, in the 1819 Royal Academy summer show at Somerset House (whereabouts now unknown). Further evidence of her closeness to the *London Magazine* circle is the fact that, via John Taylor, she contributed two guineas to the subscription to support the widow and children of the paper's editor John Scott, after he was killed in a duel provoked by the attacks in *Blackwood's* on Keats, Leigh Hunt and other 'Cockney' authors. She was beautiful, she was literary, she was kind, she vanished out of their lives. That is all we know.

Biographers have assumed that Mrs Jones was a widow, but no one has been able to track down her late husband. It should, however, be remembered that in the eighteenth century 'Mrs' denoted not a married woman but a woman of some status or means. The title continued to be attached to older unmarried women well into the nineteenth century. But Mrs Jones was *not* an older woman. Keats explicitly says that she and his sister-in-law Georgiana are 'à peu près de mon age', about his age. He was twenty-two and Georgiana was eighteen. Mrs

Jones was not an older woman; if she was a widow, she must have been a very young one.

There was, however, another kind of woman who was given the title Mrs, even when unmarried and when young. It was bestowed on singers and actresses to confer a degree of respectability upon them. The confidence and independence of Mrs Jones, the taste with which she decorated her apartment, her sheet music and Aeolian harp, the histrionic quality of her prose in the letters to Taylor, her love of entertaining and her ease in literary salons, not to mention her beauty, are all compatible with the possibility that she moved in the theatrical world. After all, the second time that Keats saw her was on an evening when he went to the English Opera at the Lyceum. Taylor, Hessey and Reynolds always refer to her as 'Mrs Jones', despite her youth: this is exactly what they would have done if it was her professional name as a public performer. There was indeed a stage-singer called 'Mrs Jones', who debuted at the Theatre Royal Cheltenham in 1816, performed on the same night as Edmund Kean, and appeared three times at Drury Lane, before she disappeared from public view, but perhaps continued to make a professional living through appearances at private parties. She is a plausible candidate, save that her first name is unknown.

*

Whoever she was, Mrs Jones steered Keats well by suggesting 'The Eve of St Agnes' as the topic for a new narrative poem. In its mingling of romantic atmosphere, bright imagery and adroit wit, it is the poem in which he truly finds his voice. The legend that drives the story is explained in an early stanza. By performing certain rituals before bed, a young woman could supposedly conjure up a dream of her future husband. She must fast, lie naked on her back in bed and not turn her head:

> They told her how, upon St Agnes' Eve,
> Young virgins might have visions of delight,
> And soft adorings from their loves receive
> Upon the honey'd middle of the night,
> If ceremonies due they did aright;
> As, supperless to bed they must retire,
> And couch supine their beauties, lily white;
> Nor look behind, nor sideways, but require
> Of Heaven with upward eyes for all that they desire.

In the manner of *Romeo and Juliet*, Porphyro is from a rival household to that of Madeline. During a feast of 'argent revelry' on St Agnes' Eve, he enters her home, with its Gothic chapel and baronial hall, and with the assistance of her aged attendant Angela (the equivalent of Juliet's nurse) hides in a closet in her bedroom. By the light of the moon shining through a triple-arched casement window 'garlanded with carven imageries / Of fruits, and flowers, and bunches of knot-grass', he peeps out to see her saying her bedtime prayers and then getting undressed:

> Full on this casement shone the wintry moon,
> And threw warm gules on Madeline's fair breast,
> As down she knelt for heaven's grace and boon;
> Rose-bloom fell on her hands, together prest,
> And on her silver cross soft amethyst,
> And on her hair a glory, like a saint:
> She seem'd a splendid angel, newly drest,
> Save wings, for heaven: – Porphyro grew faint:
> She knelt, so pure a thing, so free from mortal taint.

> Anon his heart revives: her vespers done,
> Of all its wreathed pearls her hair she frees;

Unclasps her warmed jewels one by one;
Loosens her fragrant boddice; by degrees
Her rich attire creeps rustling to her knees:
Half-hidden, like a mermaid in sea-weed,
Pensive awhile she dreams awake, and sees,
In fancy, fair St Agnes in her bed,
But dares not look behind, or all the charm is fled.

Stirred by the sight of Madeline's empty dress on the floor
and her soft breathing as she sleeps, Porphyro whisks an exotic
feast out of the closet:

And still she slept an azure-lidded sleep,
In blanched linen, smooth, and lavender'd,
While he from forth the closet brought a heap
Of candied apple, quince, and plum, and gourd;
With jellies soother than the creamy curd,
And lucent syrops, tinct with cinnamon;
Manna and dates, in argosy transferr'd
From Fez; and spiced dainties, every one,
From silken Samarcand to cedar'd Lebanon.

His calculation is that the food will be seductive, since the need
to fast has kept her from the feast downstairs. He then proceeds
to serenade her with a rendition of 'La belle dame sans merci'.
When she opens her eyes, at first she still believes that she is
in her dream, but then the mortal Porphyro seems a pale thing
in comparison to the dream figure. She asks him to become
the 'immortal' of the dream again, so he takes advantage of
the moment:

Beyond a mortal man impassion'd far
At these voluptuous accents, he arose

> Ethereal, flush'd, and like a throbbing star
> Seen mid the sapphire heaven's deep repose;
> Into her dream he melted, as the rose
> Blendeth its odour with the violet –
> Solution sweet: meantime the frost-wind blows
> Like Love's alarum pattering the sharp sleet
> Against the window-panes; St Agnes' moon hath set.

Keats at one point revised his original draft of this stanza to make it more sexually explicit. Porphyro encircles Madeline's body as she speaks: 'See while she speaks his arms encroaching slow / Have zon'd her, heart to heart'. Richard Woodhouse objected to this. He thought that the original version could be read as if it suggested that Porphyro merely persuaded Madeline to run off with him, without having sex before marriage. 'But, as it is now altered,' he remarked to Taylor, 'as soon as M. has confessed her love, P. winds by degrees his arm round her, presses breast to breast, and acts all the acts of a bonâ fide husband, while she fancies she is only playing the part of a Wife in a dream.' This, Woodhouse feared, might 'render the poem unfit for ladies'. When he put this to Keats, he got a robust reply:

> He says he does not want ladies to read his poetry: that he writes for men – and that if in the former poem [i.e. the first draft] there was an opening for doubt what took place, it was his fault for not writing clearly and comprehensibly – that he would despise a man who would be such a eunuch in sentiment as to leave a maid, with that Character about her, in such a situation: and should despise himself to write about it.

Keats was not being entirely serious here – Woodhouse describes his response as 'rhodomontade', bluster. He left it to Taylor and Hessey to decide which version to publish. They reverted to the original, but even in this version it is pretty clear that Porphyro and Madeline are having sex: 'arose', 'flush'd', 'throbbing' and 'melted' leave little to the imagination. However, as in the movies produced under the Hays code when Fitzgerald was working in Hollywood, the camera pans away to the sleet pattering against the casement. To a modern sensibility, the problem is not so much the sex as the fact that Porphyro has tricked Madeline into it, using the legend of St Agnes' Eve in the manner of a date rapist's Rohypnol.

More profoundly, Madeline's dream is like Keats's account of Adam's in *Paradise Lost*: she awakes and finds it true. She and Porphyro slip out of the house, fleeing away into the storm. She has found her future husband. But so as not to end on a note of easeful romance, Keats revised his final stanza by bringing back old Angela and making her die 'palsy-twitched, with meagre face deform'. Though sexual passion warms the core of the poem, the night begins and ends with cold. 'The Eve of St Agnes' was written at a time when Keats was wrestling with extreme emotions. With love and death.

Madeline undressing as moonlight shines in 'warm gules' through
the casement: engraving after painting by John Everett Millais,
exhibited at the Royal Academy in 1863. Millais' model was his wife
Effie. To set the scene, he took her to the great Jacobean manor house,
Knole in Kent, and stood her in front of a bed in which
King James I was supposed to have slept.

Scott Fitzgerald also loved a casement: 'The wind shivered
over the leaves, over the white casements – then as if it was
beauty it could not stand, jumped out the window and
climbed down from the cornice on the corner.'

10

'OR IF THY MISTRESS SOME RICH ANGER SHOWS'

Scott and Zelda on the cover of *Hearst's International* (1923)

Fitzgerald cashed in on his celebrity by writing story after story and accepting numerous commissions for newspaper pieces. In May 1923 he and Zelda appeared on the front cover of *Hearst's International*, to mark his signing of a deal to give them first option on all his new fiction. Mrs F. Scott Fitzgerald was described as the person who started the flapper movement, her husband as the best-loved novelist of the younger generation. Magazine readers lapped up stories about fortune and fame. He wrote stories with titles such as 'The Popular Girl' and

'Rags Martin-Jones and the Pr-nce of W-les'. The association of his name with conspicuous expenditure was cemented by the title that was highlighted on the front cover of H. L. Mencken's magazine *The Smart Set* in June 1922: 'The Diamond as Big as the Ritz', the flash headline describing it as 'A Complete Novelette by the Author of "The Beautiful and Damned"'.

They had gone briefly to New York in March 1922 for the publication of *The Beautiful and Damned*. While they were there, Zelda had an abortion because she did not want a second child so soon. In his ledger, Scott merely recorded 'Zelda & her abortionist'. In a much later notebook entry, he was more explicit: 'His son went down the toilet of the XXXX hotel after Dr X – Pills.' By that time, he felt resentment towards Zelda that she had never given him a son.

His second novel, meanwhile, was born into the world to a more muted reception than that of *This Side of Paradise*. Fitzgerald's name and a strong publicity campaign helped it to sell 50,000 copies, but the critical reception was epitomized by a newspaper review headline that reads 'FITZGERALD'S LATEST NOT FOR ALL PALATES – "The Beautiful and Damned" a Story of Deterioration, Brilliantly Written'. Like many readers, the reviewer for the *New York Tribune* was at once 'surprised, amused, and vexed' by the novel. The three layers of his headline chart the sense of disappointment. In large type: 'An Ironic Story of a "Flapper"' – flappers were what was wanted from Fitzgerald, but not necessarily ironically portrayed ones. Below, in slightly smaller type: 'A Man and a Maid Tread The Maze of Modern Life' – promising, answering to the public image of Fitzgerald as the voice of the post-war era to which in the collection of tales published later that year he would affix the name *The Jazz Age*. Descending, in smaller type still and a less bold face, to: 'F. Scott Fitzgerald, in His Latest Novel, "The Beautiful and Damned", Satirizes Modernity'.

The trouble was, the novel gave the appearance of glamorizing and satirizing at the same time, a difficult act to pull off, and one that Fitzgerald would achieve only when he developed the less flashy prose style and narrative techniques of *The Great Gatsby*.

Bunny Wilson, whom Fitzgerald would call his 'intellectual conscience', sent his review to his friend in advance. It proposed that two of the three principal influences shaping Fitzgerald's work were his Irishness and the Midwest. Hence his status as an outsider looking in, anatomizing the modernity of New York with a mixture of longing and disgust. Liquor, said Wilson, was the third influence. Fitzgerald asked him not to print that claim, even as he acknowledged that it was true. He also told Wilson that 'the most enormous influence on me in the four + ½ years since I met her has been the complete fine and full-hearted selfishness and chill-mindedness of Zelda'. Wilson took out the reference to alcohol; he did not add any mention of Zelda. His unsigned review-essay quoted a remark of the poet Edna St Vincent Millay, his lover at the time, anticipating the title of the story that would soon appear in *The Smart Set*: Fitzgerald resembled 'a stupid old woman with whom someone has left a diamond' – an old woman who loved showing off her jewel and who caused amazement that someone so stupid should possess something so beautiful. This gave Wilson the cue for the judgment that 'he has been given imagination without intellectual control of it; he has been given the desire for beauty without an aesthetic ideal; and he has been given a gift for expression without very many ideas to express'. This was harsh but penetrating. They were, however, good enough friends for Scott and Zelda to roar with laughter at Wilson's burlesque of the novel's description of the final meeting between Anthony Patch and his friend Maury Noble: 'It seemed to Anthony that Maury's eyes had a fixed glassy stare; his legs moved stiffly as he walked and when he spoke his voice had no life in it. When Anthony came nearer, he saw that Maury was dead!'

They made a more permanent move back to New York in October, just before Scottie's first birthday. Renting a house in Great Neck on Long Island, they embarked on a year of drinking and partying. The North Shore of the island was known as the Gold Coast. It was where millionaires built gaudy retreats in the style of French chateaux and mingled with movie stars and Broadway producers. The Fitzgeralds began to move in a new set. They were befriended by Gene Buck, songwriter and assistant to Florenz Ziegfeld, impresario of the Follies, and Ring Lardner, the best-paid sports columnist in the land, whose house had a view of the vast estate of Herbert Bayard Swope, executive editor of the *New York World* and party-giver extraordinaire.

In the course of their year in Great Neck, the Fitzgeralds spent $36,000. This was rather more than Scott's earnings of just under $29,000 (mainly from the stories for *Hearst's*, the sale of the movie rights for *This Side of Paradise* and an advance on a promised third novel). In a magazine article called 'How to Live on $36,000 a Year' – which would be the equivalent of an article today headed 'How to Live on Half a Million Dollars a Year' – Fitzgerald boasted jokingly, 'I had just received a large check from the movies and I felt a little patronizing towards the millionaires riding down Fifth Avenue in the limousines – because my income had a way of doubling every month.' Money, he believed, had to be spent, 'So we went to wait there until enough money accumulated for a trip abroad.' He and Zelda were so good at spending money that within six months of writing this article he found himself writing a follow-up called 'How to Live on Practically Nothing a Year'.

By then, they had left Long Island for France, seeking a quieter and less costly lifestyle that would enable Scott to concentrate on the new novel. The absence of Prohibition was also an attraction. The latest moneymaking scheme had failed. Moving in the theatrical crowd, Fitzgerald had come up with the idea of making serious dollars by writing a play. He dashed off a comedy called *The Vegetable, or from President to Postman,* in which a postman with the simple ambition of being the best postman in the world is held back by his wife's obsession with money. There is mild resentment towards Zelda in the joke: a postman is, after all, a man of letters. In the second act, he has a drunken fantasy of becoming president of the United States – Fitzgerald's attempt at a satire on the political class. The play bombed at its try-out in New Jersey; Zelda said that it flopped 'as flat as one of Aunt Jemima's pancakes'. It was, however, published by Scribner's with an explanatory epigraph on the title page: 'Any man who doesn't want to get on in the world, to make a million dollars, and maybe even park his toothbrush in the White House, hasn't got as much to him as a good dog has – he's nothing more or less than a vegetable.' For once, Bunny Wilson's judgment was trumped by his affection: he described the play as the best American comedy ever written and tried without success to generate interest in it among the theatrical producers he had got to know during his latest affair, which was with a glamorous and talented young actress called Mary Blair.

*

Early in 1924 Fitzgerald wrote a mischievous essay that was syndicated in various newspapers under such titles as 'Making Monogamy Work' and 'Why Blame It on the Poor Kiss if the Girl Veteran of Many Petting Parties Is Prone to Affairs After Marriage?' A series of subheadings whetted the reader's appetite: 'Utilizing Jealousy As "the Greatest Prop to Love" – Most

Potent Factor in Matrimony – The Mooted Effects of the "Petting Party" – Racial Experience With the Mating Instinct – the Baffling Formula of "Intellectual Compatability" – Essentials to Successful Matches – The Roving Tendency'. Fitzgerald argues that the 'racial experience' of his culture – as opposed, he implies, to cultures where polygamy is practised – has been that monogamy is the simplest solution to the problem of 'the mating instinct'. But monogamy is cultural, not natural. And the fact is that, 'despite the angry denials of thousands of pew-holders', more often than not at least one party within a marriage is unfaithful. The best way of dealing with this difficulty, he suggests, is for both parties to start seeing other people, thus torturing each other into mad jealousy, at which point they will 'decide that the only sensible course was to remain always together'.

The theory did not work out in practice. That May they sailed to Europe on a liquor-free ship, accompanied by seventeen pieces of luggage, '100 feet of copper screen against the mosquitoes' and a complete set of the *Encyclopaedia Britannica*, for which Fitzgerald owed Scribner's $700. After a brief stop in Paris, where they met the wealthy Gerald and Sara Murphy, who would eventually introduce them to a new world of sophistication, they headed south to Hyères on the Riviera. Fitzgerald absorbed himself in biographies of Byron and Shelley, fellow Romantics who had come in exile to the Mediterranean. Then they moved along the azure coast to Saint-Raphaël, where they rented Villa Marie, a 'clean, cool villa' in Valescure, a suburb perched above the town, with a view from Scott's workroom of Fréjus, famous for its Roman amphitheatre and aqueduct.

His ledger entry for July begins: 'The Big crisis – 13th of July'. The crisis was in the marriage. He wrote about it obliquely in his fiction, Zelda more directly. In her highly autobiographical novel *Save Me the Waltz*, the golden couple David and

Alabama – an artist and a Southern girl who are the thinnest disguises for Scott and Zelda – take a stormy first-class Atlantic crossing to Europe, then a train to the French Riviera. They find a house to rent in Saint-Raphaël. It is called Les Rossignols, the nightingales.

'The cream calcimined walls of the villa with its painted windows stretched and yawned in the golden shower of late sun', wrote Zelda in her forceful, sometimes forced, prose, accurately describing the Villa Marie. The husband is determined to stay in the cool of the house, beginning work each day after an early morning swim, wrapping up at four o'clock in the afternoon, in time for a return to the beach. Left alone for much of the time, Alabama reads Henry James – as Zelda did that summer – and befriends a group of French aviators. One of them, Jacques, looks like a Greek god. He resembles her husband, save that 'he is full of the sun', whereas David is a moon person. 'Haply the Queen-Moon is on her throne', wrote Keats in the nightingale ode, 'Clustered around by all her starry fays'. Moonlight and a person called 'fay' were prominent in the novel that Scott was working on in the villa in Valescure.

Jacques performs aerobatics above their villa. He dances with Alabama: 'He drew her body against him till she felt the blades of his bones carving her own. He was bronze and smelled of the sand and sun; she felt him naked under the starched linen. She didn't think of David. She hoped he hadn't seen; she didn't care.' Before long, her husband does see them together. Taking a swim during a break from his work, he looks back towards the beach and they are whispering to each other as a mistral stirs. When there is news of an aviator's death and Alabama thinks it might be Jacques, she cannot help revealing the depth of her passion for him. There is a showdown, a threatened fight. Jacques departs. 'I am very sorry for you', says an intermediary as she hands Alabama her lover's long farewell letter,

'We had not thought that it was so serious an affair – we had thought it was just an affair.' She tears the unread pages into a hundred pieces and casts them upon the waves, together with a picture of the charming and handsome aviator.

His real name was Edouard Jozan; he went on to a distinguished war record and the rank of vice admiral in the French navy.

Within a matter of weeks, Scott professed in his ledger that he and Zelda were close again. Jozan later said that there was never anything more than a flirtation, but in Scott's accounts to Hemingway of the affair, in *Tender is the Night* and in Zelda's unfinished second novel, *Caesar's Things*, there is high drama: a demand for divorce, a duel, the wife locked in the villa. Such details are probably the exaggerations of romantic storytellers, but there is no question that Zelda later confessed to Scott that he was justified in his anger over the affair, nor that in his notebook he professed that in September 1924 he knew 'something had happened that could never be repaired'. His notebook also contains a collage of snapshots of the affair: 'The table at Villa Marie. The attempt at adjusting swimming time. The aviation field. The garden in the morning . . . Night in St Maxime. Feeling of proxy in passion strange encouragement . . . He was sorry, knowing how she would pay.'

This was the summer during which he completed his third novel. Its burden, he said in a letter written at the time, was 'the loss of those illusions that give such color to the world that you don't care whether things are true or false as long as they partake of the magical glory'. To adapt the words of William Wordsworth, who so profoundly shaped the imagination of Keats, there had passed away a glory from the marriage of Scott and Zelda.

He had begun the novel two years earlier, back in the Midwest at White Bear Lake, Minnesota, while he was correcting the proofs of his second short-story collection, *Tales of the Jazz Age*, which he dedicated 'quite inappropriately' to his mother. He told his editor Max Perkins that he was planning a novel set in the Midwest and New York in the Gilded Age of the 1880s. 'It will concern less superlative beauties than I run to usually & will be centered on a smaller period of time.' It would also have a Catholic element. By the following summer, he had produced nearly 20,000 words, of which only two pages of manuscript survive. They are enough to give the flavour of his maturing prose: 'It was a dark sad face with bright things in it like children playing in a house of death.' Against that, he wrote 'SAVE!', though he does not appear to have reused the sentence. He evokes, too, the musical voice of a woman, a voice in which one suspects there is money.

He salvaged a short story from the draft. It was published in an American magazine in June 1924, the month when he and Zelda settled in Saint-Raphaël and he began to work in earnest on the revised version of the story, which now brought its upper-class characters from the Midwestern origin that they all share to the New York not of the Gilded Age but of his own time. In the end, the narrator melts back indistinguishably into the west. While the Midwestern setting was turned from a location to an origin and a destination, one thing that Fitzgerald did retain from the original plan was the centring of his story on a small period of time: though narrated from the retrospective vantage point of a two-year aftermath, the action of *The Great Gatsby* takes place over a single summer, that of 1922.

Fitzgerald said later that the boy in the short story he salvaged, which had the very Catholic title 'Absolution', was Gatsby at the age of twelve. The boy tells a small lie in the confessional, which prompts a train of events that leads to a kind of confession on the part of the priest. Father Schwartz's complete mystical union with God is thwarted by the sight and sound of beautiful Swedish girls laughing on the path beside his window. The beautiful blue eyes of the beautiful child in search of absolution are also a distraction.

To the puzzlement of the boy in the confessional, the priest blurts out that 'When a lot of people get together in the best places things go glimmering.' He starts talking about parties and amusement parks where everything twinkles. He tells the boy to stand in the dark under trees at a distance, looking at the lights of the big wheel – 'But don't get up close,' he warns, 'because if you do you'll only feel the heat and the sweat and the life.' Out under the moon, the handsome youths and blonde Northern girls will lie together in the wheat fields, while for the tortured priest and the wondering boy the bright lights will always be at a distance. Yet they will take comfort in the knowledge that 'There was something ineffably gorgeous some-where that had nothing to do with God.' The ground is laid for Gatsby as Fitzgerald shares the apprehension of Keats's friend Hazlitt in his essay 'Why Distant Objects Please': 'Passion is lord of infinite space, and distant objects please because they border on its confines and are moulded by its touch.'

The memory of distant times also pleases. In 'The Sensible Thing', another story that paved the way for *The Great Gatsby*, a young man has a brief romance with a Southern girl, but they do the sensible thing and part because he is not rich enough to marry her. When he returns to her house the following year, a place that once had 'a cloud of magic hovering over its roof and issuing from the windows of the upper floor' (i.e. the girl's bedroom) becomes mundane. The sitting room ceases to be the 'enchanted chamber' it was when he had been there before, his imagination colouring everything because he was in love. The girl agrees to sit on his lap and kiss him one more time, but as he kisses her he recognizes that 'though he search through eternity he could never recapture those lost April hours'. He is not granted the eternal youth, the always-about-to-kiss, of the lovers on Keats's 'Grecian Urn'. The Keatzian song of spring has vanished: 'He might press her close now till the muscles knotted on his arms – she was something desirable and rare that he had fought for and made his own – but never again an intangible whisper in the dusk, or on the breeze of the night.' 'Let it pass', he then thinks: 'April is over, April is over. There are all kinds of love in the world, but never the same love twice.'

Fitzgerald was still haunted by the memory of Ginevra King.

Scott and Zelda on the Riviera with Scottie during the composition of *The Great Gatsby*

11

'SHALL I GIVE YOU MISS BRAWN?'

Having told his brother and sister-in-law about the charms of Jane Cox and (without naming her) Isabella Jones, Keats reassured them that he enjoyed his solitude. He claimed that he did not want to follow their example and get married, however comfortable the home and beautiful the wife. 'The roaring of the wind is my wife and the Stars through the window pane are my Children. The mighty abstract Idea I have of Beauty in all things stifles the more divided and minute domestic happiness.' He needed the 'particles' of beauty to fill his life. He did not need domestic ties because as his imagination strengthened he felt more and more that he did 'not live in this world alone but in a thousand worlds – No sooner am I alone than shapes of epic greatness are stationed around me':

According to my state of mind I am with Achilles shouting in the Trenches, or with Theocritus in the Vales of Sicily. Or I throw my whole being into Troilus, and repeating those lines, 'I wander like a lost Soul upon the stygian Banks staying for waftage,' I melt into the air with a voluptuousness so delicate that I am content to be alone.

He can overcome loneliness by projecting his 'whole being' into the epic poetry of Homer, or the pastoral lyrics of Theocritus, above all the plays of Shakespeare such as *Troilus and Cressida*. These things seem grander to him than the trivial parlour conversations of women, 'who appear to me as children to whom I would rather give a sugar Plum than my time'. All that matters to him is his ability to write: 'The only thing that can ever affect me personally for more than one short passing day, is any doubt about my powers for poetry.'

Keats goes on to say that he is like a child in matters of the world, and there is indeed an adolescent defensiveness about the attitude to relationships on display here. He has met two beautiful and highly charismatic women. Sensing that he is out of his league, he vows to have nothing to do with women and to concentrate instead on writing poetry. But the quotation that comes to his mind is from a scene in which Troilus is consumed with as yet unconsummated desire for Cressida. The line preceding the quotation is 'I stalk about her door' and the character's following speech, which Keats heavily underlined in his facsimile of the First Folio, is one of Shakespeare's most intense hymns to the power of *eros*:

I am giddy; expectation whirles me round,
   Th'imaginary relish is so sweete
   That it inchants my sence: what will it be,
   When that the watry pallats taste indeede
   Loves thrice reputed Nectar? Death I feare me
      woon [Keats's emendation]
   ~~Sound~~ing distruction, or some joy too fine,
   Too subtile, potent, and too sharpe in sweetnesse,
   For the capacitie of my ruder powers.

The language of this speech – especially once Keats has altered 'sounding' to 'swooning' – is a template for that of the odes he would compose the following spring. Technically, they are renowned in the classroom for their sibilance and assonance; Scott Fitzgerald took imaginary relish in the sound of the nightingale ode, as if tasting its sensuous words on his palate. These features might be said to have their origins in this speech of Shakespeare's Troilus.

The reality does not live up to the dream: Troilus discovers that Cressida is unfaithful. He blames her, as men do, ignoring the fact that she has been traded as a commodity in the Trojan war and gives up her body only as a means of survival. Keats was shying away from love because domestic reality could never match the ethereal ideal of poetry. He was afraid that a genuine relationship would become as monochrome as the figure of Porphyro seems to Madeline when she awakes from her technicolor dream.

Besides, there was an overwhelming priority. Keats was a semi-trained doctor. His love and his duty were owed to his brother. The letter to George and Georgiana, finished on his twenty-third birthday, ends with Tom. He is 'rather more easy than he has been: but is still so nervous that I can not speak to him of these Matters . . . I cannot even now ask him for any Message – his heart speaks to you – Be as happy as you can.' This is Keats at his most real, projecting himself into his ailing brother instead of the fictional Troilus. Speaking from his own heart, he says that Tom's heart is speaking to George and Georgiana, asking them to be happy, or at least as happy as they could be, given the knowledge of what they knew to be all but inevitable.

In the small hours of the morning of 1 December 1818, he wrote to his little sister Fanny, preparing her for the worst: 'he is in a very dangerous state – I have scare any hopes of him'. 'Scare' is a – Freudian? – slip of the pen for 'scarce'.

Tom Keats died of consumption at eight o'clock that morning. John Keats walked the half-mile from the lodgings in Well Walk, Hampstead, where he had nursed his brother for the previous three months, to Wentworth Place, the home of Charles Brown. He probably posted his brief letter to Fanny on the way. He woke his friend with a gentle touch on his hand. He told him that his brother was dead. Brown said nothing. They both remained silent for a while, their hands locked fast together. Then Brown said 'Have nothing more to do with those lodgings, – and alone too. Had you not better live with me?' Keats paused, pressed his friend's hand warmly, and replied 'I think it would be better.'

Wentworth Place was a handsome villa, newly built in 1815 and divided into two, with Charles Wentworth Dilke of the Navy Pay Office in one half and Brown in the other. The postman with whom Keats and Tom had been lodging in Well Walk had noisy children. It was agreed that Keats would occupy the front parlour of Brown's half of Wentworth Place to give him quiet for his work. The postman carried down his library of books in a clothes basket.

Wentworth Place in Hampstead as it is today, now the Keats House Museum

Between Tom's death and his burial, Keats distracted himself by going down into the country to watch a prize fight featuring Jack Randall, the most celebrated boxer of the day, who defeated his Welsh rival Ned Turner in thirty-four rounds, a match of nearly two and a half hours. Describing the fight to his old friend Charles Cowden Clarke, Keats tapped his fingers on a windowpane in imitation of 'the rapidity of the blows of the one, while the other was falling'. After the funeral, he willed himself to move on: 'I must work – I must read – I must write.'

It is always hard when a loved one dies just before Christmas. The Reynolds family invited him for Christmas Day. But he had already accepted another invitation. This was from a widow called Mrs Brawne. She and her three children had rented Brown's half of Wentworth Place when he had vacated it for the summer walking tour. Now they were in a nearby cottage. The oldest daughter, eighteen years old, was called Frances, always known as Fanny. Keats had met them a few times, initially at the Dilkes'. In his next journal-letter to George and Georgiana, he casually mentioned that he thought her 'beautiful and elegant, graceful, silly, fashionable and strange', adding that 'we have a little tiff now and then'. Reverting to the thought of her two days later, he gave a not entirely complimentary description of her:

Shall I give you Miss Brawn? She is about my height – with a fine style of countenance of the lengthen'd sort – she wants sentiment in every feature – she manages to make her hair look well – her nostrills are fine – though a little painful – he[r] mouth is bad and good – he[r] Profil is better than her full-face which indeed is not full [b]ut pale and thin without showing any bone – Her shape is very graceful and so are her movements – her Arms are good her hands baddish – her feet tolerable – she is not seventeen [*sic*] – but she is ignorant – monstrous in her behaviour flying out in all directions, calling people such names – that I was forced lately to make use of the term *Minx* – this is I think no[t] from any innate vice but from a penchant she has for acting stylishly – I am however tired of such style and shall decline any more of it.

This sounds half-hearted, perhaps because Jane Cox and Mrs Jones were still on his mind. Or he might have been consciously or subconsciously suppressing the strength of his feelings. It does not sound like a very promising beginning. Furthermore, in a letter to America written on Valentine's Day, he merely said that 'Miss Brawne and I have every now and then a chat and a tiff.' And yet seven months later he told her that 'the very first week I knew you I wrote myself your vassal; but burnt the Letter as the very next time I saw you I thought you manifested some dislike to me'. As for Fanny, she described that Christmas Day as the happiest of her life.

Silhouette of Fanny Brawne, cut by Auguste Edouard
a few years after Keats's death

She loved fashion, she sang in a sweet voice, she was funny and sociable, she liked books – romantic novels, but also Byron's poetry (for its humour) and Mary Shelley's *Frankenstein*. Keats's financial prospects were poor – the business around Mr Abbey's control of his late parents' estate was rumbling towards the Court of Chancery – and his health was precarious. A persistent cough that troubled him in the new year was a worrying sign, given that his mother had probably died of tuberculosis and that he had nursed Tom through his last months. It was known that TB had a tendency to run in families. Mrs Brawne was accordingly cautious about allowing any public recognition of the relationship, though Fanny seems to have had expectations. On the feast day of St Agnes, 21 January, she copied out a light-touch love poem that Keats had given her. Whether she had visions of delight in her dreams the previous night is not known.

*

His moods swung wildly that spring. Sitting in the front parlour of Wentworth Place, he struggled with *Hyperion*, the draft of an epic poem about the Greek gods that he had begun the previous autumn. He deeply appreciated the friendship of Brown and of the Dilkes next door. At teatime, Mrs Dilke would knock on the wall to tell him that a brew was ready. He went to evening parties, relishing the cool taste of claret on the tongue and throat. He wrote punning letters to family and friends. He walked for exercise and tried his hand at cricket – only to get a black eye the first time he picked up a bat. But he worried about his finances: perhaps he should return to Teignmouth and become a country doctor, or even serve as a medical man on an East Indiaman. And on darker days he thought about death:

Why did I laugh to-night? No voice will tell:
   No God, no Daemon of severe response
Deigns to reply from heaven or from Hell. –
   Then to my human heart I turn at once –
Heart! thou and I are here sad and alone;
   Say, wherefore did I laugh? O mortal pain!
O Darkness! Darkness! ever must I moan,
   To question Heaven and Hell and Heart in vain!
Why did I laugh? I know this being's lease
   My fancy to its utmost blisses spreads:
Yet could I on this very midnight cease,
   And all the world's gaudy ensigns see in shreds.
Verse, fame and Beauty are intense indeed,
But Death intenser – Death is Life's high meed.

Tom's death still haunted him, and yet he recognized that to
have seen death at close hand could potentially make him a
better, an 'intenser', poet.

On a memorable April day, while walking on Hampstead
Heath, along the edge of the park of Kenwood House, the
estate of Lord Chief Justice Mansfield, he bumped into one of
his medical demonstrators from Guy's Hospital days, who
happened to be in the company of Samuel Taylor Coleridge.
They walked together for two miles and Coleridge, as was his
wont, talked. And talked:

> he broached a thousand things – let me see if I can give you a
> list – Nightingales, Poetry – on Poetical sensation – Metaphysics
> – Different genera and species of Dreams – Nightmare – a dream
> accompanied by a sense of touch – single and double touch – a
> dream related – First and second consciousness – the difference
> explained between will and Volition – so m[an]y metaphysicians
> from a want of smoking the second consciousness – Monsters

– the Kraken – Mermaids – [S]outhey believes in them –
[S]outheys belief too much diluted – a Ghost story – Good
morning – I heard his voice as he came towards me – I heard
it as he moved away – I had heard it all the interval.

Years later, Coleridge remembered the encounter:

A loose, slack, not well-dressed youth met Mr Green and myself
in a lane near Highgate. Green knew him, and spoke. It was
Keats. He was introduced to me, and stayed a minute or so.
After he had left us a little way, he came back, and said, 'Let
me carry away the memory, Coleridge, of having pressed your
hand!' 'There is death in that hand,' I said to Green, when Keats
was gone; yet this was, I believe, before the consumption showed
itself distinctly.

There was, he recalled, a peculiar heat and dampness in the hand.

*

Hyperion was Keats's attempt to advance from romance to
epic. He shared Hazlitt's view that Milton ranked second only
to Shakespeare in the pantheon of English poets. To write a
long poem in the style of *Paradise Lost* would be the next step
on the ascent of Mount Parnassus, home of the Muses. By
combining a homage to Milton with a further foray into what
in the preface to *Endymion* he had called 'the beautiful
mythology of Greece', he could write at a distance from himself
in a manner that was negatively capable rather than egotistic.

The thirty-three poems in the 1817 collection were rhymed.
The 4,000 lines of *Endymion* were rhymed. 'Isabella' and,
naturally, all his sonnets were rhymed, as were the unpublished
early works and the occasional poems he had slipped into his

letters or handed to friends. Having written 110 poems in rhyme, it was time to try his hand at blank verse, the medium of Milton and Shakespeare.

Closer to home, there were the examples of Wordsworth's *Excursion* and another work published in 1814, which was among the few books that Keats took in his knapsack on the Scottish tour: *The Vision; or Hell, Purgatory, and Paradise, of Dante Alighieri*, newly translated by the Reverend Henry Cary and published by his own firm of Taylor and Hessey. 'Nel mezzo del cammin di nostra vita', Dante had begun his epic of damnation and salvation. Cary abandoned Dante's melodious terza rima for the Shakespearean-Miltonic-Wordsworthian flow of blank-verse iambic pentameter:

> In the midway of this our mortal life,
> I found me in a gloomy wood, astray
> Gone from the path direct.

'Astray / Gone': by abandoning the chime of rhyme, Keats could play with the potential of the pause at the line ending. Those moments of suspension were one of Wordsworth's greatest gifts, ripe for imitation even as Wordsworth the man had become a political apostate. But Keats's musical ear could not do without rhyme altogether, so he found it internally within his lines and created rhyme-like harmonies through the echoing of his vowel sounds.

The academical Bailey recalled that one of Keats's favourite topics of conversation was 'the principle of melody in Verse': 'Keats's theory was, that the vowels should be so managed as not to clash with one another so as to mar the melody – & yet that they should be interchanged, like differing notes of music to prevent monotony.' Bailey exemplified this art by quoting the opening lines of *Hyperion*:

Deep in the shady sadness of a vale
Far sunken from the healthy breath of morn,
Far from the fiery noon, and eve's one star,
Sat gray-hair'd Saturn, quiet as a stone,
Still as the silence round about his lair;
Forest on forest hung about his head
Like cloud on cloud. No stir of air was there,
Not so much life as on a summer's day
Robs not one light seed from the feather'd grass,
But where the dead leaf fell, there did it rest.

'Shady sadness', 'Healthy breath', 'round about', 'stir of air
was there', 'cloud on cloud': later in the nineteenth century,
theorists of prosody laid down the rule that 'assonance'
required 'the repetition of the same vowels in the assonant
words, from the last accented vowel inclusive', but Keats's
melodies are subtler and more varied than this. Bailey was
closer to the mark in recognizing that the alternation of long
and short vowels was also a key technique, which he illustrated
by marking up the lines:

> "Dēep ĭn thĕ shādy sādness ŏf ă vāle,
> Fār sūnken from the hēalthy brēath of morn—
> Fār from thĕ fiĕry mōōn & ēve's ōne stār—

The movement of the verse slows with the monosyllables of
'eve's one star', bright Venus solitary in the sky at dusk serving
as a projection of the loneliness of the fallen Saturn. The
melancholy beauty of the scene is in its stillness, captured by
the image of a summer's day so tranquil that there is neither
the rustle of a fallen leaf nor movement in the feather-thin
grass.

Epic poems traditionally begin *in medias res*, in the middle

of the story. As *Paradise Lost* began with the fallen angels
plotting their revenge after the war in heaven, so *Hyperion*
begins with its pagan equivalent: the fallen Titans, led by Saturn,
discussing what they should do after being defeated by the new
and younger gods led by Jupiter. As the poem unfolds, there
are several set pieces inspired by Milton: the rebellious energy
of Hyperion as he flares through the darkness in imitation of
the blaze of Satan; a catalogue of exotic names of all the gods;
a palace akin to that of *Paradise Lost*'s Mulciber. At the same
time, Keats develops his own voice, particularly in a speech by
the character of Oceanus, who, in contrast to Hyperion's spirit
of resistance, argues for the need to accept that all things pass.
The Titans have fallen 'by course of Nature's law', not through
the force of their opponents. As they were not 'the first of
powers', so they are not the last. Oceanus offers Saturn a
narrative of creation and ripening:

> From chaos and parental darkness came
> Light, the first fruits of that intestine broil,
> That sullen ferment, which for wondrous ends
> Was ripening in itself. The ripe hour came,
> And with it light, and light engendering
> Upon its own producer, forthwith touch'd
> The whole enormous matter into life.
> Upon that very hour, our parentage,
> The Heavens and the Earth, were manifest:
> Then thou first-born, and we the giant-race,
> Found ourselves ruling new and beauteous realms.

The logic of his argument is that as the realm ruled by Saturn
and his fellow Titans is more beautiful than the 'Chaos and
blank Darkness' out of which the world was created, so they
must acknowledge the painful truth that

So on our heels a fresh perfection treads,
A power more strong in beauty, born of us
And fated to excel us, as we pass
In glory that old Darkness: nor are we
Thereby more conquer'd, than by us the rule
Of shapeless Chaos.

In *Endymion*, Keats had expressed the fear that 'the count / Of mighty Poets is made up; the scroll / Is folded by the Muses'. How could any English poet who came after the mighty Chaucer, Spenser, Shakespeare and Milton dare to rival their titanic power? Oceanus' narrative of change offers hope instead: if a principle of evolution drives divine and by implication earthly history, then literary history will follow the same course, allowing the younger generation to ascend Mount Parnassus. As Apollo replaced Hyperion and became the god of poetry, so perhaps Keats could outdo Milton. Then he would be ready for his match with the greatest of them all, Shakespeare.

Book three of *Hyperion* turns from the old gods to the new. Apollo confronts Mnemosyne, mother of the nine Muses, and learns from her that in order to become a god – the god of poetry – he must gain knowledge of not only heroic but also tragic things, 'agonies, / Creations and destroyings'. The argument is in line with that in the letter about the need to enter the darkened chamber and take on 'the burden of the mystery'. And yet, at the very moment when Apollo has passed his initiation and is about to become a god, the manuscript of the poem breaks off, mid-sentence. Keats had suffered a crisis of confidence.

'ALL BREATHING HUMAN PASSION FAR ABOVE'

On the last day of April 1819, the month in which he gave up on the first *Hyperion*, Keats ended one of his long journal-letters to George and Georgiana with a burst of poetry: two sonnets on fame and one addressed to sleep, but then a longer piece in the more complex form of an ode. This is a form of poetry that reaches back to Pindar in ancient Greece; the stanzas of an ode, known technically as strophes, are irregular verse-paragraphs with lines of varying lengths and a complex interwoven rhyme scheme that sometimes embeds a sonnet pattern within the block of verse. Classically versed eighteenth-century poets such as Thomas Gray and William Collins had followed the tradition of writing odes to a person, a thing or an abstraction. The latter published a collection of *Odes on several Descriptive and Allegoric Subjects* in 1747. Wordsworth's 'Ode: Intimations of Immortality from Recollections of Early Childhood' was, for Keats, the most notable contemporary revival of the form.

Keats had tried his hand at the form a year before, but not got beyond the first fourteen lines. This time, he made a breakthrough. He had found the form that suited his skill in harmonizing emotions and ideas in a soft-vowelled soundscape of varied tempo. This first major ode is addressed to Psyche. Keats learned from Lemprière's *Classical Dictionary* that she was a nymph whom Cupid married and that she was usually represented with the wings of a butterfly to intimate the lightness of the soul, which was the meaning of the Greek word *psyche*. By way of preface to the poem, he explained to his brother and sister-in-law that Psyche was not embodied as a goddess in the ancient Greek pantheon; the story of Cupid's love for her seems to have originated in the *Golden Ass* of the second-century CE Platonist writer Apuleius. Conscious of his own belatedness in the poetic tradition and eager to embody in verse the ideas about imagination (his version of the psyche or soul), Keats saw how apt it would be to make his own mind into a temple dedicated to the belated goddess. He told George and Georgiana that for the most part he had dashed off his lines in a hurry, but that he had taken his time over this poem: 'I think it reads more richly for it and will I hope encourage me to write other thing[s] in even a more peacable and healthy spirit.'

By this time, he was in love with Fanny, though he had probably not yet kissed her. He was ready, as the closing line of the poem puts it, 'To let the warm Love in'. The ode begins with Cupid and Psyche in the dawn of their love, their arms (and wings) entwined in a post-coital slumber that feels pre-coital. The atmosphere evoked by the setting has the freshness of morning dew (present in Keats's mind, to judge from his spelling of 'adieu'):

> I wander'd in a forest thoughtlessly,
> And on the sudden, fainting with surprise,
> Saw two fair Creatures couched side by side
> In deepest grass beneath the whisp'ring roof
> Of leaves and trembled blossoms, where there ran
> A Brooklet scarce espied

'Mid hush'd, cool-rooted flowers, fragrant-eyed,
Blue, freckle-pink, and budded syrian,
They lay, calm-breathing on the bedded grass.
Their arms embraced and their pinions too;
Their lips touch'd not, but had not bade adiew,
As if disjoined by soft-handed slumber,
And ready still past kisses to outnumber,
At tender eye-dawn of aurorian love.

Keats's judgment of his own work was impeccable: these are some of the best lines he had yet written. Sometimes in the past his compound adjectives had been either lazy or self-indulgent. Here they are delicately weighted: 'cool-rooted', 'freckle-pink', 'calm-breathing'. The risk that the reader might be lulled towards 'soft-handed slumber' is mitigated by rousing word choices ('disjoined' and the dizzying coinage 'eye-dawn').

Over the course of the next few weeks, Keats wrote the odes 'to a Nightingale', 'on a Grecian Urn', 'on Melancholy' and 'on Indolence'. Years later, his housemate Charles Brown gave a romantic description of how the first of these came to be written:

In the spring of 1819 a nightingale had built her nest in my house. Keats felt a tranquil and continual joy in her song; and one morning he took his chair from the breakfast-table to the grass-plot under a plum-tree, where he sat for two or three hours. When he came into the house, I perceived he had some scraps of paper in his hand, and these he was quietly thrusting behind the books. On inquiry, I found those scraps, four or five in number, contained his poetic feeling on the song of our nightingale. The writing was not well legible; and it was difficult to arrange the stanzas on so many scraps. With his assistance I succeeded, and this was his *Ode to a Nightingale*, a poem which has been the delight of every one.

Charles Dilke, who lived in the other half of the house, called this story a 'pure delusion'. 'We do not usually thrust waste paper behind books', he scribbled sarcastically in his copy of the biography of Keats in which Brown's account was quoted. Brown was certainly misremembering the details: the surviving holograph of the ode has only two sheets, with a clear progression from stanza to stanza. The ode with a confusing arrangement of stanzas – different in Brown's transcript from Woodhouse's – was that on 'Indolence'. There is, however, no reason to doubt that Keats did indeed take his chair from the breakfast table and write the poem on a patch of grass under a plum tree in the garden of Wentworth Place. Since it was written in the morning, it was a memory of the previous night's song of their nightingale.

On the last line of his first page of manuscript, Keats made an insertion and a correction:

spectre
Where youth grows pale and ^ thin, ~~and old~~
and dies

Haydon recorded in his diary that Keats said of this line that he was thinking of Tom, wasted thin by tuberculosis, never growing old. The removal of 'old' from the line also served to make it less imitative of a passage in Wordsworth's *Excursion* which haunted Keats:

While Man grows old, and dwindles, and decays;
And countless generations of Mankind
Depart, and leave no vestige where they trod.

The nightingale, by contrast, is an image of endurance: 'Thou wast not born for death, immortal bird! / No hungry generations tread thee down.' The nesting bird in the eaves of Wentworth Place will die, but its young will sing the same notes to future generations, just as the 'selfsame ~~voice~~ notes' were heard 'in ancient days by Emperour and Clown', and perhaps in biblical times 'Through the sad heart of Ruth, when sick for home / She stood in tears amid the alien corn'. The particular nightingale in Hampstead represents all nightingales: in this sense, the title in Keats's original manuscript, 'Ode to the Nightingale', is more apt than 'Ode to a Nightingale', as the poem was called when it was published, first in the magazine *Annals of the Fine Arts* (where the 'Grecian Urn' would also reach print) and then in the 1820 collection of his mature poems.

Keats wishes to escape what the ode calls his 'sole self', partly as relief from the sorrow of Tom's death and George and Georgiana's distance from home amidst the alien corn of Kentucky, but also out of his desire to avoid the 'wordsworthian or egotistical sublime'. In the opening stanzas, he toys with opiates or alcohol – 'a draught of vintage that hath been / Cooled a long age in the deep-delvèd earth' – as the means of escape, but then he suggests that instead 'the viewless wings of Poesy' will enable him to take flight with the nightingale.

Coleridge had talked about nightingales and poetry in that on-the-hoof monologue when he met Keats out on the heath; he had also contributed 'The Nightingale, a Conversational Poem' to the collection of *Lyrical Ballads* that he co-authored with Wordsworth (it ends with a repeated 'farewell', as Keats ends his ode with a repeated 'adieu'). There, Coleridge had written about the way that many poets had invoked the song of the nightingale in the context of the desire that their 'fame / Should share in nature's immortality' and their 'song / Should make all nature lovelier, and itself / Be lov'd, like nature!' This is Keats's aspiration in his ode, driving him towards the penultimate stanza in which he imagines how nightingales of old have 'Charmed magic casements, opening on the foam / Of perilous seas in fairy lands forlorn'. But then the very word 'forlorn' rings out like a funeral knell, tolling him back to his own forlornness, at which point he recognizes that his imagining of an immortality like that of the nightingale's song is but a dream, even a deception: 'The fancy cannot cheat so well / As she is famed to do'.

Keats had addressed these themes before, not least in the sonnets on fame written a few days earlier, but there is a new music to his language in the 'Ode to a Nightingale'. Instead of the Miltonic grandeur of the abandoned *Hyperion*, he finds a voice that is at once intense and conversational. His rhythms feel Shakespearean, as never before. The first phrase that he underlined in his pocket edition of *Hamlet* was 'I am sick at heart'; he had gone on to underscore such passages in Hamlet's soliloquies as 'O, that this too too solid flesh would melt, / Thaw, and resolve itself into a dew!' and such words as 'weary, stale, flat, and unprofitable'. This is the mood that he channels in the opening of the ode: 'My heart aches, and a drowsy numbness pains / My sense'. The rhythm echoes Hamlet's 'The heartache and the thousand natural shocks / That flesh is heir to' in 'To be or not to be', his perennially quoted meditation on mortality in general and suicide in particular.

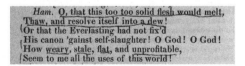

Keats underlines Hamlet's musings on death

Hamlet is literature's most famous melancholic. Ophelia describes his appearance in her chamber – distracted, dishevelled, wild-eyed and sleepless – in a way that suggests the symptoms of what Robert Burton in *The Anatomy of Melancholy* called love-melancholy. The *Anatomy* was one of Keats's favourite books. He annotated his copy especially heavily in the chapter on the 'Symptoms or Signs of Love-Melancholy, in Body, Mind, good, bad, etc.', where Burton gathered hundreds of references in ancient literature to passionate kisses and other manifestations of extreme passion. So, for example, Keats ran a marginal line beside a reference to an Arabian sultaness who thought a man (not her husband) so beautiful that she gazed at him for two full hours. On the opposite page of his Burton, he lingered over the following passage:

> *Dentes illidunt saepe labellis,*
>   *Atque premunt arcte adfigentes oscula.*
> [Often the teeth hurt the lips, pressing them tight in the act of kissing.]
> They cannot, I say, contain themselves, they will be still not only joining hands, kissing, but embracing, treading on their toes, etc., diving into their bosoms, and that *libenter, et cum delectatione* [lasciviously and voluptuously], as Philostratus confesseth to his mistress; and Lamprias in Lucian, *mamillas premens, per sinum clam dextra*, etc., feeling their paps, and that scarce honestly sometimes.

Keats put another line down the margin and underscored 'diving into their bosoms' and 'that scarce honestly sometimes'.

He also paid particular attention to Burton's chapter on how melancholy can lead to suicide. The first draft of the 'Ode on Melancholy' begins in Burtonesque vein with a death-ship that has the smack of Coleridge's 'Ancient Mariner':

Though you should build a bark of dead men's bones,
And rear a phantom gibbet for a mast,
Stitch creeds together for a sail, with groans
To fill it out, blood-stained and aghast . . .

Rejecting this as altogether too Gothic, Keats started instead
with an injunction against suicide: 'No, no, go not to Lethe,
neither twist / Wolf's-bane, tight-rooted, for its poisonous
wine'. As a trained apothecary, he knew the poisonous quality
of aconite, known colloquially as wolf's-bane. But no, he
says, deny death. When a fit of depression falls, indulge your
senses in the beauty of nature and submit to that intensity
of passion which Burton had anatomized in his chapter on
love-melancholy:

Then glut thy sorrow on a morning rose,
    Or on the rainbow of the salt sand-wave,
        Or on the wealth of globed peonies;
Or if thy mistress some rich anger shows,
    Emprison her soft hand, and let her rave,
        And feed deep, deep upon her peerless eyes.

She dwells with Beauty – Beauty that must die;
    And Joy, whose hand is ever at his lips
Bidding adieu; and aching Pleasure nigh,
    Turns to poison while the bee-mouth sips.

Delight and Melancholy go together because intensity of passion
consumes itself, so is perforce short-lived. Joy is momentary,
so always signals its own farewell. Pleasure turns to poison,
which may be why, as Galen, the father of classical medicine,
allegedly proclaimed, *post coitum omne animal triste est*, all
creatures are sad after sexual union.

In the months ahead, Keats would articulate similarly strong mixed emotions in the love letters he began writing to Fanny Brawne.

*

He claimed that the ode he most enjoyed writing was the one that he subsequently decided was poetically inferior to the others, with the result that he omitted it from his 1820 collection. Entitled 'Ode on Indolence', it celebrates the state of passiveness he described at one point in his long journal-letter to George and Georgiana:

> the fibres of the brain are relaxed in common with the rest of the body, and to such a happy degree that pleasure has no show of enticement and pain no unbearable power. Neither Poetry, nor Ambition, nor Love have any alertness of countenance as they pass by me: they seem rather like three figures on a greek vase – a Man and two women – whom no one but myself could distinguish in their disguisement. This is the only happiness; and is a rare instance of advantage in the body overpowering the Mind.

The ode describes the passing by of these three figures of Love, Ambition and the 'demon Poesy'. Keats is content to let them remain carved on a 'dreamy urn' while 'The blissful cloud of summer indolence' benumbs him, his pulse slows, 'Pain has no sting, and pleasure's wreath no flower'. The sentiment is the exact opposite of that in the 'Ode on Melancholy'. There, it is the very sting that gives the poem energy; here, 'the drowsy hour' and 'honeyed indolence' fail to arouse the reader's engagement. Keats did well to drop the poem.

However, he had more to say about the figures of men and

women 'on a marble urn'. Since one of his great themes – and his most ambitious hope – was the immortality afforded by art, he was compelled by the endurance of the art of ancient Greece.

In 1808, Benjamin Robert Haydon saw the Parthenon friezes that Lord Elgin had stolen from the Acropolis in Athens and brought to London. Haydon was riveted by their representation of human anatomy. He spent months sketching them and came to the conclusion that they were the finest artworks ever created. Three years later, Elgin offered to sell them to the British government. Lovers of Greece such as Lord Byron vehemently opposed the idea, denouncing Elgin as a vandal and a thief. Figures in the art establishment sneered that the marbles were Roman copies, not original. But Haydon was their champion. He argued the cause for five years and was eventually vindicated when they were declared genuine and a government committee agreed on the purchase. This was at exactly the time that Keats met Haydon. He wrote sonnets that praised his new friend not only for his own art, but also for his campaign on behalf of the marbles. In early March 1817, Keats accompanied Haydon to see them in their new home, the British Museum. Upon gazing at them, he compared himself to 'a sick eagle looking at the sky'. 'These wonders', he wrote in his sonnet 'On Seeing the Elgin Marbles', gave him 'a most dizzy pain' as he contemplated the survival of 'Grecian grandeur' despite 'the rude / Wasting of old Time'. The thought was almost too much for him: the marbles offered 'a shadow of a magnitude', an achievement so great that it could hardly be comprehended. Keats returned to the museum again and again to sit and contemplate the marbles. His eye might have been caught by an exquisitely executed figure on the south frieze of a heifer looking skyward.

'Who are these coming to the sacrifice?' Sources for the composite imaginary creation of the Grecian Urn: 'heifer lowing at the skies' on the Elgin Marbles in the British Museum, together with leaf-fringed legend, pipes and timbrels on the Sosibios Vase, and wild ecstasy from the Townley Vase, as seen by Fitzgerald in his copy of Colvin's biography

His visits to the British Museum also introduced him to Greek and Roman antiquities on a more manageable scale, such as the Townley Vase, a perfectly preserved neo-Attic marble urn dating from the second century CE, decorated in high relief with figures of Pan and followers of the wine-god Bacchus dancing in drunken revelry. He would also have seen Greek painted vases from the collection of Sir William Hamilton, which had been acquired by the museum. And engravings of Grecian vases were available in various printed portfolios. There survives a drawing or tracing of the Sosibios Vase, pillaged for the Louvre by Napoleon, which, according to Charles Dilke, was executed by Keats himself. Around its neck is a band of ornament in a leaf pattern.

The 'Ode on a Grecian Urn' is addressed not to a particular object, but to an imagined urn, with composite elements: 'that heifer lowing at the skies' is from the Elgin Marbles, the 'leaf-fringed legend' from the Sosibios Vase and the 'pipes and timbrels' and 'wild ecstasy' from the Townley. Sidney Colvin surveyed this array of sources in his biography of Keats, then explained that 'the sculptured forms of such an imaginary antique, visualized in full intensity before his mind's eye, have set his thoughts to work, on the one hand asking himself what living, human scenes of ancient custom and worship lay behind them, and on the other speculating upon the abstract relations of plastic art to life'. Colvin was unstinting in his praise: 'The second and third stanzas express with full felicity and insight the differences between life, which pays for its unique prerogative of reality by satiety and decay' – a theme that picks up where the 'Ode on Melancholy' left off – 'and art, which in forfeiting reality gains in exchange permanence of beauty, and the power to charm by imagined experiences even richer than the real.'

Had Scott Fitzgerald been in the habit of marking his books, as Keats was, he would have highlighted this passage in his copy of Colvin's Keats. The two stanzas in question were, for him, the high point of Keats's art and the chief inspiration for his repeated images of the 'perfect hour' that vanishes in life but endures in the lover's memory and the writer's art:

Heard melodies are sweet, but those unheard
    Are sweeter; therefore, ye soft pipes, play on;
Not to the sensual ear, but, more endear'd,
    Pipe to the spirit ditties of no tone:
Fair youth, beneath the trees, thou canst not leave
    Thy song, nor ever can those trees be bare;

Bold Lover, never, never canst thou kiss,
Though winning near the goal – yet, do not grieve;
She cannot fade, though thou hast not thy bliss,
For ever wilt thou love, and she be fair!

Ah, happy, happy boughs! that cannot shed
Your leaves, nor ever bid the Spring adieu;
And, happy melodist, unwearied,
For ever piping songs for ever new;
More happy love! more happy, happy love!
For ever warm and still to be enjoy'd,
For ever panting, and for ever young;
All breathing human passion far above,
That leaves a heart high-sorrowful and cloy'd,
A burning forehead, and a parching tongue.

Just a few months before he died, Scott Fitzgerald wrote to his daughter Scottie:

The Grecian Urn is unbearably beautiful with every syllable as inevitable as the notes of Beethoven's Ninth Symphony or it's just something you don't understand. It is what it is because an extraordinary genius paused at that point in history and touched it. I suppose I've read it a hundred times. About the tenth time I began to know what it was about, and caught the chime in it and the exquisite inner mechanics. Likewise with The Nightingale which I can never read through without tears in my eyes.

'WHILE HE FROM FORTH THE CLOSET BROUGHT A HEAP'

think the novel is a wonder . . . It is a marvelous fusion, into a unity of presentation, of the extraordinary incongruities of life today. And as for sheer writing, it's astonishing.

(Max Perkins to Scott Fitzgerald,
on receiving the typescript of *The Great Gatsby*)

Though the writing of *The Great Gatsby* belongs to the summer of 1924, its content derives from Fitzgerald's experience living in Great Neck on Long Island during the year and a half before he and Zelda sailed for Europe. Late in life, he scribbled a list of real-life correspondences on the end leaf of a book by the French writer André Malraux. Chapter one: 'Glamor of Rumsies + Hitchcoks.' Charles C. Rumsey, famous sculptor and polo player, son-in-law of 'robber baron' E. H. Harriman, was killed in a car crash not far from Great Neck, shortly before the Fitzgeralds moved there. They attended parties on the estate of his widow, Mary Harriman, where they met Tommy Hitchcock, a polo celebrity whose first name would be given to polo-playing Tom Buchanan. Chapter two: 'Ash Heaps. Memory of 125th Gt Neck'. There were indeed ash heaps between posh Manhasset, home of the old New York money (East Egg in the novel), and slightly less fashionable Sands Point (West Egg), where the Fitzgeralds rented their place among the new money that came from Hollywood and the west.

Chapter three: 'Goddards. Dwanns Swopes.' A mansion called Great Neck House, on which Ring Lardner looked out from his yard, was where Herbert Bayard Swope held his lavish parties. People weren't invited; they just turned up. Guests would sometimes stay for weeks, even months, in one case years. 'Dwanns' is one of Fitzgerald's many misspellings. Barring a missing apostrophe, his ledger for July 1923 gets the surname right: 'Parties at Allen Dwans. Gloria Swanson and the movie crowd.' Allan Dwan was a pioneering director, producer and screenwriter who often worked with Swanson. They are models for 'the moving-picture director and his Star' under the white-plum tree at Gatsby's party. It had to be a white plum tree, not a coloured one: 'We're all white here,' murmurs Jordan Baker later in the novel.

'Goddards' is a more sinister name:

> 'Civilization's going to pieces,' broke out Tom violently. 'I've gotten to be a terrible pessimist about things. Have you read "The Rise of the Colored Empires" by this man Goddard?'
>
> 'Why, no,' I answered, rather surprised by his tone.
>
> 'Well, it's a fine book, and everybody ought to read it. The idea is if we don't look out the white race will be – will be utterly submerged. It's all scientific stuff; it's been proved.'

The book to which Tom refers was published by Scribner's in 1920. Written by Theodore Lothrop Stoddard, it was called *The Rising Tide of Color* and was adorned with a garishly alarmist dust-jacket illustration and a strapline reading 'The Threat against White World Supremacy'. Stoddard was a 'scientific racist' who argued that, unless stringent immigration controls were introduced and elements of the Treaty of Versailles reversed, the white Western world would be overwhelmed by a tide of black, brown and yellow people. The book became an international bestseller.

Fitzgerald was perfectly capable of including correct book titles in his works, and using them for symbolic purposes. In chapter two, he cites *Simon Called Peter*, a runaway bestselling novel about a priest's adulterous affair, published in 1921 and enlivened by some very explicit sex scenes. It is exactly the novel one would expect to find on the scantily clad bookshelf of a love nest in a scene set in the hot summer of 1922. Nick Carraway flicks through it in the sweltering New York apartment as Fitzgerald's way of indicating that Tom Buchanan is having vigorous adulterous sex with Myrtle Wilson in the room next door.

It may therefore be assumed that he is adding ignorance to Tom's boorishness by deliberately having him get the names of both the author and the title of his racist bible wrong. If Tom had been reading more widely in the white supremacist literature that proliferated in the years after the First World War, he might have muddled up Lothrop Stoddard with the eugenicist H. H. Goddard, author of *Human Efficiency and Levels of Intelligence*, a series of lectures delivered at Princeton in 1919 and published the following year. Goddard used dubious psychological data to 'prove' that 'feeble-mindedness' was hereditary and especially prominent among immigrants.

By the time Fitzgerald scribbled his note about the sources of *Gatsby* in Malraux's book, his memory was addled by liquor. Now he is the one who gets the name wrong. He appears to have forgotten that Tom's outburst occurs in chapter one, not chapter three, and that Stoddard, not Goddard, was the name of the author of the source material for the novel's engagement with the race question. He should have written 'Stoddards'.

Why plural? Because of a detail in chapter three when Nick Carraway and Jordan Baker meet 'Owl-eyes', a literary man who is the spitting image of Ring Lardner, in Gatsby's library, which is panelled with carved English oak and modelled on that of Merton College, Oxford. They wonder whether Gatsby's books, like Gatsby himself, are real or fake, prompting Owl-eyes to take down a volume of the 'Stoddard Lectures'. Fitzgerald is asking his readers to imagine a row of fourteen volumes with 'Stoddard Lectures' on their spines. When Owl-eyes opens up one of the volumes, he will have seen the title page: 'John L. Stoddard's Lectures: Illustrated and Embellished with Views of the World's Famous Places and People: Being the Identical Discourses Delivered During the Past Eighteen Years Under the Title of the Stoddard Lectures'. This was a popular and respectable series of illustrated volumes about different parts of the world, lavishly illustrated with photographs. The author, John Lawson Stoddard, was the father of Lothrop Stoddard. Hence the plural Goddards, meant for Stoddards.

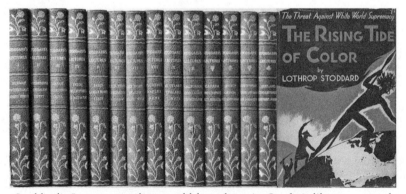

Stoddard's Lectures, as they would have been in Gatsby's library . . . and Stoddard Jr, the reading matter of white supremacist Tom Buchanan

Why is this important? In the case of the white-supremacist son, Fitzgerald is guiltily projecting onto the novel's most antagonistic character his own racism, which he revealed in the letter to Bunny Wilson written during that first trip to Europe, back in 1921 when Lothrop's book was creating a stir. Fitzgerald's self-description at the time – 'philistine, anti-socialistic, provincial + racially snobbish' – had been borne out by subsequent events. An avid consumer of the newspapers, he would have known that later in 1921 in a pro-segregation speech in Zelda's home state of Alabama, President Warren G. Harding said 'Whoever will take the time to read and ponder Mr Lothrop Stoddard's book on *The Rising Tide of Color* ... must realize that our race problem here in the United States is only a phase of a race issue that the whole world confronts.'

Fitzgerald was not a fan of President Harding, contrasting him unfavourably with the charismatic playboy the Prince of Wales (the future abdicator Edward VIII) in his memorable essay 'Echoes of the Jazz Age': 'It was an age of miracles, it was an age of art, it was an age of excess, and it was an age of satire. A Stuffed Shirt, squirming to blackmail in a lifelike way, sat upon the throne of the United States; a stylish young man hurried over to represent to us the throne of England.' Closer to home, he would also have known that in 1923, at exactly the time he was signed up by *Hearst's International*, the magazine published an investigation revealing that Lothrop Stoddard was a member of the Ku Klux Klan. The leaders of the KKK advised that every Klansman should read his book.

Anti-Semitism was endemic to the racism of the age. In the draft manuscript of the novel, Tom Buchanan sneers in passing, 'one Jew is all right, but when you get a crowd of them . . .' Lothrop Stoddard denounced *Hearst's International* as a 'radical-Jew outfit' that was out to get him. This was ironic, because his father was notable as an early Zionist. Owl-eyes pulls volume one of the Stoddard Lectures off Gatsby's shelf, but the most celebrated passage of the series came in volume two. In the section on Jerusalem, Stoddard proposed what he called 'a final solution of the "Eastern Question"'. He suggested that the world powers should gather together and resolve to restore the Jews to their historic homeland:

> Conceive that those Christian nations, moved by magnanimity, should say to this race which they, or their ancestors, have persecuted so long: 'Take again the land of your forefathers. We guarantee you its independence and integrity. It is the least that we can do for you after all these centuries of misery. All of you will not wish to go thither, but many will. At present Palestine supports only six hundred thousand people, but, with proper cultivation it can easily maintain two and a half millions. You are a people without a country; there is a country without a people. Be united. Fulfil the dreams of your old poets and patriarchs. Go back, – go back to the land of Abraham.'

Lothrop went on to disabuse any readers who doubted the ability of the Jews to become a nation and govern themselves by listing the great statesmen they had produced.

Gatsby has not cut the pages of his set of the Stoddard Lectures – in this respect, his library is only for show, as Nick and Jordan suspect – but Fitzgerald's decision to name this particular author must have symbolic significance. After all, Owl-eyes could equally well have gone to some other set of volumes betokening culture, a row of Shakespeare, say, or Goethe. By placing the older Stoddard in Gatsby's library and having Tom read the younger Stoddard, Fitzgerald establishes a deliberate and striking coded opposition within the novel. Tom Buchanan: White Supremacist. Jay Gatsby: Jewish Connection.

Zelda Fitzgerald said that the character of Gatsby was based on a neighbour in Great Neck: 'a Teutonic-featured man named Von Guerlach or something', who was 'in trouble over bootlegging'. In the 1950s, the man in question, a used car salesman who had by that time blinded himself in a suicide attempt, telephoned Fitzgerald's first biographer and announced that he was Gatsby. The identification is confirmed by a newspaper clipping pasted into the Fitzgeralds' scrapbook in the summer of 1923. Headlined '"THE BEAUTIFUL AND DAMNED" DOES NOT LOOK ALL OF THAT', it shows Scott, Zelda and two-year-old 'Scotty' on the lawn of their Long Island home, all three of them looking beautiful but not damned. The cutting had been given to them with a scrawled note that reads 'Enroute from the coast – Here for a few days on business – How are you and the family old Sport? Gerlach.' It must have been from Gerlach that Fitzgerald derived the term of address that Gatsby uses over forty times as he tries to represent himself as a proper Oxford-style Anglo-Saxon gentleman: 'old sport'.

The question of Gatsby's backstory troubled both Fitzgerald and his editor. When Max Perkins read the draft of the novel, his main criticism was the character of Gatsby himself. Congratulating Fitzgerald on his 'extraordinary book, suggestive of all sorts of thoughts and moods', Perkins singled out for particular praise the technique of having the peripheral character of Nick as narrator, the symbolism of the eyes of Dr Eckleburg, and the character of Daisy's husband ('I would know Tom Buchanan if I met him on the street and would avoid him'). But he found Gatsby 'somewhat vague'. He granted that it was probably Fitzgerald's artistic intention to leave the character 'more or less a mystery', but felt that readers would be dissatisfied. They would want to know more about the source of Gatsby's wealth than the mere fact that it came through his connection with Meyer Wolfshiem. Though professing himself mildly ashamed to be making any criticisms, given the 'general brilliant quality' of the book, Perkins proposed that the truth or fabrication of Gatsby's biography – his claims about Oxford and his war service, for example – should 'come out bit by bit in the course of actual narrative'. Fitzgerald responded that he didn't want to break up, or indeed sacrifice any of, the long narrative of Gatsby's past that was in chapter eight of the draft, but he agreed to add in some extra details making it clear that the money came from bootlegging.

Scott, probably not thinking about road safety, and Zelda in Italy with Scottie during the final revision of *The Great Gatsby*

After sending the typescript of the novel to Perkins, the Fitzgeralds drove down from the French Riviera to Rome. They were short of money again and the weak lire made Italy a good place to live cheaply. They spent the winter there, lodging in a hotel at 15 Piazza di Spagna. To Fitzgerald's delight, he could lean out of the bedroom window and see the house where Keats had died. In *Tender is the Night*, Dick Diver would follow in his creator's footsteps, taking a 'walk toward the American Express past the odorous confectioneries of the Via Nationale, through the foul tunnel up to the Spanish Steps, where his spirit soared before the flower stalls and the house where Keats had died'.

It was here that Fitzgerald reworked *The Great Gatsby*. He told Perkins that he had spent 'six weeks of uninterrupted work' handwriting extensive revisions on the galley proofs. 'Uninterrupted' is not strictly true. During their time in Rome, Fitzgerald was moved by a glimpse of the Pope and socialized with the cast and crew who were there filming *Ben-Hur*. He flirted with one of the stars, Carmel Myers, who was playing an Egyptian vamp. Another distraction from the revision of his novel was an incident in which he was beaten up in jail after being arrested for refusing to pay a taxi fare. This misadventure prompted Scott and Zelda to decamp to the calmer setting of the isle of Capri. On leaving Rome he dispatched the heavily marked-up proofs to Perkins, explaining that he had 'brought Gatsby to life', accounted for his money, and broken up the long backstory.

As always, he had heeded much of Perkins' advice, while remaining insistent about details that he believed in. Yes, it is horrifying that Myrtle Wilson's breast is ripped off when she is run over, but it was 'exactly the thing' that the scene needed; no, 'orgastic' was not a misspelling of 'orgiastic', it was 'the adjective from "orgasm" and it expresses exactly the intended ecstasy'. His main innovation was to move the account of Gatsby's meeting with the wealthy adventurer Dan Cody forward in the narrative. (The Malraux note gives 'Bob Kerr's story' as the source for Cody and his yacht – as a teenager Kerr, a neighbour in Great Neck, had seen an opulent yacht drop anchor in a bay in a place where he knew it would run aground when the tide turned; he had rowed out to warn the wealthy yachtsman, who hired him out of gratitude.)

Even in the final version, the air of mystery surrounding the

eponymous hero is retained. We learn that Jay Gatsby's real
name was James Gatz, that he was brought up by 'shiftless and
unsuccessful farm people' in North Dakota, dropped out after
two weeks at a small Lutheran college in Minnesota, and got
his first break from Cody on Lake Superior. From there, he
became involved in the running of alcohol across the Canadian
border via the Great Lakes. His shady business dealings are
conducted in close cahoots with Meyer Wolfshiem, 'the man
who fixed the World's Series back in 1919'. It has long been
recognized that Wolfshiem, unpleasantly represented as the
stereotypical Jew, was based on Arnold Rothstein, the racketeer
and gambler who allegedly did just that. We are to assume
from these connections that there is no truth to the rumour
reported early in the book that Gatsby owes his fortune to his
being a nephew or a cousin of Kaiser Wilhelm, though the hint
of a Germanic origin is no doubt derived from the element of
Max Gerlach in the creation of the character.

Zelda knew Gerlach as 'von Gerlach', but he wasn't really
a German baron. He gave himself the title to add an air of
grandeur when he set himself up in New York. This was not
uncommon among immigrants. Jonas Sternberg, for example,
arrived in America as the child of an impoverished Orthodox
Jewish family from Vienna, but reinvented himself as Josef von
Sternberg and became the most brilliant movie director in 1920s
Hollywood. Changing your name was more or less synonymous
with concealing your Jewishness.

Gatsby has the taint of racial impurity from the outset. Before
Nick Carraway hears about his origins in North Dakota, he
'would have accepted without question the information that
Gatsby sprang from the swamps of Louisiana or from
the lower East Side of New York', which is code for 'he might
have been mixed race or Jewish'. Tom Buchanan, furthermore,
says that Gatsby, Mr Nobody from Nowhere, making love to

his wife is only one step away from 'intermarriage between black and white'. Jews were regarded as Nowhere people, wanderers without a homeland.

The association of Gatsby with North Dakota – now one of the whitest states in the Union – might give the appearance that Gatsby is a regular Midwestern farm boy. But here are some facts that have been curiously neglected by Fitzgerald scholars. Gatz was a Jewish surname in the form of an acronym derived from the Hebrew *gabbai tzedakah*, meaning 'the communal official in charge of charity and almsgiving'. Goetz, Gotz and Getz are variants on the same family name. All these names were common among the Ashkenazi – the large community of Jews who settled in the Rhineland and elsewhere during the diaspora of the Middle Ages. Thousands of Ashkenazi Jews emigrated from Germany to America in the nineteenth century. Many of them ended up farming in homesteads on the Great Plains. Nearly a thousand Jewish individuals filed for land in North Dakota between 1880 and 1916, often through the good offices of the Jewish Agricultural and Industrial Aid Society. Few were 'shiftless', but most were 'unsuccessful', enduring great hardship and much prejudice. There were, however, many synagogues in North Dakota, where they could find a sense of community.

Beside the close connection with Meyer Wolfshiem and the signal provided by the older Stoddard's presence in the library, all this circumstantial evidence strongly suggests that – consciously or not – Fitzgerald was imagining that Gatz/Gatsby could have been an Ashkenazi Jew passing as a pure-blooded white man, though finding himself out of place when making his first attempt at assimilation by attending a Lutheran college. James is the anglicized form of the archetypal Jewish name Jacob. Had Fitzgerald given Jay Gatsby's original name as Jacob Gatz, it would have been self-evident that he was a Jew. In order to retain the character's mystery and to make him into an archetypal outsider, not one identified too explicitly with a single ethnicity, James is chosen instead, so the implication of Jewishness is left vague. In the imaginary pre-life of the character, one could suppose his parents changing Jacob to James on arriving in America, perhaps along with his father changing a Germanic Heinrich to an Anglo-Saxon Henry. We never hear his mother's name – and of course Jewishness was inherited on the maternal, not the paternal, side.

Shortly after the novel's publication, Fitzgerald told his Princeton friend John Peale Bishop that he was 'right about Gatsby being blurred and patchy'. 'I never at any one time saw him clear myself,' he continued, 'for he started out as one man I knew' – presumably Gerlach – 'and then changed into myself.' His own Irish ancestry and Midwestern origins also contributed to the sense of the outsider.

The Jewish element, it seems to me, is an essential part of the blurry patchwork that is Gatsby. On the penultimate page of the novel, Nick uses his shoe to erase 'an obscene word, scrawled by some boy with a piece of brick' on the white steps of Gatsby's now deserted mansion. We are not told the word: the blank makes Gatsby into a generic scapegoat for the havoc that has come to West Egg. But the emphasis on a defacement of the *white* steps of the mansion strongly suggests a notion of racial impurity. The attentive reader might well wonder whether the word was a derogatory term for a Jew, perhaps the one used by the 'shrill, languid, handsome and horrible' Mrs McKee in the seedy New York party scene: 'I almost married a little kyke who'd been after me for years.' Are we to imagine Gatz as another 'little kyke', who has been after the supremely white Southern belle Daisy for years? Was his ethnic impurity the reason why she of the 'beautiful white girlhood', the white dresses and the 'little white roadster', wouldn't marry him in the first place, choosing instead the bigoted WASP Tom Buchanan?

Myrtle Wilson replies ambiguously to Mrs McKee: 'Well, I married him.' The ambiguity is whether she means that she married the man in question or married someone like him who was perceived to be below her, whom she mistakenly believed was a 'gentleman' that 'knew something about breeding'. The latter is more likely: there is no indication that George Wilson is Jewish. But what he and Gatsby have in common is that they are men of questionable breeding each of whom unreservedly loves a woman who sleeps with the pure-blooded Tom Buchanan. At the end of the novel, they are the sacrificial victims, while the white and prosperous Daisy and Tom get off scot-free. As the chauffeur, the butler, the gardener and Nick are carrying Gatsby's body from the pool to the house, 'the gardener saw Wilson's body a little way off in the grass, and the holocaust was complete'.

The Jew as scapegoat: there is proleptic irony in that word 'holocaust', given the new meaning it took on after Fitzgerald's death, just as there is in the fact that Wolfshiem's front organization is called The Swastika Holding Company.

Lothrop Stoddard, apologist for eugenics, virulent opponent of miscegenation and colored immigration, member of the KKK, followed up *The Rising Tide of Color* with another book, *The Revolt Against Civilization: The Menace of the Under-man*. It was published in a German translation in the year of *Gatsby* under the title *Der Kulturumsturz: Die Drohung des Untermenschen*. Though the term *Untermensch* was already in circulation, Stoddard's use of it was a major influence on Hitler's racial theorist Alfred Rosenberg and his propagandist Julius Streicher. Equally, the Nazis were initially keen to adopt Stoddard Sr's benignly intended 'final solution' to the Eastern Question: whereas he proposed the voluntary patriation of Jews to Palestine, they sought to make it compulsory. When that proved impossible because of the war, they came up with their own 'final solution to the Jewish Question'.

*

Fitzgerald's list of sources for the later chapters of the book range from personal recollections to cultural references. So, for example, chapter four draws on 'Vegetable days in NY' while chapter five makes use of '*Mary*', a hugely successful Broadway musical of the time. Its signature number was called 'The Love Nest'. This is the tune that Klipspringer plays on Gatsby's piano when he is showing Nick and Daisy round the mansion. The chapter has begun with Gatsby meeting Daisy in Nick's cottage, with the intention that it might become his love nest.

There were other real-life correspondences that Fitzgerald did not mention in the list. In a letter to Max Perkins, he explained that Jordan Baker, close friend of Gatsby's long-lost love Daisy, was based on celebrity golfer Edith Cummings, the first female athlete to appear on the cover of *Time* magazine. He did not mention that Edith was a close friend of his long-lost love Ginevra. Gatsby's war exploits and his medal from 'little Montenegro' are closely modelled on the heroism of Sergeant Alvin York in the Argonne Forest during the climactic offensive of autumn 1918. York's exploits were much trumpeted in the newspapers and Fitzgerald namechecked him in his 1920 story 'Dalrymple Goes Wrong'. These two 'sources' are perfect examples of Fitzgerald's gift of taking a prominent Jazz Age type from the newspapers and magazines – the war hero and The Fairway Flapper, as Edith was known – and linking it to his own sense of loss and inadequacy: the memory of Ginevra, his disappointment at not having had the chance to fight in Europe despite joining the army.

The murder and the shabby funeral were 'invention'. Though Perkins was characteristically astute in describing the novel as a 'marvelous fusion, into a unity of presentation, of the extraordinary incongruities of life today', *The Great Gatsby* is not a documentary of the Jazz Age. The real advance was Fitzgerald's growth into Keatzian negative capability. *This Side of Paradise* was a modern transposition of the Romantic egotistical sublime; *The Beautiful and Damned* might be described as an egotistical satire (akin to Lord Byron's Romanticism that mocks Romanticism). In each case, the protagonist is manifestly a version of the author himself, whereas in *Gatsby* Fitzgerald is 'capable of being in uncertainties, Mysteries, doubts, without any irritable reaching after fact & reason'. The novel is romantic *and* ironic; Gatsby (and Nick himself) are to be admired *and* despised; Gatsby's infinite capacity for hope is delusional *and* to be wondered at. 'The test of a first-rate intelligence', Fitzgerald wrote some years later, in his reformulation of the principle of negative capability, 'is the ability to hold two opposed ideas in the mind at the same time, and still retain the ability to function. One should, for example, be able to see that things are hopeless and yet be determined to make them otherwise.'

Fitzgerald was adamant that, like Keats, he should be admired for negative capability and not merely for sensuousness. Matthew Arnold had claimed that Keats would always be remembered because his poetry was 'enchantingly sensuous', but with the qualification that there was perhaps nothing more to him than that: 'Many things may be brought forward which seem to show him as under the fascination and sole dominion of sense, and desiring nothing better.' Against this, Fitzgerald wrote in the margin of his copy of Arnold's *Essays in Criticism*, 'Later ages have entirely disagreed with this. It shows Victorian stiffness and primness in its most unattractive pose.'

He also followed Keats's edict that what the imagination

seizes as beauty must be not only beautiful but also true: true to that 'honesty of imagination' which recognizes illusion and doubt as well as enchantment and faith in beauty. As Fitzgerald wrote in his introduction to the reprint of the novel in the 'Modern Library' series of contemporary classics, 'the author would like to say that never before did one try to keep his artistic conscience as pure as during the ten months put into doing it'. There was no 'discrepancy from the truth, as far as I saw it; truth or rather the *equivalent* of the truth, the attempt at honesty of imagination'.

The claim may even be applied to the question of race: Fitzgerald was honest in confronting his own instinctive prejudice, but he was negatively capable in projecting it onto Tom Buchanan. Intriguingly, one reason for the virulence of Tom's white supremacism, toyed with by Fitzgerald but removed when he revised the novel in proof, may have been a fear that his own blood was tainted: in the original version of the novel, there is a reference to the possibility of the Buchanans' daughter inheriting a 'curse' from her father's genes and then an exchange in which, having murmured 'We're all white here,' Jordan Baker adds 'Except possibly Tom.' In his revision on the galleys, Fitzgerald cut the aspersion, but at some level he was acknowledging out of his own Irishness that to speak of an all-white America was, given the nation's history of immigration, a dishonesty of imagination.

*

In one of the first reviews upon the novel's publication, Carl Van Vechten wrote shrewdly that Gatsby 'invented an entirely fictitious career for himself out of material derived from inferior romances'. Gatsby's creator did the same. He took the adultery theme out of popular romance novels such as Robert Keable's

Simon Called Peter and raised it to the level of high tragedy. The novel has all the elements that Aristotle in his *Poetics* prescribed as the recipe for classical tragedy: a hero who is somehow greater than us, but not so great that we fail to identify with them; a sense of inevitability (cause and effect) combined with surprise; a unity of plot, character and thought; moments of reversal of fortune and recognition of disastrous mistakes; a climactic scene of suffering; harmony and rhythm in both structure and language; perspicuity in the writing; above all, the creation in the audience of a mixture of pity and awe, creating an emotional catharsis and a sense of wonder.

Van Vechten also made a smart comparison between Gatsby and the protagonist of Henry James's signature novella, *Daisy Miller*: 'the theme of a soiled or rather cheap personality transfigured and rendered pathetically appealing through the possession of a passionate idealism'. A key element of Fitzgerald's advance upon his first two novels is the device of having Nick as narrator. It was from Henry James and Edith Wharton that he learned the technique of writing scenes through the eyes of a narrator who stands on the fringe of the main action and who considers himself more important than he is.

Comparing himself to 'the casual watcher in the darkening streets', looking in on human secrecy, Nick Carraway is 'within and without, simultaneously enchanted and repelled by the inexhaustible variety of life'. This is Fitzgerald as well as Nick. As the critic Malcolm Cowley put it in a review of Fitzgerald's next novel: 'Part of him has been a little boy peeping in through the window and being thrilled by the music and the beautifully dressed women – a romantic but hardheaded little boy who stops every once in a while to wonder how much it all cost and where the money comes from.' This is Nick and it is Scott, but it is also Keats, as seen by W. B. Yeats in a poem that Fitzgerald shared with Sheilah Graham:

His art is happy, but who knows his mind?
I see a schoolboy when I think of him,
With face and nose pressed to sweet-shop window . . .
Shut out from all the luxury of the world,
The coarse-bred son of a livery stablekeeper.

Whereas Amory and Anthony had overt resemblances to Fitzgerald himself, in *Gatsby* he projected himself covertly, with a subtle mix of empathy and irony, into both Nick and Gatsby, the two outsiders. He had also been reading the novels of Joseph Conrad, where he again found great sophistication of narrative voice. And, he told H. L. Mencken, he had benefited from the 'masculine' influence of Dostoevsky's *The Brothers Karamazov*, which he read in Great Neck: 'a thing of incomparable form, rather than the feminine one of *The Portrait of a Lady*'.

The reference to Henry James's greatest novel is a reminder that the intimidating shadow of 'the Master' of modern fiction hung over the literary culture of the age. It accordingly gave Fitzgerald an enormous sense of pride when another modern master, T. S. Eliot, graciously thanked him for the copy of the novel that he had sent. It was inscribed 'For T. S. Elliott / Greatest of Living Poets / from his enthusiastic / worshipper / F. Scott Fitzgerald. / Paris. / Oct. / 1925'. Eliot read the novel three times, tactfully ignored the misspelling of his name, and replied: 'it has interested and excited me more than any new novel I have seen, either English or American, for a number of years . . . In fact it seems to me to be the first step that American fiction has taken since Henry James.'

Fitzgerald made his high ambition for the novel clear from the very beginning, writing to Perkins with respect to the aborted first version of 1922 that was going to be set in the Gilded Age: 'I want to write something *new* – something extraordinary and beautiful and simple + intricately patterned.' To be both new and beautiful, the book would have to conceal its principal literary influences beneath the surface. 'All you can get from books is rhythm and technique', he wrote in his notebook. The problem with *This Side of Paradise* was, he came to recognize, that it was 'A Romance and a Reading List' (as opposed to his friend and rival Hemingway's *The Sun Also Rises*, which was 'A Romance and a Guide Book'). *The Beautiful and Damned* was also too self-consciously literary, as Zelda smartly perceived in her review of friend husband's latest: 'The other things I didn't like in the book – I mean the unimportant things – were the literary references and the attempt to convey a profound air of erudition. It reminds me in its more soggy moments of the essays I used to get up in school at the last minute by looking up strange names in the *Encyclopaedia Britannica*.'

H. L. Mencken, as astute in his criticism as he was reactionary in his political and racial views, saw the improvement in the writing: in his first novel Fitzgerald was merely 'a bright college boy' with a good eye for character and incident, but slipshod in style and 'devoid of any feeling for the color and savor of words'. The progression to *Gatsby* was so extraordinary as to be barely imaginable. It wasn't the management of the action or the handling of the characters that made the novel so distinguished, 'it is the charm and beauty of the writing'.

That beauty would not have been possible without Keats. Fitzgerald said that 'The Eve of St Agnes' contained 'the richest, most sensuous imagery in English, not excepting Shakespeare'. That was what he absorbed in *The Great Gatsby*.

Gatsby is both a dreamer like Madeline and a pursuer of his ideal like Porphyro. When the thought of Madeline comes to Porphyro like a full-blown rose his 'pained heart / Made purple riot'. Gatsby in his youth has both a riotous heart and dreams that stimulate his imagination in a bedroom that, like

Madeline's, is flooded with moonlight shining upon a heap of clothes on the floor:

> But his heart was in a constant, turbulent riot. The most grotesque and fantastic conceits haunted him in his bed at night. A universe of ineffable gaudiness spun itself out in his brain while the clock ticked on the wash-stand and the moon soaked with wet light his tangled clothes upon the floor. Each night he added to the pattern of his fancies until drowsiness closed down upon some vivid scene with an oblivious embrace. For a while these reveries provided an outlet for his imagination; they were a satisfactory hint of the unreality of reality, a promise that the rock of the world was founded securely on a fairy's wing.

This lighting effect remembered by Gatsby from his youth anticipates that of the moon on the Sound when he looks out towards Daisy's dock, while also echoing 'The lustrous salvers' that 'in the moonlight gleam' in Madeline's chamber. Porphyro, anticipating Gatsby, stands in the moonlight and implores the saints to

> give him sight of Madeline
> But for one moment in the tedious hours,
> That he might gaze and worship all unseen;
> Perchance speak, kneel, touch, kiss.

The most striking parallel comes when, as Madeline sleeps in 'blanched linen, smooth, and lavendered', Porphyro 'from forth the closet brought a heap' of seductive 'candied apple, quince, and plum, and gourd', along with 'spiced dainties' from 'silken Samarcand'. Fitzgerald gives both laundered linens and rich silks to Gatsby when he from forth his closet brings a heap of shirts, coloured as brightly as Porphyro's fruits of the East:

He took out a pile of shirts and began throwing them, one by one, before us, shirts of sheer linen and thick silk and fine flannel, which lost their folds as they fell and covered the table in many colored disarray. While we admired he brought more and the soft rich heap mounted higher – shirts with stripes and scrolls and plaids in coral and apple-green and lavender and faint orange, and monograms of Indian blue. Suddenly, with a strained sound, Daisy bent her head into the shirts and began to cry stormily.

'They're such beautiful shirts,' she sobbed, her voice muffled in the thick folds. 'It makes me sad because I've never seen such – such beautiful shirts before.'

Madeline weeps when she sees the pale reality of Porphyro as opposed to the gaudily coloured figure of her dream; Daisy weeps because beauty – but, with finely tuned irony, also vulgar ostentation – is incarnated in Gatsby's silk shirts.

Though Keats said that he wanted his readers to assume that Porphyro and Madeline have sex, his language was, as Woodhouse saw, not entirely explicit. Similarly, Gatsby's act of getting rid of all his servants and bringing in others whose discretion can be trusted because Daisy has started coming round in the afternoons leaves the extent of their renewed liaison deliberately vague. The difference between the poem and the novel is that the lovers do not finally flee together into the storm of the world at the close of the narrative.

In the original typescript, Gatsby tells Nick that Daisy wants them to run off together. She has her suitcase packed and ready in the car. But Gatsby has explained that they can't do that, making her cry. 'In other words you've got her – and now you don't want her,' replies Nick. No, says Gatsby, that's not the thing at all: the reason is that it is not enough to have her, he must also have the belief that she has always loved him and never loved Tom. Gatsby wants her to go to Tom and tell him this. Only then will they return to Louisville and get married, as if they had done so the first time around. To which Nick replies with the most sensible thing he says in the entire novel: 'Daisy's a person – she's not just a figure in your dreams.' In 'The Eve of St Agnes', the figure in the dream melts into the real person; here the two are kept apart. Gatsby will never have the real person. All that remains, through Nick's narrative, is Gatsby's longing and his 'extraordinary gift for hope'.

*

To evoke that longing as opposed to the having, Fitzgerald's imagination turned from 'The Eve of St Agnes' to the odes.

He knew that he was under the influence of his favourite poet. Early in the novel, Daisy says 'There's a bird on the lawn that I think must be a nightingale come over on the Cunard or White Star Line. He's singing away – '. Her voice sings, as if in answer: 'It's romantic, isn't it, Tom?' 'Very romantic,' replies the unromantic Tom, not meaning it. We may assume that before stowing away on a transatlantic liner, this nightingale flew in from the leafy Romantic garden of Keats's ode. Writing to Scottie late in life, Fitzgerald instructed his daughter to 'Read carefully Keats's Ode to a Nightingale'. He explained that she would find there a phrase that would immediately remind her of his work: 'tender is the night', of course. Having found that: 'In the same stanza is another phrase which I rather guiltily adapted to prose in the 2nd paragraph on p. 115 of The Great Gatsby.' Then 'The question': 'When you have found what I refer to have you learned anything about the power of the verb in description?'

The lines in question are in stanza four of the 'Ode to a Nightingale', immediately after the phrase that eventually gave him the title for his next novel and the image of the Queen-Moon clustered around by all her starry Fays – Fay being both Daisy's name and that of the Monsignor whom Fitzgerald worshipped as a youth. The stanza continues:

> But *here there is no light*,
> *Save what* from heaven is with the breezes blown
> Through verdurous glooms and winding mossy ways.

As Klipspringer is playing 'The Love Nest' from the musical *Mary*, Gatsby turns on a solitary light in the music room. Then 'He lit Daisy's cigarette from a trembling match, and sat down with her on a couch far across the room, *where there was no light save what* the gleaming floor bounced in from the hall.' I have italicized the borrowed phrase, but the detail to which Fitzgerald drew attention was the verb choice. How can light be 'blown' by the wind? The power of the verb in Keats's description comes from the synaesthesia, the novel application to light of a verb associated with movement and sound. Fitzgerald's description is more naturalistic, in that light does seem to bounce from a gleaming floor. The verb creates energy and also answers to the bounce-back that Gatsby is seeking in his attempt to rekindle his relationship with Daisy. *The High-Bouncing Lover*, a half-echo of the 'Bold Lover' on Keats's 'Grecian Urn', was among Fitzgerald's many ill-chosen potential titles for his novel (along with *Among Ash-Heaps and Millionaires*; *Gold-Hatted Gatsby*; *On the Road to West Egg*; *Trimalchio*; *Trimalchio in West Egg*; *Under the Red, White, and Blue* – a particular favourite of his – and plain *Gatsby*).

The bounce is retained in the title-page epigraph, written in the style of a fragment from a Keatzian ode and attributed to Thomas Parke D'Invilliers, the fictional poet of *This Side of Paradise* who is actually Fitzgerald himself:

Then wear the gold hat, if that will move her;
  If you can bounce high, bounce for her too,
Till she cry 'Lover, gold-hatted, high-bouncing lover,
  I must have you!'

This is Keatzian not only by way of its compound adjectives and metrical scheme, but also in its gift of an impassioned voice to the lover, as in the 'let her rave' sequence of the ode on Melancholy.

The Keatzian glimmer returns time after time. The 'Ode on a Grecian Urn', which Fitzgerald read again and again, kept echoing in his head. Keats: 'What mad pursuit? What struggle to escape?' Fitzgerald: 'There are only the pursued, the pursuing . . . What was it up there in the song that seemed to be calling her back inside? What would happen now in the dim, incalculable hours?'

Gatsby first meets his Southern belle when he is a young officer in training in the South towards the end of the war. In this respect, she is Zelda. The elegiac tone of *The Great Gatsby* was inevitably shaped by her affair with Jozan that unfolded as Fitzgerald was writing the novel in the Villa Marie in Valescure in the summer of 1924. When a marriage is disrupted by an affair, the injured party may be forgiven for a nostalgic yearning for the time before it happened. Fitzgerald wishes to erase the affair, as Gatsby wishes to erase Daisy's years with Tom. Little Pammy is in the novel, neglected by her mother, not least because Fitzgerald, who was always a devoted father, was angry with Zelda for gadding around with Jozan instead of caring for Scottie.

Another effect of an affair is for the person who feels that their marriage is slipping away from them to think 'if only I'd married my first love instead'. Throughout the hectic first four years of their marriage, Scott and Zelda had given every impression of being soulmates. But what if his true soulmate had been Ginevra instead? When the imagination dwells on what might have been, instead of what is, the possibilities for idealization are boundless. Fitzgerald listed 'Memory of Ginevras Wedding' among his sources for the novel. His self-plagiarism of the kiss on the porch from the Ginevra-inspired story 'Winter Dreams' is only the most obvious instance of her shadow flickering across the pages of the novel.

> 'I wouldn't ask too much of her,' I ventured. 'You can't repeat the past.'
>
> 'Can't repeat the past?' he cried incredulously. 'Why of course you can!'

Disillusioned with Zelda, Scott repeats the past by recreating his first kiss with Ginevra in two paragraphs of limpid prose-poetry that are his equivalent of the second and third stanzas of Keats's 'Grecian Urn':

> One autumn night, five years before, they had been walking down the street when the leaves were falling, and they came to a place where there were no trees and the sidewalk was white with moonlight. They stopped here and turned toward each other. Now it was a cool night with that mysterious excitement in it which comes at the two changes of the year. The quiet lights in the houses were humming out into the darkness and there was a stir and bustle among the stars. Out of the corner of his eye Gatsby saw that the blocks of the sidewalks really formed a ladder and mounted to a secret place above the trees – he could climb to it, if he climbed alone, and once there he could suck on the pap of life, gulp down the incomparable milk of wonder.
>
> His heart beat faster and faster as Daisy's white face came up to his own. He knew that when he kissed this girl, and

forever wed his unutterable visions to her perishable breath, his mind would never romp again like the mind of God. So he waited, listening for a moment longer to the tuning-fork that had been struck upon a star. Then he kissed her. At his lips' touch she blossomed for him like a flower and the incarnation was complete.

The breathless lover on the Grecian urn will never get his kiss, but never lose his girl. Gatsby's tragedy is that he did not freeze the frame of his life the moment before he touched the lips on Daisy's marble-like face. With the kiss, the incarnation is complete. But momentary. For ever he will love; she will fade from him in reality as the memory of her grows and takes possession of his imagination. Breath is perishable; only in art can the unutterable vision endure.

For a moment, the narrative viewpoint has shifted from Nick to Gatsby. In the version of this passage in the original type-script sent to Max Perkins, Nick speaks of Gatsby performing a 'fantastic communication with space and time'. That is what Fitzgerald performs here. For Nick, there is an inarticulable echo of something in his own past:

> Through all he said, even through his appalling sentimentality, I was reminded of something – an elusive rhythm, a fragment of lost words, that I had heard somewhere a long time ago. For a moment a phrase tried to take shape in my mouth and my lips parted like a dumb man's, as though there was more struggling upon them than a wisp of startled air. But they made no sound, and what I had almost remembered was uncommunicable forever.

It would have been too easy to bring in Nick's own (rumoured) broken engagement here. But Fitzgerald was right not to do so. The 'elusive rhythm', the struggle for the memory to escape, the words that 'made no sound', have the effect of universalizing instead of personalizing the feeling. 'Heard melodies are sweet,' wrote Keats in the ode, 'but those unheard / Are sweeter'.

Dust jacket of *The Great Gatsby*

14

'WHERE ARE THE SONGS
OF SPRING?'

Fanny Keats regarded her childhood and teenage years under the guardianship of Mr Abbey as an imprisonment. George Keats had claimed his portion of the family inheritance before leaving for America, and John had lent him a proportion of his own. Now, the widow of their uncle, Captain Jennings, who had been one of the other trustees of their grandmother's estate, was suing Abbey over the administration of the trust. The remaining funds had provided Keats with a modest income, which was now blocked. Another trust, left by their grandfather for the benefit of the Keats siblings, was tied up in an investment that could not be drawn down and distributed until Fanny came of age in 1824. Keats, ever generous, had lent some money to Haydon, who did not repay it when asked.

In the face of these financial difficulties, Keats began to think again about becoming a surgeon aboard one of the ships of the East India Company. He suggested to Sarah Jeffrey, a young woman who had befriended him in the West Country, that it might be a productive move for his poetry. She told him that such a move would destroy 'the energies of Mind'. He disagreed: 'on the contrary it would be the finest thing in the world to strengthen them':

To be thrown among people who care not for you, with whom you have no sympathies, forces the Mind upon its own resources, and leaves it free to make its speculations of the differences of human character and to class them with the calmness of a Botanist. An Indiaman is a little world. One of the great reasons that the English have produced the finest writers in the world is, that the English world has ill-treated them during their lives and foster'd them after their deaths. They have in general been trampled aside into the bye paths of life and seen the festerings of Society.

But he wasn't really serious. In a letter to his sister Fanny, posted the same day, he said that he had given up on the idea. He did not really want to leave his friends in the London literary world. Or Fanny Brawne.

Another friend, James Rice, whom he had met through Reynolds, invited him to spend a month back on the Isle of Wight, where they could live cheaply and benefit from the sea air – Rice was an invalid. It was from Shanklin, on the south side of the island, looking out over the English Channel, that Keats began writing love letters to Fanny. He destroyed the first one that he wrote, because he felt that it was too much in the style of the most widely read romantic novel of the age, Rousseau's *La Nouvelle Héloïse*. His second attempt was hardly more restrained:

The morning is the only proper time to write to a beautiful Girl whom I love so much . . . Ask yourself my love whether you are not very cruel to have so entrammelled me, so destroyed my freedom. Will you confess this in the Letter you must write immediately and do all you can to console me in it – make it rich as a draught of poppies to intoxicate me – write the softest words and kiss them that I may at least touch my lips where yours have been. For myself I know not how to express my devotion to so fair a form: I want a brighter word than bright, a fairer word than fair. I almost wish we were butterflies and liv'd but three summer days – three such days with you I could fill with more delight than fifty common years could ever contain.

The language of the odes has worked its way into his prose: the poppies are a variant on the 'draught of vintage' in the 'Nightingale', while the image of cruelty and entrapment echoes 'Melancholy'. Keats also makes use of his favourite linguistic resource, Shakespeare: 'a brighter word than bright, a fairer word than fair' adapts *Love's Labour's Lost*: 'truth itself that thou art lovely: More fairer than fair; beautiful than beauteous; truer than truth itself'. In the flush of love, Keats seems to have forgotten that this is from a letter written by the bombastic character of Don Armado, in which Shakespeare is parodying the language of the kind of lover who declares himself his lady's 'vassal'.

Keats goes on to say that some lines from a play by one of Shakespeare's contemporaries have been ringing in his ears, reminding him of the horror of the thought that 'those sweet lips (yielding immortal nectar)' might 'Be gently press'd by any but myself'. More mundanely, he begged her not to dance with other men at parties. Always conscious of his diminutive stature and physical frailty, he was developing a jealous disposition, sometimes verging on paranoia about infidelity, that was wholly at odds with the confidence of his male friendships and his bantering epistolary relationships with other women such as Sarah Jeffrey.

They had reached an understanding before he departed for the Isle of Wight: she would marry him if and when he could afford to support her. Despite this, Keats was still uncertain as to whether his affections were fully returned. This first letter is addressed to 'My dearest Lady' and signed off 'Be as kind as the distance will permit to your J. Keats'. Fanny's reply, which does not survive, reassured him. A week later, he wrote to her as 'My sweet Girl' and told of his delight in receiving her letter. Then he let loose his ardour:

> I never knew before, what such love as you have made me feel, was; I did not believe in it; my Fancy was affraid [*sic*] of it, lest it should burn me up . . . Why may I not speak of your Beauty, since without that I could never have lov'd you – I cannot conceive any beginning of such love as I have for you but Beauty.

This time he signs off 'Ever yours my love – John Keats!' He took the next letter that he received from her to bed with him, and was dismayed in the morning to find that his body heat had obliterated her name from the sealing wax.

By the end of the month, his mind was full of her – stuffed as tight as a cricket ball.

> I am in deep love with you . . . the very first week I knew you I wrote myself your vassal; but burnt the Letter as the very next time I saw you I thought you manifested some dislike to me. If you should ever feel for Man at the first sight what I did for you, I am lost. . . . I am not a thing to be admired. You are, I love you; all I can bring you is a swooning admiration of your Beauty. . . . I have two luxuries to brood over in my walks, your Loveliness and the hour of my death. O that I could have possession of them both in the same minute.

His (ungrounded) anxiety about infidelity fed into the new narrative poem that he was working on by the sea. Entitled 'Lamia', it was a versification of a story he read in Burton's *Anatomy of Melancholy* in which a young man named Lycius marries an extraordinarily beautiful woman, only for the philosopher Apollonius, a guest at the wedding, to reveal that she is really 'a serpent, a lamia'.

Keats embroidered the story with his usual array of mythological and floral drapery. It begins with the Greek god Hermes striking a deal with the serpent: in return for him giving her the female form that will enable her to ensnare Lycius, she brings to material form a wood-nymph, also of great beauty, who has been rendered invisible so as to protect her from the advances of assorted Wood-Gods and Satyrs. The nymph appears, then fades, then is warmed by Hermes' hand, at which point she opens her eyes and 'gave up her honey to the lees'. She and Hermes make an escape akin to that of Endymion and the Indian Girl, Porphyro and Madeline: 'Into the green-recessed woods they flew; / Nor grew they pale, as mortal lovers do.' Like the figures on the Grecian urn, they are vouchsafed an immortality, whereas Lycius suffers the fate of mortal lovers, descending from ecstasy to arms 'empty of delight' – and to death. Psychologically, Keats was balancing his hope that he and Fanny might be united in the manner of Hermes and the nymph against his fear that she might be a snake – the traditional misogynistic image of woman as temptress – and that he might be left to die without her.

To have any chance of persuading Mrs Brawne to agree to a marriage, Keats needed money. Charles Brown arrived on the Isle of Wight with a plan. He had made a decent sum from his Drury Lane opera *Narensky* and historical drama in the Shakespearean style had the potential for even greater success – the Gothic fiction writer Charles Maturin had made £1,000 for his *Bertram*, starring the box-office giant, diminutive Edmund Kean. So why not co-author a play? Brown had expertise in plotting and construction; Keats in blank-verse iambic pentameter of the kind that could be turned into Shakespearean dramatic dialogue. Off they went:

OTHO THE GREAT
A TRAGEDY IN FIVE ACTS
ACT I
Scene I. – *An Apartment in the Castle*
Enter CONRAD

Conrad. So, I am safe emerged from these broils!
Amid the wreck of thousands I am whole;
For every crime I have a laurel-wreath,
For every lie a lordship. Nor yet has
My ship of fortune furl'd her silken sails, –
Let her glide on! This danger'd neck is saved . . .

It does not get any better. The lead role, Ludolph, son of
Otho the Great, Emperor of Germany, mad with love for
Conrad's sister Auranthe, was written for Kean. Keats's ambition was 'to make as great a revolution in modern dramatic
writing as Kean has done in acting'. 'If he invokes the hot-
blooded character of Ludolph, – and he is the only actor that
can do it, – he will add to his own fame and fortune', wrote
Keats to his publisher, willing himself into optimism. But
Ludolph's big soliloquy is desperately forced, the lamest pastiche
of *Romeo and Juliet*:

Auranthe! My Life!
Long have I lov'd thee, yet till now not lov'd . . .
O unbenignest Love, why wilt thou let
Darkness steal out upon the sleepy world
So wearily; as if night's chariot wheels
Were clogg'd in some thick cloud. O, changeful Love,
Let not her steeds with drowsy-footed pace
Pass the high stars, before sweet embassage
Comes from the pillow'd beauty of that fair
Completion of all delicate nature's wit.

Pout her faint lips anew with rubious health
And with thine infant fingers lift the fringe
Of her sick eyelids; that those eyes may glow
With wooing light upon me, ere the Morn
Peers with disrelish, grey, barren, and cold.

Keats and Brown tried to think of ways of making the play a stage spectacular – a scene with an elephant, perhaps – but then lost faith in the project when they heard a rumour that Kean might soon be leaving for America.

The house where Keats was staying was exposed to the sea. Rice had left the island and Brown went gadding about the countryside, feeling that he had done his part by furnishing his writing partner with the plot. Morning mists shrouded Shanklin, afflicting the lonely Keats with the damp. He decided to move inland to the picturesque medieval town of Winchester, where there was a library that could help him with historical details for the play, along with reading for his leisure hours. On the short crossing back to the mainland, the ferry was nearly sunk by a navy ship.

*

He loved Winchester, with its magnificent cathedral, fresh-looking surrounding countryside and quiet streets. 'The whole town is beautifully wooded. From the Hill at the eastern extremity you see a prospect of Streets, and old Buildings mixed up with Trees. Then there are the most beautiful streams about I ever saw – full of Trout.' He wandered down cobbled lanes, noticing well-scrubbed doorsteps and black front doors with brass knockers in the shape of lions' or rams' heads; he breathed the clean country air on the dry chalky downland on the edge of the city, valuing it at 'six pence a pint'. Reunited with Brown, he found tolerably good cheap lodgings near the cathedral, disturbed only by their landlady's son's screechy violin practice.

'The great beauty of Poetry is, that it makes every thing in every place interesting', he wrote. 'The palatine [V]enice and the abbotine Winchester are equally interesting.' The thought sent him back to 'The Eve of St Mark', an unfinished poem he had begun earlier that year 'in the spirit of town quietude'. It evokes a calm Sunday evening atmosphere as a prelude to a tale that remains untold. Scott Fitzgerald listed it among the poems of Keats for Sheilah Graham to read. His interest in it had been sparked by a lyrical passage in the novel that inspired *This Side of Paradise*, Compton Mackenzie's *Sinister Street*:

> It happened that year St Mark's Eve fell upon a Sunday, and Michael, having been reading the poems of Keats nearly all the afternoon, was struck by the coincidence. Oxford on such an occasion was able to provide exactly the same sensation for him as Winchester had given to the poet. Michael sat in his window-seat looking out over the broad thoroughfare of St Giles, listening to the patter and lisp of Sabbath footfalls, to the burden of the bells; and as he sat there with the city receding in the wake of his window, he was aware more poignantly than ever of how actually in a few weeks it would recede. The bells and the footsteps were quiet for a while: the sun had gone: it was the vesper stillness of evening prayer: slowly the printed page before him faded from recognition. Already the farther corners of the room were black, revealing from time to time, as a tongue of flame leaped up in the grate, the golden blazonries of the books on the walls. It was everywhere dark when the people came out of church, and the footsteps were again audible.

Winchester, with its ancient college and quiet nooks, was for Keats as Oxford was for Compton Mackenzie and Princeton for Fitzgerald. Furthermore, it was from Keats more than any other writer that Mackenzie and then Fitzgerald learned the art of both bewitching the present and summoning up the past through art:

> Michael envied Keats the power which he had known to preserve forever that St Mark's Eve of eighty years ago in Winchester. It was exasperating that now already the footfalls were dying away, that already their sensation was evanescent, that he could not with the wand of poetry forbid time to disturb this quintessential hour of Oxford. Art alone could bewitch the present in the fashion of that enchantress in the old fairy tale who sent long ago a court to sleep.

*

Keats had at last found a place that he could bewitch into the most serene of his poems, one which evokes an atmosphere that creates in the reader a sensation akin to the peace of sleep whilst simultaneously stimulating the sense of beauty. He was cheered not only by his own productivity – 'The Eve of St Agnes' and 'Isabella' both done, 'Lamia' half finished, four acts of the tragedy and a measure of progress on *Hyperion* – but also by the unseasonable warmth of the September air. He suggested to his publisher that 'Our health temperament and disposition are taken more from the air we breathe, than is generally imagined.' His mind was readying itself for a weather poem.

On the other side of the world in April 1815, a few weeks before Keats published his first poem, there was a huge eruption of the long-dormant volcano Mount Tambora on one of the Lesser Sunda Islands of Indonesia. The top was blasted off Tambora, reducing its elevation by 5,000 feet. The explosion was heard in Sumatra, over 1,000 miles away. More than 70,000 people were killed. Volcanic ash rained down as far away as Borneo and lingered in the stratosphere, causing global disruption to weather patterns. 1816 became known as 'the year without a summer' because of the perpetual cloud and vapours. Crops failed across Europe, leading to food riots amid the worst famine for a century. In early September that year, when Keats returned from the seaside to London, the noon temperature rarely rose above fifty degrees Fahrenheit. Now, three years on, there was at last a long stint of warm dry weather. Walking in the meadows and fields around Winchester, Keats basked in temperatures close to seventy degrees Fahrenheit as workers gathered in the first good harvest for years. 'The delightful Weather we have had for two Months is the highest gratification I could receive', he wrote to his little sister,

no chill'd red noses – no shivering – but fair Atmosphere to think in – a clean towel mark'd with the mangle and a basin of clear Water to drench one's face with ten times a day: no need of much exercise – a Mile a day being quite sufficient – My greatest regret is that I have not been well enough to bathe though I have been two Months by the sea side and live now close to delicious bathing – Still I enjoy the Weather – I adore fine Weather as the greatest blessing I can have. Give me Books, fruit, French wine and fine weather and a little music out of doors, played by somebody I do not know – not pay the price of one's time for a jig – but a little chance music: and I can pass a summer very quietly without caring much about Fat Louis, fat Regent or the Duke of Wellington.

He did care about politics – the restoration of the reactionary Bourbon monarchy in France (Fat Louis), the dissipation of the very fat Prince Regent during the madness of King George, the role of the Duke of Wellington as Master-General of the Ordnance in the Tory government of Lord Liverpool that was cracking down on political dissent and public assembly – but the good weather made him forget those cares. He wrote at length to George and Georgiana about the cycle of history – the way that nations changed for the better, then the worse, then the better again – and his hope that the quelling of the 'Peterloo' riot in Manchester would lead to new reform, not old tyranny.

But he was content for now to live in the moment and to take pleasure in solitude (Brown had left Winchester for Chichester, leaving him alone for three weeks): 'I think if I had a free and healthy and lasting organisation of heart and Lungs – as strong as an ox's – so as to be able [to bear] unhurt the shock of extreme thought and sensation without weariness, I could pass my Life very nearly alone though it should last eighty years.' All he cared for and all he lived for, he told Reynolds, was the state of mind that would create poetry. But poetry of a less enervating kind than had been his habitual mode:

> Some think I have lost that poetic ardour and fire 'tis said I once had – the fact is, perhaps I have; but, instead of that, I hope I shall substitute a more thoughtful and quiet power. I am more frequently now contented to read and think, but now and then haunted with ambitious thoughts. Quieter in my pulse, improved in my digestion, exerting myself against vexing speculations, scarcely content to write the best verses for the fever they leave behind. I want to compose without this fever.

That is what he did, following an autumn walk.

'Now the time is beautiful', he continued his letter to America, 'I take a walk every day for an hour before dinner, and this is generally my walk.' He asks George and Georgiana to follow his footsteps in their imagination. Out through the back gate of his lodgings, across one street, into the cathedral yard, under the trees along a paved path, past the beautiful front of the cathedral, turn left under a stone doorway, continue 'through two college-like squares seemingly built for the dwelling place of Deans and Prebendaries – garnished with grass and shaded with trees'. Then through one of the old city gates, along College Street, and out of town across the water meadows. Beyond 'a country alley of gardens', 'I arrive, that is, my worship arrives, at the foundation of Saint Cross, which is a very interesting old place, both for its gothic tower and alms square and for the appropriation of its rich rents to a relation of the Bishop of Winchester.' The Hospital of St Cross and Almshouse of Noble Poverty – two ancient quadrangles built around an entrance tower, a dining hall and a magnificent stone-vaulted Norman-Gothic church – was founded by the brother of King Stephen, a grandson of William the Conqueror. It was an embodiment of both the endurance of things that are beautifully made and the corruption that comes with power. As a historian explained some years later, 'Gross mismanagement of this grandly conceived foundation, and the alienation of so large a share of its funds from the poor to wealthy pluralists, which made the mastership of St Cross a scandal and a byword for full six centuries, began at an early date.'

'Then I pass across St Cross meadows till you come to the most beautifully clear river – now this is only one mile of my walk.' At this point, Keats broke off his journal-letter in order to have his supper and he did not return to it in order to describe the remaining two miles of his walk, but the likelihood is that he turned east and contoured round St Catherine's Hill, on which the sheep that had been reared as lambs among the water meadows in the spring were now grazing. Then he would have walked north to admire the prospect of the city from St Giles's Hill, which by the end of the third week of September had returned to peace after having been the site of the busy autumnal fair that came to the city each year. From the top of St Giles's, Keats would have seen a varied landscape of town and country. As a contemporary guidebook had it, 'Being arrived thus far, the curious stranger will not fail to mount up to the top of that white cliff, which overhangs the city, and once formed part of it, called *St Giles's Hill*, either by the long circuit of the high road or by the short but steep ascent which he sees immediately before him.' Keats the walker to the north would not have been daunted by the brief climb.

> Having attained to that point of the summit which is in a line with the High-street, he will certainly confess himself richly repaid for his labour in mounting hither. In fact, we have here the whole city under our feet, and command a bird's eye view of all the objects that we have described, consisting of streets, fortifications, palaces, churches, and ruins, with intermingled gardens, fields, groves, and streams.

Descending the hill, he would have passed through a stubble-field – the hill was partially under corn – and into an area called 'the Soke' beside the river Itchen, where there was a granary.

On the same day that he conjured up his walk for George and Georgiana in their American exile, he wrote more briefly to Reynolds:

> How beautiful the season is now – How fine the air. A temperate sharpness about it. Really, without joking, chaste weather – Dian skies – I never liked stubble-fields so much as now – Aye better than the chilly green of the Spring. Somehow, a stubble-field

looks warm – in the same way that some pictures look warm. This struck me so much in my Sunday's walk that I composed upon it.

And for Woodhouse, following some ribald remarks about girls he met on the road, he copied out the poem:

Season of mists and mellow fruitfulness,
    Close bosom friend of the maturing sun;
Conspiring with him how to load and bless
    With fruit the vines that round the thatch eves run;
To bend with apples the moss'd cottage trees,
    And fill all fruit with ripeness to the core;
        To swell the gourd, and plump the hazle-shells
    With a white kernel; to set budding more,
And still more later flowers for the bees
Until they think wa[r]m days will never cease
        For summer has o'er brimm'd their clammy Cells.

Who hath not seen thee oft, amid thy stores?
    Sometimes, whoever seeks abroad may find
Thee sitting careless on a granary floor,
    Thy hair soft-lifted by the winmowing wind;
Or on a half reap'd furrow sound asleep,
    Dased with the fume of poppies, while thy hook
        Spares the next swath and all its twined flowers;
And sometimes like a gleaner thou dost keep
    Stready thy laden head across a brook;
    Or by a Cyder press, with patient look,
        Thou watchest the last oozings hours by hours –

Where are the songs of spring? Ay, Where are they?
    Think not of them, thou hast thy music too.

While barred clouds bloom the soft-dying day
    And touch the stubble plains with rosy hue:
Then in a wailful choir the small gnats mourn
    Among the river sallows, borne aloft
        Or sinking as the light wind lives and dies;
And full grown Lambs loud bleat from hilly bourne:
    Hedge-crickets sing; and now with treble soft
    The Red breast whistles from a garden Croft
        And gather'd Swallows twitter in the Skies.

Keats's sound-system, so admired by his friend Bailey, is tuned here to perfect pitch. The repeated 'm's of the first two lines set the imagination buzzing in preparation for the arrival of the bees at the end of the stanza. Where most of the May odes had turned on Keats's feelings, now he further develops the impersonal gaze that he had lodged in the 'Grecian Urn'. His self is entirely absorbed in the landscape as the three stanzas follow his walk via sound, then sight, then back to sound. In the first, there is no human figure, just the hum of the bees signalling the natural processes of fruitfulness enabled by their work of pollination. In the second, the eye falls on a sequence of still lifes in nature: autumn is personified in the form of female labourers momentarily resting in the afternoon warmth amid the stubbled corn, in the granary and the apple-pressing barn, and midstream in one of the brooks that Keats may have crossed himself. In the third, the dawn chorus of spring is replaced by the autumnal evening sound of gnats, hedge-crickets, the bleating from the flock on St Catherine's Hill, and finally two species of bird that signify constancy and change: the robin redbreast that stays all year, and will cheer the winter months, and the swallows preparing to migrate southward, where Keats would soon be forced to follow.

'To Autumn' is, rightly, one of the most anthologized poems

in the English language. The anthology especially loved by F. Scott Fitzgerald was F. T. Palgrave's much-reprinted *The Golden Treasury of the Best Songs and Lyrical Poems in the English Language*. In the copy that he gave to his lover Sheilah Graham, he marked the poem as deserving of special attention, ideally to be learnt by heart. In the letter on poetry that he wrote to his daughter Scottie shortly before his death, he wrote, unconsciously echoing the bee-hum and swallow-twitter of 'To Autumn', 'For awhile after you quit Keats all other poetry seems to be only whistling or humming.'

The autumn walk: Winchester and the water meadows seen from St Giles's Hill, with the Hospital of St Cross in the distance, towards the left

15

'A BEAKER FULL OF THE WARM SOUTH'

'There are no second acts in American lives.' For Fitzgerald, *The Great Gatsby* was the climax of act one. Knowing it was his best work to date, he waited eagerly for the reviews. And he started immediately on his next novel. Entitled *Our Type*, it would focus on 'an intellectual murder on the Leopold–Loeb idea'. Nathan Freudenthal Leopold Jr and Richard Albert Loeb were two wealthy University of Chicago students who in 1924 kidnapped and murdered a fourteen-year-old boy merely to prove that they were so clever that they could commit the perfect crime and get away with it. They were caught and sentenced to life imprisonment. The case became a press sensation and would inspire the British author Patrick Hamilton's stage play *Rope*, which was made into a film by Alfred Hitchcock. Fitzgerald's protagonist was going to be a clever but hot-tempered young American who travels to France with his mother and murders her. The protagonist's curious name was Francis (Scott's first name) Melarky: 'me'/'larky', suggesting not only the neologism 'malarkey', coined around this time, but perhaps also 'I am larking about with aspects of my own identity'. Including, it would seem, alcoholism: the murder was going to be executed under the influence. The novel would incidentally, he told Perkins, be 'about Zelda + me + the hysteria of last May + June in Paris. (Confidential)'.

Three chapters survive in draft, enough to bring Francis and his mother to the Riviera and to reveal that there would be plenty of autobiographical elements – such as being beaten up by the police in Rome. The cast list includes a rich and hospitable American couple on the Riviera and an alcoholic composer. There was going to be a duel. It would be nine years before the novel was published, having taken on a very different form and theme. After the achievement of writing three novels in five years, Fitzgerald completed only one and a half more in his remaining fifteen years. His second act was a downward spiral.

The Great Gatsby was published in April 1925, with a dedication 'ONCE AGAIN TO ZELDA'. It was priced at $2 and Scribner's printed 20,000 copies. An early review did not augur well: 'F. Scott Fitzgerald's Latest a Dud' announced the *New York World*. Sales were slower than for the first two novels, but most of the reviews were excellent. Four in particular were notable. H. L. Mencken praised the brilliant finish of the writing, suggesting that 'Fitzgerald the stylist' had risen up to challenge 'Fitzgerald the social historian'. Conrad Aiken argued that the novel achieved its distinction through a combination of the twin but diverse influences of Henry James and the cinema. Gilbert Seldes, in a review in the influential literary magazine *The Dial* headed 'Spring Flight', proposed that Fitzgerald had 'more than matured', had indeed 'mastered his talent and gone soaring in a beautiful flight, leaving behind him everything dubious and tricky in his earlier work, and leaving even farther behind all the men of his own generation and most of his elders'. He praised the 'concentration of the book' in language akin to that of Keats's ethereal chemicals: 'so intense that the principal characters exist almost as essences, as biting acids that find themselves in the same golden cup and have no choice but to act upon each other'. And in the opening paragraph of a review headed '*The Great Gatsby*: Bagdad-on-Subway', Thomas Caldecot Chubb, a prolific poet, biographer and book reviewer, managed both to praise the novel and sum up Fitzgerald's vertiginous progress:

> In a short career, even now amounting to only five years, Scott Fitzgerald has already found time to do a great many things. He has written the most brilliant novel of the younger generation. He has written one of the two best novels of the younger generation. He has written probably the worst play of any generation. He has scattered very close of half a hundred short stories in all the better-paying receptacles for facile fiction. He has told – and presumably based the telling on his own experience – how it is possible to live on $30,000 a year. Latterly, he has been responsible for *The Great Gatsby*, a fable in the form of a realistic novel, an Arabian Night's tale of the environs of what O. Henry used to call Bagdad-on-Subway, a hasheesh dream for a romantic-minded inhabitant of Nassau County, and incidentally his most attractive book.

*

'The hysteria of May and June' occurred when they returned to France from Capri, taking an apartment in Paris on the rue de Tilsitt, a block away from the Arc de Triomphe. The hysteria revolved largely around the drinking that their new acquaintance Ernest Hemingway immortalized in *A Moveable Feast*.

Scott met him in the Dingo bar on the Left Bank. Unlike Fitzgerald, Hemingway had seen active service in the war. He had driven a Red Cross ambulance in the Italian campaign and been seriously wounded by mortar fire. Now he was in Paris, twenty-five years old to Fitzgerald's twenty-eight, working as a journalist and beginning to publish short stories in the spare prose style that would become his signature. Hemingway was the epitome of manliness: tall, dark, brown-eyed and muscular. He described Fitzgerald as 'a man who looked like a boy', halfway between handsome and pretty: 'He had very fair wavy hair, a high forehead, excited and friendly eyes and a delicate long-lipped Irish mouth that, on a girl, would have been the mouth of a beauty.' His prettiness came from the blond hair and the mouth. In a classic Hemingway sentence: 'The mouth worried you until you knew him and then it worried you more.'

As Hemingway remembered his first encounter with the writer whose prose was the polar opposite of his own, Fitzgerald walked into the bar sporting a suit by Brooks Brothers, a white shirt with a buttoned-down collar and a tie of the British regiment the Guards, which he should not have been wearing. He was accompanied by a celebrated Princeton baseball pitcher. He introduced himself to Hemingway, ordered champagne and never stopped talking. He asked incessant questions – 'You don't mind if I call you Ernest, do you?' and 'did you and your wife sleep together before you were married?' – until he had to be put in a taxi. There may be a little retrospective embroidery in this account.

Hemingway moved in a circle of American expatriate writers presided over by the queenly Gertrude Stein. He took Fitzgerald to meet her and she handed down her judgment on *The Great Gatsby*:

Here we are and have read your book and it is a good book. I like the melody of your dedication it shows that you have a background of beauty and tenderness and that is a comfort. The next good thing is that you write naturally in sentences and that too is a comfort . . . You are creating the contemporary world much as Thackeray did his in *Pendennis* and *Vanity Fair* and that isn't a bad compliment. You make a modern world and a modern orgy.

She appears to have assumed that the 'orgastic future' at the climax of *Gatsby* referred to orgies rather than orgasms, but Fitzgerald would have been pleased by the notion that his dedication of the book to Zelda was a sign of 'tenderness'. It was not only Keats who cared for tender nights; tenderness, like kindness, was very important to Stein. 'The teasing is tender and trying and thoughtful' she wrote in the fragment on sugar in *Tender Buttons*, her tender, trying, thoughtful and anything but saccharine collage of stream-of-consciousness meditations on objects, food and rooms.

In Paris, Fitzgerald spent most of his time, sometimes in company and sometimes alone, crawling from bar to bar. He told Perkins that he was excited about his work in progress, that 'it is something really NEW in form, idea, structure – the model for the age that Joyce and Stien [*sic*] are searching for, that Conrad didn't find'. But its progress was impeded by the drinking. Hemingway loved the 'moveable feast' of being in Paris while you were young, the memory of it staying with you all your life. Fitzgerald less so: he preferred the Riviera.

In the summer of 1925, he and Zelda returned to the south, joining Gerald and Sara Murphy on the Cap d'Antibes. Gerald was an aesthete and an intellectual, a lover equally of luxury and avant-garde artists. He laboured over precise, geometric paintings in the cubist style. Sara, the daughter of a self-made millionaire who did not approve of her marriage, was the perfect hostess. At Villa America, their exquisitely appointed home on the Cap, they gathered around them a stellar group of creatives ranging from Pablo Picasso to Cole Porter. The Fitzgeralds were enchanted.

Dick Diver on his beach: Gerald and Sara Murphy on La Garoupe, during the time when they entertained the Fitzgeralds at Villa America

In the opening scene of Fitzgerald's Riviera novel, when it finally appeared under the title *Tender is the Night*, Dick Diver swims alone in the early morning light off the 'bright tan prayer rug of a beach' below the hotel on the Cap d'Antibes, with its view across to the pink and cream of the old fortifications of Cannes. Fitzgerald's scene was a careful blend of observation and invention. It really was the case that there was no summer season on the Riviera until a small group of Americans – first Cole Porter and his wife, then the Murphys, then their guests such as the Fitzgeralds – began going there in the early 1920s. And Gerald Murphy really did clear the little beach of La Garoupe with his own hands. His striped bathing wear sparked a Paris fashion, as Dick Diver's does in the novel. But Fitzgerald's art was to reshape the untidiness of reality, to give it the sharp edges and bright light of myth. Just as he fused the Murphys with the Fitzgeralds in order to create the Divers, so he adjusted the real place: if you go to the Cap d'Antibes, you will find that the 'large, proud, rose-coloured hotel' is still there (though it is now white), but that the 'short dazzling beach' is not, as the novel recreates it, immediately adjacent to the hotel on the side of the cape from which you look over to Cannes – La Garoupe is actually tucked away, now rather gone to seed, on the rockier, more secluded eastern side. But for the sake of art it was better that the hotel and the beach should have been as one.

Riviera summers at the Murphys' Villa America were a moveable feast of warm days that never seemed to cease:

Shortly before noon Gerald would emerge from the studio, and everyone – the children, Mam'zelle, any guests staying in the *bastide*, and Gerald and Sara – would pile into cars or make their way on foot down the winding road to the little beach at La Garoupe. There the children did exercises with Gerald – head and leg lifts, yogic plows, and toe touches. Everyone sunbathed and swam. The water, clear enough for you to see your feet on the sandy bottom, was salty and just cold enough to be refreshing . . . After a while everyone went back to the villa for lunch. They ate at the big table on the terrace under the linden tree – an omelette and salad from the garden, or poached eggs on a bed of creamed corn with sautéed Provençal tomatoes on the side, or a plain dish of potatoes, freshly dug, with butter from the villa's cows and fresh parsley, and simple local wine to wash it all down. The sky would harden into an intense blue, the earth would give back the smell of bracken and eucalyptus, and the air would throb with the shrilling of cicadas.

With Gerald and Sara, the company was always good, but the assemblage of self-confident artists heightened Scott's anxiety. He always felt insecure around those who wore their talents with ease.

His sociability, accelerated into overdrive by Zelda, took him away from the quiet space and concentrated hours that he needed for his writing. Beneath his pose of charm and insouciance, he was a grafter, a craftsman, who worked and reworked his sentences. *Gatsby* was his best novel not least because it was shorter than the first two. Like Gustave Flaubert, whom he considered one of the masters of fiction, Fitzgerald believed that in good writing less was always more. 'The novel of selected incidents has this to be said [for it]', he would advise the prolix genius Thomas Wolfe, 'that the great writer like Flaubert has consciously left out the stuff that Bill or Joe, (in his case Zola) will come along and say presently'. He continued, with his usual barrage of spelling mistakes:

> He will say only the things that he alone see. So Mme Bovary becomes eternal while Zola already rocks with age. Repression itself has a value, as with a poet who struggles for a nessessary ryme achieves accidently a new word association that would not have come by any mental or even flow-of-consciousness process. The Nightengale is full of that.

As well as incidentally achieving a deep insight into the relationship between rhyme and word association in Keats, this is possibly the best advice that Fitzgerald ever gave to a fellow writer. The greatness of *Gatsby* is not least in the selection of its incidents and the repression of excessive autobiographical detail. The problem with the new novel was that it was going in too many different directions.

Looking back on his thirtieth year, which they had divided between the Riviera and Paris, with excursions to London, Biarritz and the battlefields of Verdun and the Somme, Scott wrote in his ledger: 'Futile, shameful useless but the $30,000 rewards of 1924 work. Self disgust. Health gone.' The financial reward for past efforts came from a substantial advance on royalties for his third story collection, *All the Sad Young Men*, which included many of his very best pieces ('The Rich Boy', 'Winter Dreams', 'Absolution', 'The Sensible Thing'), together with a successful stage version of *The Great Gatsby*, and the sale of the novel's movie rights. Hollywood now had its eye on the most celebrated writer of the younger generation. Fitzgerald was accordingly invited to go to the coast and write a flapper comedy for Constance Talmadge, one of the brightest stars of the silent screen.

*

He and Zelda were given a suite in a bungalow at the Ambassador Hotel, 'just between the leading vamps of the cinema: Pola Negri on one side and John Barrymore on the other'. Among their other neighbours was someone they knew from New York, the bisexual writer and photographer (and patron of the 'New Negro Renaissance') Carl Van Vechten. The Fitzgeralds had still been in France when the *Gatsby* film was released, so they now took the opportunity to go to a screening in Hollywood. Zelda wrote to Scottie that it was 'ROTTEN and awful and terrible and we left'.

Scott and Zelda belonged to the first generation to have their dreams shaped by the movies and musicals. He began 'My Lost City', his beautifully nostalgic elegy for his early days in New York, with two symbolic memories: the ferry boat 'moving softly from the Jersey shore at dawn' when he was ten, and a visit into the city from school when he was fifteen. He saw Ina Claire in *The Quaker Girl* and Gertrude Bryan in *Little Boy Blue*: 'Confused by my hopeless and melancholy love for them both, I was unable to choose between them so they blurred into one lovely entity, the girl. She was my second symbol of New York. The ferry boat stood for triumph, the girl for romance.' They gave the city that he would conquer and lose 'all the iridescence of the beginning of the world'.

The script for First National, a production company that was soon to be taken over by Warner Brothers, was commissioned with an advance of $3,500 and the promise of a further $12,500 if the finished version was accepted. Calling it *Lipstick*, Fitzgerald gave Talmadge the lead as a girl who starts out in prison and escapes to high society with the help of a magic lipstick that makes every man want to kiss her. The script was rejected. Fitzgerald was too focused on stylish prose as opposed to comic action and scenic setting. His first foray into the movie world did, however, introduce him to two figures who would be converted into future fictional characters.

One was at the very top of the ladder. Irving Thalberg was known as the Boy Wonder of Hollywood. At the age of just twenty-six he had become head of production at MGM. He was a man who got things done. Sitting in the commissary at MGM, he gave Fitzgerald an allegory of leadership. Suppose you want to drive a railroad tunnel through a mountain. The surveyors tell you there are half a dozen possible routes. If you're the top man, do you weigh up all the possibilities slowly and rationally? No, you make an arbitrary decision and stick to it, and pretend that you had a good reason for it. Nobody must know or guess that there was no particular reason, nor should they be allowed to imagine that you had any doubt about your decision.

Lois Moran, the original for Rosemary Hoyt in *Tender is the Night*,
photographed by Carl Van Vechten

The other person was, like a hundred other young women, hoping to climb the ladder, propelled by her beauty. Two years earlier, Lois Moran had made her Hollywood debut at the age of sixteen, beside Ronald Colman and Douglas Fairbanks Jr in a Samuel Goldwyn film called *Stella Dallas*, based on a novel by Olive Higgins Prouty. She played the daughter of a small-town girl who has married and then fallen out with a rich man. By the time the Fitzgeralds arrived in Hollywood, the name of Lois Moran was appearing above the title in pictures such as *The Whirlwind of Youth*, *The Music Master* (an Allan Dwan production) and *Publicity Madness* (inspired by the flight of the Lindberghs, story by Anita Loos). Scott met her when Douglas Fairbanks and Mary Pickford, Hollywood's leading celebrity couple, invited him and Zelda to lunch at their mock-Tudor mansion 'Pickfair', set on an eighteen-acre Beverly Hills estate. Lois was flattered by Scott's fame and brilliance, he by her youth and beauty. She spoke perfect French, loved reading and music, copied poetry into a chapbook, and adored *The Great Gatsby* – she had indeed been considered for a part in the film. She was always chaperoned by her widowed mother, so they were never alone together, but Scott started visiting her apartment where they shared strawberries and caviar. At crowded parties, they would slip out onto the stairwell and just talk. Lois dreamed of them starring together in her next movie. She even arranged a screen test for him, which did not go well.

Interviewed by one of Fitzgerald's biographers half a century later, Moran remembered that when she and her mother invited Scott and Zelda to a tea party he collected the watches, purses and wallets of all the guests and tried to make a soup out of them. Zelda was not impressed by the flirtation, especially when Scott chided her for not making more of herself in the way that Lois had. She burnt her clothes in the bathtub of their villa and threw her platinum wristwatch – her wedding present from Scott – out of the train on the way back east. Although the screenplay had been aborted, this first trip to California gave him material for several short stories about the allure of Hollywood in general and Lois Moran in particular. The best of them was called 'Magnetism', featuring among its cast Helen Avery, a starlet based on Lois, and Kay, a wife who, like Zelda, fears that she is ageing and losing her appeal after having a baby:

> He hadn't said a word to Helen Avery that Kay could have objected to, but something had begun between them . . . that Kay had felt in the air . . . Helen Avery's voice and the dropping of her eyes when she finished speaking, like a sort of exercise in control, fascinated him. He had felt that they both tolerated something, that each knew half of some secret about people and life, and that if they rushed towards each other there would be a romantic communion of almost unbelievable intensity.

The marriage is beginning to crack. George Hannaford, the Fitzgerald figure in the story (he is a famous actor – Scott fantasizing about the might-have-been following the screen test), has a dream set in Gatsby-like starlight and gleam upon dark water in which he remembers the early soaring flight of the love that is now crashing to earth.

*

Back in Europe, Zelda started to behave strangely. Partly, she was provoked by Scott's attention to other women. At Saint-Paul-de-Vence in the hills above Nice, he flirted with the renowned dancer Isadora Duncan. Zelda, who always wanted to be a ballet dancer, threw herself down a set of stone steps. On another occasion, she accused Scott of being gay, which infuriated him because there was a strong homophobic streak in his personality. Zelda, in turn, accepted the attentions of Oscar Wilde's daughter Dolly, the best-known lesbian in Paris. These tensions would work their way into the novel that Scott was putting through draft after draft. A scene that did not make it into the final cut involved banter between 'fairies' in a gay bar in Lausanne. The lesbian theme did reach the published version: the character of Mary North has an affair with a Dolly Wildean lesbian after the death of her alcoholic composer husband Abe North.

In 'Babylon Revisited', one of the best of Fitzgerald's later short stories, the protagonist revisits Paris in the 1930s, finds it almost emptied of Americans and without its Babylonian excess of the 1920s. He has lost money in the 1929 Wall Street Crash, but lost the things that he really values – his wife and his daughter – in the boom years. Lost them because of his drinking. The story ends with him alone in a bar: 'he wanted his child, and nothing was much good now, beside that fact'.

In the story, the wife is dead. In reality, Scott lost Zelda to mental illness. He characterized autumn 1929 to autumn 1930 in his ledger as the year of 'The Crash! Zelda & America'. There was history in her family: three sisters and a brother suffered from 'neurosis', her father Judge Sayre had had a nervous breakdown, her maternal grandmother and an aunt had committed suicide. Three years later, her brother Anthony would commit suicide, having had violent fantasies of killing his mother.

She had been taking dance classes with manic energy and passionate feeling for her instructor, Madame Egorova, formerly of the Russian Imperial Ballet, who had opened a dance school in Paris at Diaghilev's behest. She had taken up painting; she was writing fiction; she had felt utterly alienated when she and Scott made a brief trip to Algiers in the hope of some recuperative winter sun. Looking back on this time, she accused Scott of not helping her, of being absorbed in drink and tennis, of hating her for asking him to stop drinking.

On Shakespeare's birthday in 1930, she entered the Malmaison Clinic, just outside Paris, in a state of what her doctor described as acute anxiety and restlessness. She kept repeating that she needed to work, that she was going to die, that she would never be cured, but that she had to work. Madame Egorova had given her such joy, the joy of great art, a symphony of perfume; she was in love with her, but she was afraid of becoming a lesbian. After three weeks, she discharged herself, against medical advice. She began hallucinating, seeing horrific phantoms. There was a suicide attempt, the first of many. On the advice of friends, she took herself to another clinic, this one near Montreux in Switzerland. Scott's visits to her there were turbulent, with quarrels flaring over their mutual accusations of homosexuality.

The clinic did not have expertise in difficult mental health cases. They summoned Dr Oscar Forel of the renowned Les Rives de Prangins psychiatric facility on Lake Geneva. A disciple of Freud, he diagnosed schizophrenia and prescribed an intense course of psychoanalysis. Zelda moved to Prangins. Over the course of the next year, Scott commuted between Paris and Prangins, doing all he could to take care of Scottie. Zelda's diagnosis was confirmed by Dr Eugen Bleuler, the man who had named the disease of schizophrenia and become the leading authority on it (he was also an advocate of eugenic sterilization, but he did not take Zelda down that road). Fitzgerald wrote in his ledger 'A Year in Lausanne. Waiting. From Darkness to Hope'.

*

His hope was fulfilled. Zelda seemed a lot better, so they decided to move to her home town of Montgomery, Alabama, in search of a quiet life. The return to America was timely because Scott received a second Hollywood invitation in the form of a five-week contract with MGM at $1,200 per week. His job was to adapt for the screen a flapper novel by the sharp-witted best-selling novelist Katharine Brush. Entitled *Red-Headed Woman*, it begins with a girl leaving her date at a restaurant table, exiting through the powder room and meeting a rich boy in the woods, before going on to try to seduce her married boss. Despite the assistance of a co-writer, Scott did not get beyond an unfinished seventy-six pages, breaking off with the line 'You're not so bad yourself, Big Boy.' Anita Loos took over the screenplay and the movie became a very racy vehicle for Jean Harlow, full of premarital sex and adultery of the kind that would provoke the implementation of the Hays Code in 1934.

This time, Fitzgerald disgraced himself in Hollywood by turning up drunk at a party of Irving Thalberg's, where he launched, loudly and very badly, into an incoherent song about a dog. He fictionalized the incident in a story called 'Crazy Sunday': 'as he finished he had the sickening realization that he had made a fool of himself in view of an important section of the picture world, upon whose favour depended his career'. Zelda, meanwhile, wrote to him regularly, sanely and lovingly: 'Darling, my own darling. The little mossy place on the back of your neck is the sweetest place and I can rub my nose in it like a pony in his feed bag when you come home and I'm very, very lucky.'

Her healthy spell did not last. In February 1932 she was admitted to the psychiatric clinic of the Johns Hopkins University Hospital in Baltimore. Scott rented a large house nearby, while Zelda moved between inpatient and outpatient status. She was no longer dancing, but she was still painting and writing. In particular, she was writing her novel about their marriage, especially the Riviera years – exactly the material that Scott had been working on for nearly a decade. She sent the manuscript to Max Perkins without showing it to Scott, or even telling him about it.

When Scott saw the book, his fury knew no bounds. She had even called the husband Amory Blaine, making him a second-rate portrait painter. 'My God,' he wrote to Zelda's doctor, 'my books made her a legend and her single intention in this somewhat thin portrait is to make me a non-entity.' After initial intransigence on both sides, they eventually reached an agreement, thanks to some skilful mediation on the part of Perkins. Zelda would go ahead and publish, but with certain omissions and alterations insisted upon by Scott. And she would have to agree not to write any more novels based on their marriage. As far as Scott was concerned, there could be no second trespass on his domain.

16

TENDER IS THE NIGHT

'Night lends enchantment to everything.'
'It does something for a title too.'
'I owe it to Keats. He saved me at the last minute. But I had thought about it before. Scribner's didn't like it. I forced it on them.'

(Tony Buttita, remembering an exchange of dialogue
with Scott Fitzgerald in 1935)

'Plagued by the nightingale,' Abe suggested, and repeated, 'probably plagued by the nightingale.'

(Tender is the Night, Book One, Chapter IX)

Spurred by his rivalry with Zelda, he finally finished his version of the story. *Tender is the Night* was serialized in *Scribner's Magazine* in the early months of 1934 and published as a book that April. To anyone who knew the Fitzgeralds, it was obvious that the couple at the centre of the story, Dick and Nicole Diver, were a combination of Gerald and Sara Murphy and the Fitzgeralds.

The story pivots on the fragile mental health of Nicole. In this respect the character is, as Fitzgerald stated explicitly in his notes for the novel, a portrait of Zelda. One of the contributing factors to her second breakdown had been the death of her father, Judge Sayre, in November 1931. Her letters to Hollywood kept returning to the subject of her father and how much she missed him. It was at this time that Scott introduced into his story a Freudian explanation for Nicole's psychosis: 'At fifteen she was raped by her own father under peculiar circumstances.' The incestuous rape causes a mental collapse, which sends Nicole the following year to a Swiss clinic, where she falls in love with her doctor, Dick Diver. Only the psychoanalytic transference saves her from homicidal mania and the desire to kill men in revenge for her abuse.

Numerous passages in the sections of the novel devoted to Nicole's mental illness were lifted directly from Zelda's letters written in her various clinics and even from the diagnosis of her case that Scott received from Dr Bleuler. One cannot therefore help wondering whether there was any basis in fact for the rape. Unsurprisingly, Scott kept his book from Zelda for as long as he could, but when she read it, in the psychiatric clinic, she said that she was 'a little upset': 'What made me mad was he made the girl so awful and kept on reiterating how she had ruined his life and I couldn't help identifying myself with her because she had so many of my experiences.' 'She had ruined his life': Zelda's implication is that by having Nicole ruin Dick's life, Scott was accusing her of ruining his. At some level, by casting blame upon the father, Scott was trying to exculpate himself from responsibility for her breakdowns. Or was he trying not to blame Zelda herself for her mental illness? Or could he even have been telling the truth?

Zelda *was* sexually abused at the age of fifteen. In an accusatory letter, Scott wrote to one of her sisters: 'Your mother took such rotten care of Zelda that John Sellers was able to seduce her at fifteen.' Sellers was a rich boy, son of a wealthy cotton broker in Montgomery. He and his older friend, Peyton

Mathis, were known as the Gold Dust Twins. In Zelda's unfinished second novel, *Caesar's Things*, which was as autobiographical as her first, two boys clearly based on this pair force the Zelda figure to have sex in a shadowy corner of the schoolyard. She is traumatized: 'she was so miserable and trusting that her heart broke and for many years after she didn't want to live: but it was better to keep going'. Zelda said of the portrayal of Nicole's history in *Tender is the Night*, 'I don't think it's true – I don't think it's really what happened.' Her uncertainty is striking. She also said 'It was a chronological distortion': it is not impossible that she meant that Scott had fused her experience with Sellers and Mathis at the age of fifteen with an (earlier?) incident involving her father.

Fitzgerald said that the mark of the true artist was the ability to hold two opposed ideas in the mind at the same time. One might accordingly say that the rape plot in *Tender is the Night* served several opposed purposes at once: it was a painful attempt to account for Zelda's mental illness, an unforgivable act of revenge for the publication of *Save Me the Waltz*, and a purely artistic decision to cap a novel steeped in psychoanalysis with the ultimate Freudian taboo of parent–child incest.

The movie that has made the name of Rosemary Hoyt, the ingénue based on Lois Moran, is called *Daddy's Girl*. Her affair with Dick Diver is a fantasy projection of the affair Scott didn't have with Lois. But there is something more than faintly disturbing about the description of her. She

> had magic in her pink palms and her cheeks lit to a lovely flame, like the thrilling flush of children after their cold baths in the evening. Her fine forehead sloped gently up to where her hair, bordering it like an armored shield, burst into lovelocks and waves and curlicues of ash blonde and gold, her eyes were bright, big, clear, wet, and shining, the color of her cheeks was

real, breaking close to the surface from the strong young pump of her heart. Her body hovered delicately on the last edge of childhood – she was almost eighteen, nearly complete, but the dew was still on her.

Dr Diver's fellow psychoanalysts would have much to say about this.

*

Early in *Tender is the Night*, Rosemary Hoyt, Hollywood starlet, visiting the Cap d'Antibes for the first time, asks Dick and Nicole Diver whether they like the place. 'They have to like it', replies one of their party, Abe North (an alcoholic composer, loosely based on Ring Lardner, who had lapsed into depression and drinking), 'They invented it.' And he turns his noble head slowly 'so that his eyes rested with tenderness and affection on the two Divers'.

It is explained that prior to the 1920s, the French Riviera was solely a winter resort. No well-to-do European would have dreamed of spending the summer in all that heat. But then the Divers arrived and persuaded Monsieur Gausse to keep his Hôtel des Étrangers open through the summer. They built a villa nearby and Dick cleared a little beach of seaweed and rock with a rake and his own bare hands. Within a few years, fashionable Americans began visiting, a casino was built at Juan-les-Pins, and the summer season was born. This is, of course, the story of the Murphys.

Though his prose and his moral outlook could hardly have been more different, the geography of Scott Fitzgerald's imagination owed a large debt to Henry James. The essential Jamesian theme was the naïve American in sophisticated Europe. It was a subject that provided not only plotlines and character contrasts, but also a means by which to explore the delicate relationship between the American Novel as a distinctively new phenomenon and the inheritance of a long European tradition of fiction. Furthermore, James complicated his structure by introducing a north–south axis as well as the west–east journey between America and Europe. Thus in *The Portrait of a Lady*, Isabel Archer's journey from the great houses of rural England to a villa in Italy is as important as her transatlantic crossing.

In *Tender is the Night*, Scott Fitzgerald revisits the Jamesian territory of the Americans in Europe. He also hinges his novel on north and south. '*Wire, wire, wire!*' Rosemary Hoyt writes to her mother, 'Are you coming north or shall I come south with the Divers?' As in the lives of Scott and Zelda themselves, the novel includes many journeys between Paris and the south of France. An even more important north–south distinction is symbolic rather than geographic: the relationship between the Divers is formed in the Swiss Alps; it flourishes and then degenerates on the French Riviera. Though the journey between these two places is not strictly from north to south, that is how it feels in terms of emotional weather. Whereas the wealthy, the glamorous and the artistic are drawn to Nice and Cannes like bees to a honeypot, Zurich and Lausanne are the destination of misfits, the sick and the lost: 'This corner of Europe does not so much draw people as accept them without inconvenient questions. Routes cross here – people bound for private sanitariums or tuberculosis resorts in the mountains, people who are no longer *persona grata* in France or Italy.'

The symbolic geography of the novel is not confined to settings. It is also there in the names of some of the characters. It can hardly be coincidental that the mark of Dick Diver's decline at the end of the novel is his failure to execute the flashy dive into the Mediterranean that was his trademark. As Dick Diver is a diver, so Abe North stands for the world of the north and in particular the big cities that are characterized by confusion and violence – Paris, where there is an unsavoury incident involving the death of a Negro, and New York, where Abe comes to a sticky end in a speakeasy. And, in contrast, the lover for whom Nicole leaves Dick is called Tommy Barban, an American who has Europeanized himself but whose name suggests that he remains a barbarian at heart. The crucial scene in which Dick and Nicole's marriage reaches the point of no return, and the affair with Barban becomes inevitable, takes place on a boat off Cannes. A paragraph consisting of a single sentence economically evokes the end of the Divers' marriage: 'He turned away from her, toward the veil of starlight over Africa.' Before long, Nicole and Tommy are consummating their affair in a seedy hotel on the road to Monte Carlo, home of the new barbarism of brash wealth.

Dick Diver is one of the last romantics. As the novel's Keatzian title indicates, he longs within his soul for 'the warm south' of the 'Ode to a Nightingale', for 'Dance, and Provençal song, and sunburnt mirth'. But whereas Keats went to Rome to die, Dick goes there only to become involved in a drunken brawl and, like his creator, to be humiliated at the hands of the carabinieri. He returns and says farewell to the beach that he invented and then lost, just as he reinvented Nicole and then lost her: 'Let him look at it – his beach, perverted now to the tastes of the tasteless.' We wish for him to take off to some new romance further south, perhaps towards that starlight over Africa. But, pathetically, all he can do is return west and north to America, disappearing into the oblivion of small-town life in upstate New York.

The sea is at the heart of *Tender is the Night*, just as it was at the core of Keats's imagination. When Nicole contemplates her embarkation upon the affair with Tommy, 'She sat upon the low wall and looked down upon the sea. But from another sea, the wide swell of fantasy, she had fished out something tangible to lay beside the rest of her loot.' In a novel in which the protagonist is a psychiatrist, who has originally headed for Vienna in the wry hope that a passing bomb might drop on Dr Freud, leaving a vacancy for the position of top dog in the brave new world of psychoanalysis, the sea, with its 'wide swell of fantasy', is inevitably linked to the unconscious. Whatever its real-life origins may or may not have been, Dick's analysis of Nicole is the fashionable one of the Freudian age: sexual abuse in the bed of her father has made her a schizophrenic. By analogy, the novel's symbolic geography of America/Europe and north/south itself becomes a form of schizophrenia. The characters disintegrate because they are torn between two worlds.

The chronology of the story gave Fitzgerald a structural problem. He had three bodies of personal material to work with: the glamour of the Riviera, the sordid and drunken misadventures in Paris, and Zelda's treatment in a Swiss psychiatric hospital. In reality, the Riviera came first. But in the chronology of the novel, the meeting and marriage of doctor and patient come first. He decided to begin on the Riviera and to treat the psychiatric material in flashback in the middle section of the book. He was, however, never sure that this was the right way around; late in life, he left instructions that the novel should be reissued with book two as book one, which indeed it was after his death. As the story of Dick Diver's decline, it works best in the way that he published it, beginning 'On the pleasant shore of the French Riviera' with 'The hotel and its bright tan prayer rug of a beach', and ending with Diver alone, his marriage broken, far from the sophistication of Europe, practising general medicine instead of specialist psychiatry.

*

The book carries a dedication 'TO GERALD AND SARA MANY FÊTES'. It was inspired, Scott wrote to Gerald Murphy, 'by Sara and you, and the way I feel about you both and the way you live, and the last part of it is Zelda and me because you and Sara are the same people as Zelda and me'. The last part of this was patently untrue: Gerald and Sara were very different people from Scott and Zelda. Sara hated the book, and categorically rejected any resemblance to herself and her husband or anyone they knew during the Riviera years. That is hardly surprising, given the representation of Nicole and the fact that Sara had a bad relationship with her own father. Gerald, on the other hand, recognized that almost every detail – the incidents and the conversations – in the first part of the book was based on real events involving them, though 'often altered or distorted in detail'. Interviewing the Murphys thirty years later, the journalist Calvin Tomkins finely captured what Fitzgerald had done:

> 'When I like men,' Fitzgerald once wrote, 'I want to be like them – I want to lose the outer qualities that give me my indi- viduality and be like them.' Fitzgerald wanted to be like Gerald Murphy because he admired Murphy as much as any man he had ever met, and because he was thoroughly fascinated, and sometimes thoroughly baffled, by the life the Murphys had created for themselves and their friends. It was a life of great originality, and considerable beauty, and some of its special quality comes through in the first hundred pages of *Tender Is the Night*. In the eyes of the young actress, Rosemary Hoyt, the Divers represented 'the exact furthermost evolution of a class, so that most people seemed awkward beside them.' Dick Diver's 'extraordinary virtuosity with people,' his 'exquisite considera- tion,' his 'politeness that moved so fast and intuitively, that it could be examined only in its effect' all were, and still are,

qualities of Gerald Murphy's, and the Divers' effect on their friends has many echoes in the Murphys' effect on theirs.

'People were always their best selves with the Murphys', said the novelist John Dos Passos, whom they frequently entertained, while the poet Archibald MacLeish, who knew them exceptionally well, remarked that from the beginning of the Murphys' life in Europe, 'person after person – English, French, American, everybody – met them and came away saying that these people really are masters in the art of living'.

Yet there was a part of Fitzgerald that despised the cultivation that the Murphys embodied. During the many years of writing the novel, he had increasingly come under the spell of Oswald Spengler's *The Decline of the West*, which argued that all cultures undergo a rise and fall, and that the West was in its final phase. The carnage of the Great War was the principal manifestation of this. It was out of morbid Spenglerian curiosity, as well as guilt at never having reached the front line himself, that Scott toured the battlefields – Verdun, the Somme, and more – during the late 1920s. This, too, goes into the novel. When the characters visit a restored trench near Amiens, Dick mourns that 'All my beautiful lovely safe world blew itself up here with a great gust of high explosive love.'

'A "schizophrène" is well named as a split personality', he thinks, 'Nicole was alternately a person to whom nothing need be explained and one to whom nothing *could* be explained.' If Nicole is at the mercy of her dark unconscious, Dick is a physician who fails to heal himself because he suffers from an excess of self-consciousness. His analytical powers have given him an incurable sense of alienation from the modern world. We see this in his brilliant analysis of the meaning of the Great War in this key northern scene located on the battlefield of the Somme: 'This took religion and years of plenty and tremendous sureties and the exact relation that existed between the classes.' We see it in his dreams of mutilated soldiers – only half-ironically, he diagnoses his own condition as that of non-combatant shellshock – and again in the sense of loss and longing he feels when he returns to America for his father's funeral:

> He knelt on the hard soil. These dead, he knew them all, their weather-beaten faces with blue flashing eyes, the spare violent bodies, the souls made of new earth in the forest-heavy darkness of the seventeenth century.
> 'Good-by, my father – good-by, all my fathers.'

The German word that Spengler used for a culture in its decadence was *Zivilisation*. 'Civilization', that is to say, as a pejorative term. This puts a different spin on Fitzgerald's seemingly adulatory description of a day in the life of the Divers, based on a day in the life of the Murphys: 'The Divers' day was spaced like the day of the older civilizations to yield the utmost from the materials at hand, and to give all the transitions their full value, and she did not know that there would be another transition presently from the utter absorption of the swim to the garrulity of the Provençal lunch hour.' Seen from an idealizing angle, this is a supremely civilized existence. Seen from Spengler's, it is a world of hyper-refinement that is about to be lost, and perhaps deserves to be.

It certainly is lost. If you go to the Cap d'Antibes and look for the Murphys' Villa America, you can just glimpse the roof terrace and the linden tree, but now the boundary walls bristle with security systems and the gates are backed with black steel to block prying eyes. The footstepping biographer decided not to buzz for entrance. The supremely hospitable Murphys, like the fictional Divers, would have had no hesitation in inviting a passing writer to join them in one of those simple lunches. But the rich are different now. The characters in Fitzgerald smell of money but they long for love and have an openness in their hearts. The current owners of the Villa America, whoever they may be, have closed their doors and loudly proclaim their exclusivity.

When he was drunk, Fitzgerald sought to destroy the paradise, break up the party. Despite his enjoyment of caviar and champagne with Lois Moran in Hollywood, he started condemning the lifestyle it represented. Once when the Murphys and their guests were all at a restaurant, a much older man came in with an attractive young girl and sat at the next table. Fitzgerald knew what the man's money was getting him. He glared at them, then started throwing ashtrays in their direction. Gerald got up and left the party, even though he was the host. The Murphys had many a story of this kind to tell. At one of their many Villa America dinner parties, which inspired those of Dick and Nicole in the novel, Fitzgerald insulted a gay guest with a homophobic remark almost as soon as he arrived. Then over dessert, he 'picked a fig from a bowl of pineapple sherbet and threw it at the Princesse de Caraman-Chimay' – 'It hit her between the shoulder blades; she stiffened for a moment and then went on talking as though nothing had happened.' Archibald MacLeish tried to calm Scott down and was rewarded with a right hook to the jaw. 'Still feeling that not enough attention was being paid him', Scott began throwing Sara's gold-flecked Venetian wine glasses over the garden wall: 'He had smashed three of them this way before Gerald stopped him. As the party was breaking up, Gerald went up to Scott (among the last to leave) and told him that he would not be welcome in their house for three weeks – a term of banishment that was observed to the day.' Banishment of one sort or another would be the story of the remainder of Scott and Zelda's lives.

*

Matthew Arnold, Fitzgerald's touchstone for the art of criticism, described culture as the best that has been thought and said by humankind. In *Tender is the Night*, Fitzgerald sought to capture both the best and the worst of his own culture. It was his attempt at an epic of modern life, though with a wide span as opposed to the single-day concentration of Joyce's *Ulysses*. But he struggled for years with the structure and style of the book, never quite achieving the epic sweep for which he was reaching, just as Keats struggled with the structure and style of his epic of divine origins.

One of Fitzgerald's proposed titles for his novel was *The World's Fair*. This is a good pun. The novel had the potential to be the literary equivalent of those World's Fairs at which different nations and cultures came together in order to show-case their gifts and inventions. But it was also written as a testing of the proposition that the world is a fair place. The resounding conclusion is that the world is not fair: casting blame aside, it is not fair that some are rich and many are poor, that many died in the war and some did not have the chance to prove themselves heroes, that some careers end in failure and many lives are blighted by mental illness. The only consolation, the only hope, is to be tender.

For Fitzgerald, as for Keats, there was nothing more sensually tender than a kiss and yet a kiss could also be a betrayal. In Paris at the end of book one of the novel, Rosemary is maturing into screen success with its concomitant hardness of personality. She has been thinking of a poem (by Keats, perhaps?) and of rain in Beverly Hills. Dick knocks on the door and enters. Presently, she kisses him 'several times in the mouth, her face getting big as it came up to him; he had never seen anything so dazzling as the quality of her skin'. He tells her that it has stopped raining and that the sun is emerging. She replies, echoing the words of the Lois Moran character in 'Magnetism', 'Oh, we're such *actors* – you and I.' But he has stopped acting the lover. In the moment of the kiss, 'since sometimes beauty gives back the images of one's best thoughts he thought of his responsibility about Nicole, and of the responsibility of her being two doors down across the corridor'. It is the end of the affair. Dick's responsibility is to his wife, who is on the brink of a fit of madness in the bathroom. Tenderness of lips must yield to tenderness of soul. In a letter that Fitzgerald knew well, Keats wrote that poetry should strike its readers as a wording of their own highest thoughts and almost a remembrance. The numerous kisses in Keats and Fitzgerald are wordings of their imaginings and remembrances of the highest romance, but these may be in conflict with their 'best thoughts'. Like *Endymion, Tender is the Night* was subtitled 'A Romance'. But Keats and Fitzgerald knew that they had to pass beyond romance. 'Do you not see how necessary a World of Pains and troubles is to school an Intelligence and make a soul?' Keats wrote in his spring 1819 letter to America. 'A Place where the heart must feel and suffer in a thousand diverse ways!'

For the Fitzgeralds, that place was their marriage. Like Dick Diver, Scott had made his choice of a charismatic but unstable wife and now he had to live with the consequences. Keats's heartache at the beginning of the 'Ode to a Nightingale', with its echo of Hamlet's, makes him feel as if he has drunk poisonous hemlock. Dick finds a double parallel, not only with the language of the ode, but also with the fate – madness, suicide – of the woman whom Hamlet rejects: 'On an almost parallel occasion, back in Dohlmer's clinic on the Zürichsee . . . he had made his choice, chosen Ophelia, chosen the sweet poison and drunk it. Wanting above all to be brave and kind, he had wanted, even more than that, to be loved.'

TENDER IS THE NIGHT

A ROMANCE

By

F. Scott Fitzgerald

DECORATIONS BY
EDWARD SHENTON

NEW YORK

CHARLES SCRIBNER'S SONS

1934

*"Already with thee! tender is the night . . .
. . . But here there is no light,
Save what from heaven is with the breezes blown
Through verdurous glooms and winding mossy ways."*
—Ode to a Nightingale.

Title page and Keatzian epigraph

'BRIGHT STAR'

Along the Riviera of *Tender is the Night*, white Russians relive their 'lost caviare days', while the Divers dine in Nice on 'bouillabaisse, which is a stew of rock fish and small lobsters, highly seasoned with saffron, and a bottle of cold Chablis'. Shopping after lunch in the heat of the Mediterranean afternoon, Nicole buys honey, along with 'colored beads, folding beach cushions, artificial flowers . . . and three yards of some new cloth the color of prawns'. The novel rivals *The Beautiful and Damned* in its characters' alcohol intake, but far exceeds it in the realm of gastronomy. Where 'To Autumn' is the exemplary poem of ripeness, *Tender is the Night* evokes the over-ripe, the rottenness of excess: 'Along the walls on the village side all was dusty, the wriggling vines, the lemon and eucalyptus trees, the casual wheel-barrow, left only a moment since, but already grown into the path, atrophied and faintly rotten.'

'Into the dark, smoky restaurant, smelling of the rich raw foods on the buffet, slid Nicole's sky-blue suit like a stray segment of the weather outside.' Like Keats, Fitzgerald was a masterchef of the intermingled ingredients of food, colour and weather. Keats had none of the affluence of the Murphys, who entertained Scott and Zelda so royally in their warm south of Provençal song and sunburnt mirth, but for his few happy weeks of solitude in Winchester in September 1819, he took solace in food as well as weather. The day after writing out his autumnal ode, he portrayed himself in a letter: 'this moment I was writing with one hand, and with the other holding to my Mouth a Nectarine – good god how fine – It went down soft pulpy, slushy, oozy – all its delicious embonpoint melted down my throat like a large beatified Strawberry. I shall certainly breed.' In this moment, the ripened fruits of his latest ode, which would be his last, enter his very body, restoring it to short-lived health and happiness.

The morning mists and gentle breeze, the cottage gardens and water meadows, granary and cider press, swallows and robin redbreast of 'To Autumn' are suffused with the air of Merrie England. While he was living in the medieval city of Winchester, Keats thought about the teenage prodigy poet Thomas Chatterton, who had taken his own life at the age of seventeen. Chatterton achieved fame in the 1760s – and posthumously – by writing poems and verse dramas, some of them purportedly from the pen of a fictitious medieval writer called Rowley, in a pseudo-Chaucerian style, with such titles as 'The Parlyamente of Sprytes' and 'The Merrie Tricks of Lamyngetowne'. What Keats liked about Chatterton was his seeming allegiance to Anglo-Saxon as opposed to Latinate vocabulary, to the native medieval as opposed to the imported classical tradition.

Returning to the unfinished *Hyperion* when he was on the Isle of Wight, he had begun to recast it as a dream-vision (a medieval form) instead of an epic (a form always shadowed by Homer and Virgil). He divided the poem into 'cantos', as in Dante's *Divine Comedy* and the 'romance' tradition, rather than 'books', as in the first version's tracking of Milton and classical epic. He began by introducing a prelude to the story of the fall of the Titans, written in a first-person voice, in which the figure of a poet approaches the shrine of Moneta (the Latin name for the Greek Mnemosyne of the original version). On ascending the flight of steps to her temple, he feels the chill of death, at which point he hears the admonitory words of the goddess, telling him that by coming close to death, but surviving, he has achieved a special power:

> Thou hast felt
> What 'tis to die and live again before
> Thy fated hour. That thou hadst power to do so
> Is thy own safety; thou hast dated on
> Thy doom.

It is as if, having witnessed Tom's death, Keats has both seen a foreshadowing of his own demise and passed fully through the 'Chamber of Maiden-Thought' to a recognition of the world's 'Misery and Heartbreak, Pain, Sickness and oppression'. This is the achievement, Moneta tells him, that will create a true poet as opposed to a mere dreamer. 'None can usurp this height', she explains, 'But those to whom the miseries of the world / Are misery, and will not let them rest.' Keats has arrived as a dreamer, but must leave as a poet. He will make the passage by entering 'the dark secret chambers' of Memory's skull, in which the 'high tragedy' of Hyperion is enacted. At this point, the manuscript segues into a heavily cut and revised version of the original poem. Yet it too soon breaks off, as Hyperion flares across the sky.

He had not managed to de-Miltonize it sufficiently. On 21 September 1819, the day that he wrote to Reynolds, to Woodhouse, and to the George Keatses about his walk and the autumnal poem it inspired, he announced that

> I have given up Hyperion – there were too many Miltonic inversions in it – Miltonic verse cannot be written but in an artful or rather artist's humour. I wish to give myself up to other

sensations. English ought to be kept up. It may be interesting to you to pick out some lines from Hyperion and put a mark × to the false beauty proceeding from art, and one ‖ to the true voice of feeling. Upon my soul 'twas imagination I cannot make the distinction – Every now and then there is a Miltonic into-nation – But I cannot make the division properly. The fact is, I must take a walk.

He needed to clear his head of florid poetic diction and Latinate inversions of word order. Miltonic verse could be written only with conscious contrivance; in order to become a negatively capable poet, he needed to give himself up 'to other sensations', to submit to what Wordsworth had called a 'wise passiveness', to allow the Muse to come to him instead of actively striving towards her. He had achieved a more 'English' voice in 'To Autumn', but now he needed to sustain that in the more extended form of 'high tragedy'. He had matched Chatterton in lyricism, but he knew that Chatterton's fake tragedies were poor things, and that *Otho the Great* was mere Jacobethan pastiche. The task was to write a genuinely Shakespearean tragedy.

But he also needed to earn a living. He decided to return to London, find a cheap lodging and occupy himself in the literary world. Perhaps he could become a second Hazlitt: 'I will write, on the liberal side of the question, for whoever will pay me . . . endeavouring, for a beginning, to get the theatricals of some paper.' He began another tragedy, set in the twelfth-century reign of King Stephen, which had been brought to his mind by the Hospital of St Cross. He did not get beyond four short opening scenes. His commitment to liberal politics diverted him into attempting a curious comic fairy tale in his old form of Spenserian stanzas, into which he inserted tart satire directed at the matrimonial difficulties of Fat Regent and an array of topical allusions – for example, to the invention of gas lighting and the filthy condition of hackney carriages. He neither finished nor published it.

Another contemplated tragedy, set in the time of Shakespeare, was the story of Queen Elizabeth's favourite, Robert Dudley, Earl of Leicester. Keats sounded out his publisher about the topic, and scribbled a few powerful lines, probably intended for it, on one of the sheets of his comic satire:

> This living hand, now warm and capable
> Of earnest grasping, would, if it were cold
> And in the icy silence of the tomb,
> So haunt thy days and chill thy dreaming nights
> That thou would wish thine own heart dry of blood
> So in my veins red life might stream again,
> And thou be conscience-calm'd – see here it is –
> I hold it towards you.

If this is not quite Shakespearean, it certainly catches the style of John Webster, that Jacobean dramatist 'much possessed by death' who was admired in the Keats circle as one of the Bard's most accomplished successors.

When this fragment was first published, it was assumed without any evidence to be addressed to Fanny Brawne – which, given its macabre tone, would have been very cruel. Keats did, however, address a group of three love poems to her upon his return to London in October 1819. He wrote to her in ecstasy the day after their reunion:

> My sweet Girl, I am living to day in yesterday: I was in a complete fa[s]cination all day. I feel myself at your mercy. Write me ever so few lines and tell [me] you will never be less kind to me than yesterday – You dazzled me – There is nothing in

the world so bright and delicate . . . I have had a thousand kisses, for which with my whole soul I thank love – but if you should deny me the thousand and first – 'twould put me to the proof how great a misery I could live through.

The three poems linger on the music of her voice and the allure of her body, while wrestling with his sense of being trapped by his love for her:

> Sweet voice, sweet lips, soft hand, and softer breast
> Warm breath, light whisper, tender semi-tone
> Bright eyes, accomplished shape, and languorous waist!

> let me feel that warm breath here and there
> To spread a rapture in my very hair –
> Oh, the sweetness of the pain! . . .
> Touch has a memory. Oh, say, love, say
> What can I do to kill it and be free
> In my old liberty?

> Oh, let me have thee whole – all, all, be mine!
> That shape, that fairness, that sweet minor zest
> Of love, your kiss – those hands, those eyes divine,
> That warm, white, lucent, million-pleasured breast.

Published posthumously, they were gathered as 'Verses to Fanny Brawne' in Fitzgerald's edition, with a quotation from a letter in which Keats told Fanny that he hoped that the act of writing to her would enable him to free his mind from the thought of her for a short time so that he could work. His last poem to her, in the same vein, though tainted with jealous thoughts, was composed a few months later, reflecting the darkening mood of his letters, in which he spoke of his fear that she might have the infidelity of Chaucer's and Shakespeare's Cressida. His love for her was, he said, both his pleasure and his torment.

*

In the summer of the previous year, George Keats and his bride Georgiana Wylie had disembarked in Philadelphia, travelled by wagon to Pittsburgh and continued on a keelboat south along the Ohio river to Henderson, Kentucky. George had then gone to Illinois to explore the prospect of joining a group of émigré English political liberals and radicals who were experimenting with innovative farming methods, such as the cross-breeding of sheep, in a community dedicated to liberty, equality and fraternity. Once he saw that this was not a prospect for personal wealth creation, George returned to Henderson, where he and Georgiana wintered in the home of a local resident who had welcomed them to the town: John James Audubon, who would later become famous for his marvellous engravings of the birds of America. At this time, Audubon was in business in Henderson. He had purchased a flour mill and slaves to work it for him. Now he persuaded George to invest in a scheme to run a steamboat up and down the Ohio river. In old age, Audubon looked ruefully back on the venture: 'We also took it into our heads to have a steamboat, in partnership with the engineer who had come from Philadelphia to fix the engine of that mill. This also proved an entire failure, and misfortune after misfortune came down upon us like so many avalanches, both fearful and destructive.'

Audubon's brother-in-law then took his opportunity, persuading George to become a partner in his sawmill in Louisville, Kentucky. Having made this investment, and plunged into a second steamboat venture, George found himself so short of cash that he had no choice but to borrow the cost of a package back to England in the hope of extracting the remainder of his inheritance from the family trust, which would have been enlarged by Tom's death. He was reunited with his brother in early January 1820. Though there were some lively dinners and parties with old friends, about which Keats wrote warmly in letters to Georgiana, the three-week visit was marked by tensions: the finances were still deeply entangled and John felt that he was being used, while George appears not to have been impressed by Fanny Brawne.

At eleven o'clock on the evening of 3 February, six days after George left for Liverpool to take the boat back across the Atlantic, Keats suffered a severe haemorrhage. Charles Brown ran for a surgeon, who prescribed rest but declared that the lungs were uninjured. Writing to his sister Fanny, Keats underplayed the incident: 'From imprudently leaving off my great coat in the thaw I caught cold which flew to my Lungs.' Brown – whose memory was sometimes melodramatic and often faulty – recalled that Keats's reaction at the time was much more severe. Squarely facing his medical expertise, he asked Brown to bring a candle so that he could examine a single drop of blood on his sheets. Then he looked up at his friend and, if Brown is to be believed, said in a calm voice 'I know the colour of that blood; – it is arterial blood; – I cannot be deceived in that colour; – that drop of blood is my death-warrant; – I must die.'

Over the following months, he ailed, partially recovered, and ailed again. Fevers came and went, along with tightness in the chest and coughing of blood. On his better days, he watched the world go by from a sofa-bed in Brown's front parlour: the coalman's delivery, a passing pot boy, old women heading for Hampstead Heath 'with bobbins and red cloaks and unpresuming bonnets', a man with a wooden clock – striking the whole time – under his arm, an old French emigrant with 'his hands joined behind on his hips, and his face full of political schemes'. He kept his sister Fanny informed about his progress;

she was still living miserably with Mr and Mrs Abbey, so he tried to keep her cheerful with tidbits of news. The doctor assured him, rather unconvincingly, that the problem was 'nervous irritability and a general weakness of the whole system' proceeding from 'anxiety of mind' and 'too great excitement of poetry' – a diagnosis not so very different from that of the doctors of fellow poet John Clare, who was admitted to a lunatic asylum on the basis of 'years addicted to poetical prosing'.

For a time Keats was too ill to prepare his next collection of poems for the press, but he was eventually able to work through the proofs. At the end of June, he received advance copies of the new volume, given the somewhat unprepossessing catch-all title *Lamia, Isabella, The Eve of St Agnes and Other Poems*. It began with the three narrative poems, then printed six odes (four of the five written in May 1819, together with 'To Autumn' and the earlier 'Bards of passion'), three other short poems, and finally the fragmentary first version of *Hyperion*.

The reviews were mixed, but in general much more favourable than those of his first volume and *Endymion*. Charles Lamb, kind and discerning as ever, was especially generous. He singled out 'The Eve of St Agnes' for special praise: 'like the radiance, which comes from those old windows upon the limbs and garments of the damsel, is the almost Chaucer-like painting, with which this poet illumes every subject he touches. We have scarcely any thing like in modern description. It brings us back to ancient days, and *Beauty making-beautiful old rhymes*' (the quotation is a line from Shakespeare's medievalizing sonnet 106). Several other papers focused less on the virtues of the new collection than the injustice of the earlier attacks on Keats in *Blackwood's* and the *Quarterly Review*. It was the narrative poems that garnered nearly all the attention. John Scott, editor of the *London Magazine*, waxed especially lyrical about *Hyperion*; for all that it was a fragment, it constituted 'one of the most extraordinary creations of any modern imagination'. Barely anything was said about the odes which would raise Keats's reputation to its posthumous heights.

*

In early July his doctor told him that, although there had been a respite in the spitting of blood, it would take months of rest for his health to be restored and that his best course of action would be to go to Italy to avoid the cold and damp of the next English winter. Keats set about marking up 'the most beautiful passages' in the copy of his beloved Spenser to give to Fanny Brawne before leaving the country. Reflecting on a sequence in *The Faerie Queene* in which an Iron Giant representing tyranny is defeated by the knight of Justice, he scribbled a single stanza in the Spenserian form, in which he imagined books taking the place of arms as a vehicle for liberty and reform. Richard Monckton Milnes, editor of his posthumous literary 'remains', described the lines as a prophecy of Keats's 'conviction of the ultimate triumph of freedom and equality by the power of transmitted knowledge'. These nine lines – beginning 'In after-time, a sage of mickle lore / Ycleped Typographus' – were, according to Brown, the last verses that Keats ever wrote. He was awakened to poetry by his reading of *The Faerie Queene* with Charles Cowden Clarke when he was a teenage boy; his final fragment, like his first poem, was an imitation of Spenser.

His chest pains were getting worse. He began to dread the prospect of a long journey by sea. He left a rudimentary will with his publisher. He asked his loyal friend Joseph Severn to paint him in miniature for Fanny. On 16 September 1820 his passport arrived and he assigned his copyright to Taylor and Hessey. The next morning, accompanied by Severn, he boarded the *Maria Crowther*, a brig bound for Naples.

Severn's miniature for Keats to give to Fanny Brawne:
the only painting of him executed in his lifetime

The Maria Crowther by Joseph Severn

They sailed down the Thames, stopping off at Gravesend for a female passenger to come on board. While they waited, Keats dined in the cabin with the captain, to whose cat he took a liking. The lady arrived, a Miss Cotterell, also afflicted with tuberculosis and bound for Naples in the hope of weather that might ease her lungs.

They rounded the coast of Kent with a fair wind behind them and on a beautiful morning they breakfasted on deck within sight of Brighton. It was not long, however, before a bad storm blew up, confining them to their beds in the cramped cabin with six berths and the travel trunks rolling across the floor. Severn and the ladies on board were violently sick, Keats calm and uncomplaining. The squall drove them back towards the shingled coastline at Dungeness and when it died down they were becalmed for three days before they could proceed to Portsmouth, where they landed and Keats went ashore for the night. Setting sail the next day, they were confronted with contrary winds, which sent them towards his old haunt, the Isle of Wight. On 1 October they made landfall again, this time at Lulworth Cove on the Dorset coast.

Keats had with him a copy of Shakespeare's *Poems*, which had been given to him by Reynolds, and in which he had marked up many of his favourite lines in the sonnets. He intended to pass the book on to Severn, as a mark of friendship and thanks for accompanying him on the voyage. Perhaps prompted by proximity to the Isle of Wight, from where he had written his first batch of swooning love letters to Fanny Brawne, Keats copied a sonnet of his own onto the blank leaf facing 'A Lover's Complaint', the poem that had followed the sonnets in Shakespeare's original collection of 1609.

A poem for Fanny, it was long assumed to have been his last work. In Scott Fitzgerald's edition, it was labelled 'THE LAST SONNET' and given an explanatory headnote:

On his way to Italy as his last chance of life, the vessel which bore Keats had been beating about the English Channel for a fortnight, when an opportunity was given for landing for a brief respite on the Dorsetshire coast. 'The bright beauty of the day,' says Lord Houghton [Monckton Milnes], Keats's biographer, 'and the scene revived the poet's drooping heart, and the inspiration remained with him for some time even after his return to the ship. It was then that he composed that sonnet of solemn tenderness.'

He was actually copying it out, not composing it. Another surviving manuscript reveals that it was written the previous year, either in July when he was on the Isle of Wight, signing off one of his letters to Fanny with the words 'I will imagine you Venus tonight and pray, pray, pray to your star like a He[a]then. Your's ever, fair Star, John Keats', or in October along with that group of love poems in which he kept returning to the image of her 'warm, white, lucent, million-pleasured breast'.

Bright star, would I were steadfast as thou art!
    Not in lone splendour hung aloft the night,
And watching, with eternal lids apart,
    Like Nature's patient sleepless Eremite,
The moving waters at their priestlike task
    Of pure ablution round earth's human shores
Or gazing on the new soft fallen mask
    Of snow upon the mountains and the moors:
No – yet still steadfast, still unchangeable,
    Pillow'd upon my fair love's ripening breast,
To feel for ever its soft fall and swell,
    Awake for ever in a sweet unrest,
Still, still to hear her tender-taken breath,
And so live ever – or else swoon to death.

For Scott Fitzgerald, this was Keats's greatest sonnet, perhaps the greatest of all sonnets since those of Shakespeare. All the Keatzian music is there – the rhythms and repetitions, the assonance and alliteration, and especially the sibilance, the soft fall and swell that is at once like quiet breathing and the sound of the sea – but so is the image of the longed-for but unattained beloved. Sexual desire is purified into romance, the 'pure ablution' of the moving waters anticipating the 'Absolution' of Fitzgerald's first attempt at the Gatsby theme. But only in dreams and poetry is the lover's head pillowed on the beautiful breast for ever. In reality, the bright star is far from the shore.

*

Gatsby first appears on his lawn in the moonlight, watching 'the silver pepper of the stars'. Below those bright stars, he stretches out his arms towards the dark water. Across the Sound, Nick sees 'a single green light, minute and far away, that might have been the end of a dock'. Gatsby has taken the house so that he can see it. The bright star, denoting Fanny Brawne, has become the green light on Daisy's dock.

Fitzgerald believed that Keats became a great poet when he wrote the sonnet on Chapman's Homer and that 'Bright Star' was his 'Last Sonnet'. In the former, hope is represented by the image of stout Cortez and his men gazing in wild surmise on the occasion of their first sight of the Pacific. The poem was in Fitzgerald's mind when the characters in *The Great Gatsby* drive into New York and Nick says that Manhattan seen from the Queensboro Bridge is always the city 'seen for the first time in its first wild promise of all the mystery and beauty in the world'. 'Chapman's Homer' was a poem of bright beginnings. 'Bright Star', by contrast, was a poem that, like the fatal journey back from New York in *Gatsby*, 'drove on toward death through the cooling twilight'. Keats cannot be as steadfast as the star. He will not see Fanny again.

At the end of *The Great Gatsby*, Fitzgerald binds the two sonnets, the two moods, together. Nick wanders down to the beach and sprawls on the sand, as Keats may have done when he was copying out 'Bright Star' for Severn on the Dorset coast. The big shore places are closed up. A ferryboat crosses the Sound, as Keats had crossed by ferry from the Isle of Wight after writing his first love letters to Fanny. The 'ripening breast' of her sonnet, with its 'soft fall and swell', is replaced by the swell of the tide

> Until gradually I became aware of the old island here that flowered once for Dutch sailor's eyes – a fresh, green breast of the new world. Its vanished trees, the trees that had made way for Gatsby's house, had once pandered in whispers to the last and greatest of all human dreams . . .

At which point Fitzgerald segues into the watcher of the skies when a new planet swims into his ken and Cortez's stare at the Pacific, his men looking 'at each other with a wild surmise'. Nick, alone, is silent not on a peak in Darien, but on sand trodden by the Dutch sailors as they saw Manhattan for the first time, when

> for a transitory enchanted moment man must have held his breath in the presence of this continent, compelled into an aesthetic contemplation he neither understood nor desired, face to face for the last time in history with something commensurate to his capacity for wonder.

And then he thinks of Gatsby's wonder 'when he first picked out the green light at the end of Daisy's dock'. Gatsby's American dream is supposed to be of an orgastic future; he has failed to grasp that 'it was already behind him, somewhere back in that vast obscurity beyond the city, where the dark fields of the republic rolled on under the night'. Year by year the future recedes before us, always elusive, just out of reach of our outstretched arms, like those of the lovers on the Grecian urn, always in mad pursuit.

Writing 'Bright Star' into his Shakespeare at Lulworth Cove, knowing in his heart that he will never again see the girl he had hoped to marry, Keats is a boat against the current, borne back ceaselessly into the past, gazing upon the single point of light.

'Bright Star' transcribed by Keats into his copy of Shakespeare's *Poems*, with note by Dilke claiming that it was his last poem, and watercolour sketch by Joseph Severn of the bay in Dorset where they were when it was transcribed

18

'STAHR: A ROMANCE'

Fitzgerald's self-projection into the character of Dick Diver was of a piece with his research into the latest psychiatric theory and his demands of Zelda's doctors that they should give him every detail of her condition. He wanted to be her doctor himself, as Dick is Nicole's. The reception of *Tender is the Night* was lukewarm. Many of its reviewers shared Fitzgerald's dissatisfaction with the novel's structure. He took pride, however, in pasting into his scrapbook a review in the specialist *Journal of Mental and Nervous Disease* that praised him for his 'discernment in face of the balance of psychotic cause and effect':

> For the psychiatrist and psychoanalyst the book is of special value as a probing story of some of the major dynamic interlockings in marriage which, conditioned by set economic and psychobiological situations, have their innumerable counterparts in differences of degree rather than kind. After her mother's death Nicole Warren suffers intercourse with the father. The psychotic effects, accruing during adolescence and her early maturity, develop into a severe schizophrenia.

If he could not be her doctor, at least he had the satisfaction of knowing that he had given an accurate – if insufficiently tender – account of mental illness to his readers.

Fitzgerald was thinking a lot about family dynamics. Dick Diver's return to America for his father's funeral was based on the experience of his own father's death in January 1931. He was not close to his only sister Annabel, who had married a naval officer; nor indeed to his mother, who was ill and near death. And he had no brothers, no sons. Fitzgerald's heroes usually have no siblings; for all his charm and sociability, Dick Diver is deeply lonely. Just as Keats absorbed himself more and more in his poetry, with better and better results, after he lost Tom to tuberculosis and George to America, so Fitzgerald found a family in his novels: 'Books are like brothers,' he said. Gatsby was his 'imaginary elder brother', Amory his younger, Anthony his 'worry'. Dick was his 'comparatively good brother'. But all of them were 'far from home': he hoped that when he had the courage to shine 'the old white light' on the home of his heart, then he would write his greatest novel. It was not to be.

His primary concern from now on would be to earn enough money to maintain Zelda and Scottie. If he could not be his wife's doctor and his daughter's teacher, at least he would do his best to place them in the best hospitals and best schools. The month after the publication of *Tender is the Night*, Zelda was transferred to the Sheppard-Pratt hospital near Baltimore, where she made several suicide attempts. In his ledger Scott recorded that he was very unhappy. He was also concerned about his own health. Early in 1935, convinced that a tubercular infection that had been inactive was now attacking his lungs, he sought treatment at a retreat in the mountains of North Carolina. New X-rays confirmed the diagnosis. 'Debts terrible', he noted in his ledger, along with 'Went on wagon for all liquor

& alcohol' and 'Work & worry'. And a couple of months later, 'Zelda very bad'. The ledger then grinds to a halt.

That summer, he had a brief affair with a wealthy married Texan woman called Beatrice Dance. She was staying in Asheville where her sister was being treated for neurosis. When her husband arrived in town, there was a scene. Fitzgerald did the right thing, sending her a powerful 'Dear John' letter of the kind that Dick Diver might have sent to Rosemary Hoyt:

> There are emotions just as important as ours running concurrently with them – and there is literally no standard in life other than a sense of duty. When people get mixed up they try to throw out a sort of obscuring mist, and then the sharp shock of a *fact* – a collision seems to be the only thing to make them sober-minded again. You once said 'Zelda is your *love*!' (only you said 'lu-uv'). And I gave her all the youth and freshness that was in me. And it's a sort of investment that is as tangible as my talent, my child, my money: That you had the same sort of appeal to me, deep down in the gut, doesn't change the other.

The loyalty to Zelda manifested here did not stop him from having a fling with a call girl called 'Lottie Stephens' who worked the luxury hotels of Asheville, always impeccably dressed, with a book under her arm, and accompanied by her twin black poodles, Juliet and Romeo (always named in that order – one was never to call them Romeo and Juliet). When she was introduced to Fitzgerald, the book was *The Great Gatsby*. Once they got to know each other, she gave her judgment on the hero: a sweet man, but also 'a romantic sap in love with a memory'. Daisy, she thought, was 'a worthless woman'.

Fitzgerald decided to perform a *Pygmalion* upon Lottie. He began by reciting the 'Ode to a Nightingale', then recommended that she should read *Lady Chatterley's Lover*. Having become increasingly interested in radical left-wing politics, he educated her in the life and work of John Reed, the communist journalist who had witnessed the Russian Revolution and written about it in *Ten Days that Shook the World*.

He also sought reassurance that Zelda's frequent claims about his sexual inadequacy were unfounded. Hemingway told of an occasion upon which Fitzgerald had attempted to resolve his anxiety about penis size by inspecting naked statuary in the Louvre. Now Lottie reassured him, on the basis of her considerable expertise in the matter, that his endowment was within the spectrum of normal (though she did find his performance unsatisfactorily fast, as if sex was something he always felt guilty about and wanted to get over with as quickly as possible). Why then, he asked her, did Zelda persistently taunt him about his small size? Lottie replied that it could only be because she was nuts and that any woman who said such things to her man was a bitch. Daisy was merciful in comparison, she suggested: she put Gatsby out of his misery by helping to kill him, whereas Zelda was clearly trying to cripple Scott for life by humiliating him, a fate worse than death. At this, Fitzgerald, who was drunk, slapped her and called her a whore.

There had been times when, fuelled by liquor and angry at being called a 'fairy', he had hit Zelda. For a man in love with beauty, his behaviour when intoxicated could be very ugly. Lottie, nevertheless, felt sorry for him and went to see him again. He gave a sobbing apology and begged for forgiveness; their relationship endured for several months. She came to regard him as a lover and not a client, finding him 'fun and exciting, charming and lovable when sober, nasty and abusive when drunk'. She was particularly adept at nursing him into acknowledgment of his insecurities. Astutely, she saw that his homophobia and his anxiety about his manhood went back to the experience of being bullied at school for looking effeminate and being dressed in Little Lord Fauntleroy suits. Princeton had not entirely straightened him out: on the one hand, his attempts to become a footballer and his lifelong passion for the game were a mark of manliness, but on the other he could not resist the opportunity to wear drag in amateur theatricals.

Given these mitigating circumstances, she could accept the homophobia, but the relationship foundered on her lover's other blind spot: race. According to the principal witness to the affair, a highly observant if not entirely reliable writer and bookseller named Tony Buttita, who spent the summer of 1935 drinking with Fitzgerald in Asheville, the liaison came to an end when Scott revealed his deep-seated prejudice. Having expressed a good deal of sympathy for the ideals of the Communist Party of America, he told Lottie that where he differed from them was on the matter of race equality. As she recalled, 'He talked like a dyed-in-the-wool Southerner, thinking I was on his side.' At which point she revealed that she was mixed race herself. Fitzgerald stormed about the room in a blind rage, looking for a bottle, crying 'Oh God, what's happened to me?' Lottie told him that it was common knowledge in the South that 'a white boy wasn't a man till he smoked, got stinko under the kitchen table, and had himself a [black] gal in the barn'. Now, she said, he had gained all three qualifications for manhood. That was the end of the affair.

*

As usual, Scribner's followed up the new novel with a collection of short stories, which brought some additional income. But sales of *Tender is the Night* were mediocre and his agent Harold Ober, who had served him as loyally as his editor Max Perkins, was beginning to have trouble placing new stories in the magazines. The literary marketplace was suffering from the Great Depression. An exception was *Esquire* magazine, founded in 1933 with an emphasis on fashion and what would now be called lifestyle. Bypassing his agent, Fitzgerald built a relationship with the editor. He began by polishing up two essays by Zelda – one on all the hotels they had stayed in over the years and the other on their possessions – and publishing them under his own name, which earned a better price than hers.

Then in the wayward year of 1935, suffering from writer's block, he asked for an advance on future work but was told that he must produce something for the editor to show the men on the business side of the magazine. Anything would do, even some Gertrude Stein-like stream-of-consciousness spontaneity. Fitzgerald responded with a raw and confessional series of essays that began with the words 'Of course all life is a process of breaking down.' Published under the title 'The Crack-Up', they advertised his alcoholism to the American public and established the image of him as the washed-up writer, the once golden boy on the road to ruin.

It was also in 1935 that a movie with a familiar theme was released. In *The Wedding Night*, Gary Cooper played a novelist whose first novel was a huge success, but who declines in alcoholism when his next two are failures and his publisher turns down his fourth. Broke, he and his wife move to the countryside in Connecticut. When his wife goes back to New York, the writer falls in love with a much younger woman, the daughter of a neighbour, who is engaged to a wealthy man she does not love. The story was conceived by a writer called Edwin Knopf (brother of a famous publisher), who had met the Fitzgeralds in the south of France. It was intended as a vehicle for Anna Sten, a beautiful Russian actress whom Samuel Goldwyn hoped would be the next Garbo. She would play the younger woman. Knopf based the broken-down writer on his own experience of failure and liquor, but made him resemble the much better-known figure of

Scott Fitzgerald. In the original draft, the married couple are called Scott and Zelda, but by the time the movie reached the screen they had become Tony and Dora Barrett (by a bizarre coincidence, Knopf's storyline was worked up by a prolific screenwriter, no relation to Scott, called Edith Fitzgerald).

It was only when the crack-up essays were published in *Esquire* the following year that Edwin Knopf discovered just how close to the bone his portrayal of Fitzgerald had been. He decided to help out, suggesting to MGM that they should hire Scott as a screenwriter. 'Scott who?' was the response of Louis B. Mayer. Studio executive Eddie Mannix knew who Fitzgerald was, though he had to ask 'What's he done lately?', to which Knopf replied 'Not much.' But he persuaded them to take the risk. By this time, Zelda was in the Highland Hospital in Asheville. She began suffering from religious mania, a common symptom of schizophrenia. The bills from the hospital and Scottie's boarding school were racking up.

The colonnade entrance to the MGM lot where Fitzgerald worked (now Sony Studios, Culver City)

In July 1937, Scott Fitzgerald arrived in Hollywood for the third time. Knopf had wangled him an initial six-month contract with MGM. He took up residence in the Garden of Allah Hotel on Sunset Boulevard, among the movie stars and writers. Each day he would pass under the Roman colonnades at the entrance to the MGM lot in Culver City and make his way to the third floor of the writers' building, where he worked from nine till six. He was on the wagon. He got himself through the day by constantly drinking Coca-Cola, on top of the Benzedrine he took in the morning and the chloral and Nembutal at night, to which he added Digitalin when he started getting heart tremors.

His first assignment was *A Yank at Oxford*, though he ended up as a bit-part player on the writing team, rather as Gatsby's time as an 'Oggsford Man' amounted to no more than a brief post-Armistice residence opportunity for American officers. Fitzgerald said that his only contributions to make it to the screen were a scene in which Robert Taylor and Maureen O'Sullivan listen from a punt on May morning to the choirboys singing from the top of Magdalen Tower, and a single trademark line, 'Don't rub the sleep out of your eyes. It's beautiful sleep.'

The only film for which Fitzgerald got a writing credit was *Three Comrades*, based on a novel by Erich Maria Remarque. Fitzgerald hoped that it would be his screen breakthrough, a worthy sequel to the film version of Remarque's most famous novel *All Quiet on the Western Front*. The three comrades are veterans, disillusioned by war, by the rampant inflation and unemployment of Weimar Germany, and by the fighting on the streets between Nazis and communists. The protagonist is a used-car dealer on the verge of bankruptcy who meets a mysterious, beautiful young woman of a higher social class. He introduces her to gambling and drinking. She suffers a lung haemorrhage and is removed to a Swiss sanatorium. He follows her there and among the mountains in the months while she is dying his nihilism is redeemed by love. The oblique parallels with Scott and Zelda made it an excellent vehicle for him and his screenplay was remarkably faithful to the novel.

But this was Hollywood, where the writer was at the bottom of the pecking order and the producer (Joe Mankiewicz) would always insist on changes. And always get his way. Where Perkins had gently asked for rewrites, Mankiewicz barked out what they would be. Fitzgerald perceived criticism as rejection: 'Taking things hard – from Genevra to Joe Mank', he scribbled in his notebook. (By this time, his abysmal spelling extended even to the name of his first love.)

The companion he took to the premiere remembered his reaction to the final cut of *Three Comrades*:

> 'At least they've kept my beginning,' he said on the way. But as the picture unfolded, Scott slumped deeper and deeper in his seat. At the end he said, 'They changed even that.' He took it badly. 'That s.o.b.,' he growled when he came home, and furiously, helplessly, as though he had to lash out at something, he punched the wall, hard. 'My God, doesn't he know what he's done?'

The companion was Sheilah Graham, the English-born gossip columnist who had become his lover. They first met, briefly, at a party at the Garden of Allah to celebrate her engagement to the Marquess of Donegall, who had arrived in Hollywood with the intention of taking her back home. Then he had seen her at a dinner dance of the Screen Writers Guild and a passion had been kindled. She was glad to break off her engagement, despite the financial sacrifice. Hollywood was the future, the old country the past.

Sheilah reminded him of a young, beautiful and healthy Zelda. They would fight, they would break up and get back together, but she would be there for him until the end. He was deeply torn. He still loved Zelda, but she seemed irreparably damaged whereas Sheilah, who had remade herself over and over again, represented hope for a second chance at life. On the other hand, Sheilah had a ruthlessly ambitious streak and he could not help fearing that she would reject him if a better prospect came into sight. After his death, she was wounded to the quick when she took out of its frame a photograph of herself that she had given him and found the words written on the back, no doubt when he was drunk, 'Portrait of a Prostitute'.

It can hardly be a coincidence that Fitzgerald's next project was a movie with the working title *Infidelity*. This was a tricky subject in Hollywood, given the demands of the Motion Picture Production Code:

> Sex. The sanctity of the institution of marriage and the home shall be upheld. Pictures shall not infer that low forms of sex relationship are the accepted or common thing.
>
> 1. Adultery, sometimes necessary plot material, must not be explicitly treated, or justified, or presented attractively.
>
> 2. Scenes of Passion
>   a. They should not be introduced when not essential to the plot.
>   b. Excessive and lustful kissing, lustful embraces, suggestive postures and gestures, are not to be shown.
>   c. In general passion should be so treated that these scenes do not stimulate the lower and baser element.

Fitzgerald had an idea for getting round the problem. Surely the Production Code Administration Office would not be able to object to a story that had the authority of Shakespeare?

I have been playing with [an] idea [which is] utterly fantastic . . .
What would one think of Othello in modern dress on the screen?
It would be [a] fascinating job for a writer and, I should think,
for a director. Of course the great parts of the Moor, Iago, and
Desdemona belong to the ages. There is infidelity for you on a
grand scale. The more I think of it, the more I like it.

What could be a better way around the Code than a story in
which the accusation of adultery is false and the true infidelity
is that of the protagonist's apparent friend? There was only
one problem: the Code also banned miscegenation. And on
second thoughts would Joan Crawford, slated for the female
lead, go along with the idea? Besides, 'the Moor would have
to be changed for the Southern trade'. Fitzgerald abandoned
the idea and wrote instead a script, with no small measure of
guilt and autobiography, in which the marriage of a wealthy
couple is broken when the husband has a one-night stand with
a former secretary. It was his best script, but, as he reported
with 'infinite disappointment' in a letter to Scottie, they 'reached
a censorship barrier': 'It <u>won't</u> be Joan's next picture and we
are setting it aside awhile till we can think of a way of half-
witting halfwit Hays and his legion of decency.'

In the next paragraph of his letter, Scott gave his daughter
some Keatzian advice on the art of writing:

About <u>adjectives</u>: all fine prose is based on verbs carrying the
sentences. They make sentences move. Probably the finest technical poem in English is Keats' Eve of Saint Agnes. A line like:
   The Hare limped trembling through the frozen grass, is so
alive that you race through it, scarcely noticing it, yet it has
colored the whole poem with its movement – the limping,
trembling, and freezing is going on before your own eyes. Would
you read that poem for me, and report?

He was a born teacher. All through the Hollywood years, he wrote loving letters to Scottie, full of encouragement for her studies. Good writing, he told her, is like '*swimming under water* and holding your breath'. Don't give up mathematics, he told her, too; learn the basic principles of science, note the difference between nominalists and realists in the history of philosophy, and, when it came to driving lessons, remember that in wet weather one should use only the brake, 'don't depress the clutch'.

He wanted her to love literature, perhaps to be a writer, but more than that he wanted her to have a rounded education, to be prepared for whatever life might throw at her in the light of her parents' decline. As far as poetry was concerned, he would guide her but not force her. You either had a passion for it or you didn't: 'Poetry is either something that lives like fire inside you – like music to the musician or Marxism to the communist – or else it is nothing, an empty formalized bore around which pedants can endlessly drone their notes and explanations.' Anybody who has an ear and who has studied Keats's best poems – the odes, the best of the sonnets, 'Isabella' and 'The Eve of St Agnes' – would ever afterwards be able to 'distinguish between gold and dross in what one read': 'In themselves those eight poems are a scale of workmanship for anybody who wants to know truly about words, their most utter value for evocation, persuasion or charm.'

He and Zelda also kept up their correspondence, for the most part loving but sometimes accusatory. Sheilah Graham kept him from loneliness in the hills above Los Angeles, satisfied him sexually and tried to control the drinking that led to outbursts of verbal abuse and even physical violence, but she knew that his reason for being in Hollywood was the income from the studios that would support his wife and daughter. He would never divorce Zelda. Over Christmas 1937 he visited her in Asheville and took her on a vacation to Florida and a visit to her mother in Montgomery. They met Scottie at Virginia Beach, quarrelled and Scott hit the bottle on his return to LA.

The following spring, he rented a bungalow in Malibu Beach, found for him by Sheilah. They were now recognized in Hollywood as a couple. That autumn, Scottie began at Vassar College in New York State, and Scott moved to a cottage on the estate of Edward Everett Horton at Encino, just over the hill into the San Fernando Valley. He worked on a script called *The Women*, in which he created a character who was part Zelda, part Sheilah. MGM did not like the result; it was eventually rescued, a recurring pattern, by Anita Loos. Then he inherited a historical story about Marie Curie when the English writer Aldous Huxley left the studio, but it was taken from him because he wanted more science whereas MGM wanted more romance, since the movie was intended for Garbo.

At the end of the year, his contract with MGM was not renewed, so he had to freelance. He joined the team working on *Gone with the Wind* for producer David O. Selznick and director George Cukor, but his attempts to replace clichéd screen dialogue with more authentic and moving lines from Margaret Mitchell's original novel were consistently rebuffed. When Ashley conjures up for Scarlett a vision of the Confederate army with 'no arms – no foods', Scott wrote sarcastically in the margin of the draft screenplay 'It's news that the South fought without arms?' He was eventually fired after an argument about how to make the character of Aunt Pittypat funny.

By now, he was embarking on unstoppable benders. Sheilah Graham was commissioned to do a weekly version of her newspaper gossip columns on the radio. Scott helped with her scripts. She was, however, thrown off balance by the time delay caused by the distance from Chicago, where the syndicating radio station was based. Before being fired, she was given the opportunity to broadcast from Chicago, to see if this would calm her voice and stop her from stumbling. Scott flew with her, but got so drunk on the first refuelling stop in Albuquerque that he wasn't allowed back on the plane and was forced to return to Los Angeles alone. The incident was dramatized with remarkable fidelity in *Beloved Infidel*, the 1959 movie based on Sheilah's memoir of their relationship.

Another flight ended in more public humiliation. Commissioned to go to Dartmouth, New Hampshire, as research for a campus movie, he got drunk on location and was fired. He got drunk again when he took Zelda out of the hospital for a weekend in Havana. When he tried to break up a cockfight in the street, he was beaten up.

His ego was battered too. Once, he went into a Los Angeles bookshop and asked for his own work and there weren't any copies and the bookseller hadn't even heard of Scott Fitzgerald. On another occasion, he was excited to see in the *Los Angeles Times* that a dramatization of 'The Diamond as Big as the Ritz' was to open at the Pasadena Playhouse. For the opening night, he hired a limousine and took Sheilah to dinner at the top-end Trocadero restaurant. When they arrived in Pasadena, they found the theatre strangely dark. Asking in the lobby if they had got the wrong night, he was informed that it was to be an amateur student performance in the upstairs hall. They sat through it, along with a tiny audience. Fitzgerald graciously went backstage afterwards. 'They were all nice kids,' he told Sheilah in the limousine on the way home, 'they seemed a little awkward when I introduced myself. I told them they'd done a good job.' Apparently, they had assumed that the author of the story was dead.

*

His plan had been to begin and end his new novel with an airplane. His notes included an instruction to himself to craft the opening with great care: 'Landing at Glendale – and there it was again the bright California moon. (work out description of the hush of the motors, lights, etc., as elaborate settling down in the warm California night.)' The climax was to be a plane crash that killed Monroe Stahr, the boy wonder of Hollywood, the protagonist who is drawn out from the legendary figure of Irving Thalberg.

In the first chapter, the narrator, Cecilia Brady, a college student who is the daughter of a producer, finds herself in the same LA-bound plane as Monroe Stahr, who is travelling incognito. She has always been in love with him, but she remains at a distance from the main plot – 'She is of the movies but not in them', Fitzgerald explained in letters to Perkins and the editor of the magazine in which he hoped for a serialization. Cecilia has been formed by Hollywood – 'It's more than possible that some of the pictures which Stahr himself conceived had shaped me into what I was,' she says – and yet she is not a player in the world of the studios. This allows her to be a narrator from the sidelines, akin to Nick Carraway in *The Great Gatsby*.

Fitzgerald did not, however, manage to solve the problem of viewpoint in scenes where she was not present. He told his editors that he planned to grant himself the privilege of letting his narrator imagine the actions of the other characters, as Joseph Conrad had done in his stories. He hoped 'to get the verisimilitude of a first person narrative, combined with a Godlike knowledge of all events that happen to my characters'. The difficulty, though, came with the reconciliation of these two modes. His draft accordingly had several clunky transitions along the lines of 'This is Cecilia taking up the narrative in person'.

As always, Fitzgerald had trouble with his title. The half-finished typescript, together with a selection from his synopses and notes, was published by Edmund Wilson in the autumn after his death, padded out with a reprint of *The Great Gatsby* and the five short stories that Wilson regarded as his best. It was given the title *The Last Tycoon: an unfinished novel by F. Scott Fitzgerald*. A few weeks before his death, Fitzgerald had asked Sheilah Graham whether she thought 'The Love of the Last Tycoon' was a good title; he wrote it down and added the possible subtitle 'A Western'. But that is not what appears on the title page of the typescript. There, the book is called

STAHR

A Romance

by

F. Scott Fitzgerald

Hollywood was the place where you lived among the stars. On the title page, Fitzgerald's secretary scribbled by hand 'The Homes of the Stars', the title of one of his Pat Hobby stories for *Esquire*.

A star motif runs through the novel. Stahr, who is in mourning for his dead movie-star wife, first glimpses his new love interest when she floats past him on his flooded studio lot, aboard a huge head of the goddess Siva. The detail that he notices is a silver belt with stars cut out of it. What attracts him is her resemblance to Minna Davis, his lost wife who has died in a fire (Fitzgerald explained to Thalberg's widow Norma Shearer that the identification of Stahr with Thalberg, who had died in 1936 at the age of thirty-seven, should not be taken too literally). When Stahr tracks down the girl and sees her again, she has the 'starry veiled expression' of his dead wife. And on the penultimate page of the incomplete typescript, ping-pong balls lie around in the grass on Stahr's lush lawn 'like a constellation of stars'.

The lover, Kathleen, whom Stahr seduces 'because she is slipping away', as Fitzgerald put it in his working notes, was in many respects inspired by Sheilah. Their time in Malibu lay behind the best love scene that Fitzgerald ever wrote, when Stahr takes Kathleen to his half-built beach house there: 'Stahr's eyes and Kathleen's met and tangled. For an instant they made love as no one dares to do after. Their glance was closer than an embrace, more urgent than a call.'

There is a new maturity and balance to Fitzgerald's prose. Whereas the Pat Hobby stories turned on his disillusionment with Hollywood, *Stahr: A Romance* gives ample room to its dreams as well. When Fitzgerald moved to Malibu, he wryly remarked that the Pacific did not have him staring in 'wild surmise', but early in the novel there is a more positive allusion to Keats's inspirational sonnet: 'the man named Dick kept standing up in the car as if he were Cortez or Balboa, looking over that gray fleecy undulation'. Again, in his working notes for the novel, Fitzgerald wrote that 'Anything added to beauty has to be paid for', yet in the book itself Stahr is 'glad that there was beauty in the world that would not be weighed in the scales of the casting department'.

Stahr himself is developed out of Fitzgerald's slight first-hand knowledge of Thalberg – the railroad-through-the-mountain story is there – into a compelling portrait of a Hollywood mogul. 'He led pictures way up past the range and power of the theatre, reaching a sort of golden age, before the censorship'; he ruthlessly fires a director on set (causing the poor man to reflect ruefully that he won't be able to marry his third wife, as planned). He is a perfectionist, raging that a beautifully acted scene has been thrown away because the camera wasn't quite positioned to capture the beautiful top of the actress's head – it

was for the sight of the top of a beautiful actress's head that
people went to the movie theatre. What makes for the unity
of a film, he is asked? 'I'm the unity.'

He is an idealist, who believes in the endurance of great
art. In a sublimation of Keats, he quotes the French Romantic
Théophile Gautier: 'Tout passe. – L'art robuste / Seul a l'éter-
nité' ('Everything passes – only robust art lasts for eternity').
At the same time, he is half in love with easeful death. It is
death itself that haunts him, as well as his lost love Minna,
who embodies a golden age of Hollywood that is slipping
away. Gradually, though, regenerated by his fleeting affair
with Kathleen, 'his apprehension of splendor was fading so
that presently the luxury of eternal mourning would depart'.
In creating the character, Fitzgerald regained the negative
capability that eluded him when he put too much of himself
into the figure of Dick Diver. Had the novel been finished,
Thalberg would have been a more noble Gatsby and Fitzgerald
would have achieved the ambition he set himself to create
another novel that 'would be short like *Gatsby* but the same
in that it will have the transcendental approach, an attempt
to show a man's life through some passionately regarded
segment of it'.

He would also have captured, better than any other writer
(with the possible exception of Nathanael West in *The Day of
the Locust*), the world of Hollywood's first golden age, the
early 1930s. For Fitzgerald, that age was to the west coast what
his Jazz Age had been to the east a decade before. He sensed
an ending with the enforcement of the Hays Code and the
premature death of Thalberg. In one of his pages of notes for
the novel he wrote of Stahr, 'Suddenly outdated he dies.' He
continued: 'And they build the Stahr Building.' And then he
recycled a paragraph from 'Basil and Cleopatra', written a
decade before:

There was a flurry of premature snow in the air and the stars looked cold.

Staring up at them he saw that they were his stars as always – symbols of ambition, struggle and glory. The wind blew through them, trumpeting that high white note for which he always listened, and the thin-brown clouds, stripped for battle, passed in review. The scene was of an unparalleled brightness and magnificence, and only the practiced eye of the commander saw that one star was no longer there.

'One star was no longer there' could have been the mantra of his Hollywood years: the final screenplay he completed was an adaptation for Twentieth-Century Fox of a highly successful new British stage play about a once great Shakespearean actor drinking his days away in a lonely boarding house. His script was rejected for being too dark.

Another project that never got the green light from the studios was an adaptation of a Broadway play about a couple who drive each other mad in a failing marriage. When Fitzgerald saw the script, he must for a moment have wondered whether it told a different story, that of Keats and Fanny Brawne: its title was *Bright Star*.

The Hollywood years: Scott Fitzgerald in 1937, looking the worse for
wear, photographed by his friend Carl Van Vechten

'I ETERNALLY SEE HER FIGURE ETERNALLY VANISHING'

Waiting for the wind to get up, Keats wrote despairingly to Charles Brown from the cabin of the *Maria Crowther*:

I wish for death every day and night to deliver me from these pains, and then I wish death away, for death would destroy even those pains which are better than nothing. Land and Sea, weakness and decline, are great separators, but death is the great divorcer for ever. When the pang of this thought has passed through my mind, I may say the bitterness of death is passed. . . . I think without my mentioning it for my sake you would be a friend to Miss Brawne, when I am dead. You think she has many faults – but, for my sake, think she has not one – – if there is any thing you can do for her by word or deed I know you will do it.

The thought of leaving Fanny was 'beyond everything horrible'. He felt 'the sense of darkness' coming over him: 'I eternally see her figure eternally vanishing.'

Once they were underway, the wind took them south at

uncomfortable speed. Severn sketched Keats propped up on his berth (the drawing is, alas, lost). During a three-day storm in the Bay of Biscay, Keats read the cannibalistic shipwreck scene from Byron's latest poem, *Don Juan*, but threw it down, telling Severn that it gave too dark an idea of human nature. 'Byron's poetry is based on a paltry originality, that of being new by making solemn things gay and gay things solemn.' Off Cape St Vincent at the southern tip of Portugal, they were becalmed for a while; Keats delighted in the sight of a sea-shouldering whale, no doubt reminding him of the line in Spenser over which he had enthused with Charles Cowden Clarke as a boy. There was then a moment of drama when two Portuguese men-of-war sailed towards them and one of them fired a shot across their bows. They came close enough to hear the voice of the captain asking through a speaking trumpet whether they had seen the privateers they were chasing.

The *Maria Crowther* turned east into the Mediterranean. They passed through the strait at dawn, with a favourable westerly behind them and the rock of Gibraltar glowing like a vast topaz. Severn indulged his painterly eye: 'seeming close to starboard, so translucent was that fine air, the African coast, here golden, and there blue as a sapphire, stretching away into a pearly haze'. Keats, meanwhile, 'lay entranced, and with a look of serene abstraction upon his worn face'. The remainder of the voyage was calm.

Upon arrival in the Bay of Naples, they were quarantined on board for ten days. Miss Cotterell's brother, a banker based in the city, sent on fruit and flowers, passed up from small boats that clustered around the *Maria Crowther*. Keats gorged himself on grapes and wrote to Mrs Brawne, telling her of their safe arrival and of how he was taking comfort in the tokens that Fanny had given him: a paperknife in a silver case, her hair in a locket, and a pocketbook in a gold net. Once allowed ashore, Keats and Severn took lodgings in a spacious room with a view of Vesuvius. An invitation to Pisa arrived from Percy Shelley, with whom Keats had struck up a correspondence about poetry (including the advice to load every rift of his subjects with ore). He continued to yearn for Fanny: 'Every thing I have in my trunks that reminds me of her goes through me like a spear. The silk lining she put in my travelling cap scalds my head.' He sought to distract himself by reading Samuel Richardson's novel *Clarissa*. Miss Cotterell's brother, a former naval officer, showed him some of the sights of Naples, but he was uncomfortable with the atmosphere in the city, which was under the harsh control of the reactionary French Bourbon monarchy. According to Severn, it was a night at the theatre that led Keats to demand they should leave town. What appeared to be two extremely realistic-looking statues of guardsmen flanked the stage – until they moved. They were real soldiers, there for crowd control. Keats allegedly professed himself unwilling to be 'buried amid a people with such miserable political debasement'.

They hired a ramshackle carriage and headed north to Rome. It travelled so slowly that Severn was able to walk beside it, gathering wild flowers on the way. Keats was tired and listless, cast down by the poor food and lodgings at their stopping-places along the route, but uplifted by glimpses of the sea and scents from the hills. Severn 'literally filled the little carriage with flowers', bringing Keats 'a strange joy' that took him for a moment from his pain and weakness.

Severn's story about the sentries on stage was characteristically melodramatic. The intention had always been to go to Rome. Prior to their departure from England, arrangements had been made to put Keats under the care of a distinguished Edinburgh-trained doctor who was resident in Rome, James Clark (he later became physician to Queen Victoria and was granted a knighthood). Rooms had been secured at number 26 on the Piazza di Spagna, immediately below the Spanish Steps, across the square from the doctor's own house. Clark reported back to England that the disease appeared to be mostly in the stomach; he had milder concerns about the heart and the lungs, but was worried by his patient's 'mental exertions', not to mention his anxiety over the cost of treatment.

Keats lay in a dark back bedroom, unable to go out. At the end of November, he wrote, with difficulty, to Brown: 'I have an habitual feeling of my real life having past, and that I am leading a posthumous existence.' Both the memory of Fanny and the possibility of writing more poetry were slipping away from him: 'There is one thought enough to kill me; I have been well, healthy, alert, etc., walking with her, and now – the knowledge of contrast, feeling for light and shade, all that information (primitive sense) necessary for a poem, are great enemies to the recovery of the stomach.' He asked Brown to pass on news of his health to George and, especially, to send a note to sister Fanny – 'who walks about my imagination like a ghost – she is so like Tom'. He was never good at farewells, even on paper.

> I always made an awkward bow.
>
> > God bless you!
> > John Keats.

These are his last surviving written words.

Hereafter, we are reliant on Severn. He recorded a severe relapse in mid-December:

> Not a moment can I be from him – I sit by his bed and read all day – and at night I humour him in all his wanderings. He has just fallen asleep – the first for 8 nights, and now from mere exhaustion. . . . I had seen him wake on the morning of this

attack, and to all appearance he was going on merrily and had unusual good spirits – when in an instant a Cough seized him, and he vomited near two Cup-fuls of blood. – In a moment I got Dr Clarke, who saw the manner of it, and immediately took away about 8 ounces of blood from the Arm – it was black and thick in the extreme. Keats was much alarmed and dejected – O what an awful day I had with him! – He rush'd out of bed and said 'this day shall be my last,' – and but for me most certainly it would.

That closing remark is an instance of the egotism which Mrs Jones detected when she read Severn's dispatches from the deathbed.

Early in the new year, Dr Clark reported more bleeding from the lungs and complete ruin of the digestive organs. Keats was sinking daily. Severn, writing just before midnight on Sunday 14 January:

> Poor Keats has just fallen asleep – I have watched him and read to him – to his very last wink – he has been saying to me 'Severn I can see under your quiet look – immense twisting and contending – you don't know what you are reading – you are enduring for me more than I'd have you – O! that my last hour was come.'

Keats's religious scepticism meant that he could not take the 'last cheap comfort' of faith in the afterlife. Through chattering teeth, he said to Severn, 'Why is this – O! I have serv'd everyone with my utmost good – yet why is this – I cannot understand this.'

Ten days later: 'Another week and less and less hope . . . he has shewn still worse symptoms every day – clay-like expectoration – in large quantities – night sweats – a ghastly wasting-away of his body and extremities – with the approaches to a diarrhoea by laxity and griping of the bowels – his food passing through him very quick and but little digested.' He clung on into February, the weather outside cold, wet and windy:

> Four days previous to his death – the change in him was so great that I passed each moment in dread – not knowing what the next would have – he was calm and firm at its approaches – to a most astonishing degree – he told [me] not to tremble for he did not think that he should be convulsed – he said – 'did you ever see any one die' no – 'well then I pity you poor Severn – what trouble and danger you have got into for me – now you must be firm for it will not last long – I shall soon be laid in the quiet grave – thank God for the quiet grave – O! I can feel the cold earth upon me – the daisies growing over me – O for this quiet – it will be my first'.

On the afternoon of 23 February 1821, breathing with great difficulty, Keats asked Severn to lift him up in his bed. He no longer had the power to cough up his phlegm:

> an immense sweat came over him so that my breath felt cold to him – 'don't breath[e] on me – it comes like Ice' – he clasped my hand very fast as I held him in my arms – the mucus was boiling within him – it gurgled in his throat – this increased – but yet he seem'd without pain – his eyes look'd upon me with extreme sensibility but without pain – at 11 he died in my arms.

In a letter to Brown, Severn recorded Keats's last words: 'Severn – I – lift me up – I am dying – I shall die easy – don't be frightened – be firm, and thank God it has come!'

A death mask was taken the next day. Severn wrote to friends and family. When Fanny Brawne had recovered sufficiently from hearing the news, she wrote with great dignity and fortitude to Fanny Keats, the seventeen-year-old girl who would have become her sister-in-law: 'I know my Keats is happy, happier a thousand times than he could have been here, for Fanny, you do not, you never can know how he suffered. So much that I do believe, were it in my power, I would not bring him back. All that grieves me now is that I was not with him.'

*

When Dr Clark and an Italian colleague opened the body, they witnessed 'the worst possible Consumption – the lungs were intirely destroyed – the cells were quite gone'. He was buried, with a lock of Fanny Brawne's hair, and a purse and an unopened

Keats on his deathbed: engraving after drawing by Joseph Severn
(frontispiece to the first published edition of the letters to Fanny Brawne)

letter from his sister Fanny, in the Protestant (known as the English) Cemetery on the southern edge of the city, in a plot a few yards from the grave of Percy and Mary Shelley's three-year-old son. On the instruction of Dr Clark, daisy-covered turf was placed over the grave. Keats had asked Severn to include the following words on his headstone: 'HERE LIES ONE WHOSE NAME WAS WRIT IN WATER.'

*

The gravestone was set in place two years after his death. As he had requested Severn, it omits his name but includes the epitaph he wanted. Above those words, it bears an inscription dreamed up by Brown as an act of revenge against the Tory critics who had mocked and excoriated apothecary Keats in the pages of *Blackwood's Edinburgh Magazine* and the *Quarterly Review*.

As Keats was dying, their attacks had mortal consequences for his loyal supporter John Scott. In a series of editorials in the *London Magazine*, he had denounced the editors of *Blackwood's* as treacherous and cowardly lying scoundrels. And he had called out J. G. Lockhart as author of the assaults on Leigh Hunt and Keats that had been signed only with the initial 'Z'. Lockhart's proxy in London, a Mr J. H. Christie, responded by saying that honour was at stake. Threats of legal action escalated into a challenge to a duel and by moonlight on the night of 16 February 1821, Scott and Christie met with pistols in a wooded knoll on Primrose Hill. Both men fired and missed. Honour should have been satisfied, but Christie's second insisted that his man had missed deliberately whereas Scott had aimed at his opponent. There would have to be a second shot. John Scott took the bullet in his abdomen. He was removed to the nearby Chalk Farm Tavern, where he was treated by Keats's doctor, George Darling.

To no avail: he died just four days after Keats. It was merciful that Keats knew nothing of these events, but there is no doubt that Brown's grief at his friend's death was mingled with fury when he heard of Scott's. The enemies of the 'Cockney Poets' had exercised their malice in blood as well as ink.

The gravestone reads:

> *This Grave*
> *contains all that was Mortal*
> *of a*
> YOUNG ENGLISH POET
> *Who*
> *on his Death Bed*
> *in the Bitterness of his Heart*
> *at the Malicious Power of his Enemies*
> *Desired*
> *these Words to be engraven on his Tomb Stone*
>
> Here lies One
> Whose Name was writ in Water

There is no evidence that Keats was thinking about the poor reception of *Endymion* when he composed his own epitaph. He was thinking of the likelihood that he had not had the opportunity to do enough to place himself among the English poets after his death. However, the myth that he was killed by his bad reviews proved irresistible to Shelley, who made it the basis of 'Adonais', his elegy in his fellow poet's memory, written in the Spenserian stanza form that Keats loved. Shelley, whose sensibility was never restrained, burnt shame on the brow of the 'noteless blot on a remembered name' who had written the criticisms. Then he sought to immortalize Keats:

Peace, peace! he is not dead, he doth not sleep –
He hath awakened from the dream of life . . .
        . . . 'tis Death is dead, not he;
Mourn not for Adonais . . .
He is a portion of the loveliness
Which once he made more lovely.

                            *

The canonization of John Keats could not be achieved by this one poem alone. Other friends wrote eulogies too, but what was needed was a biography. Publisher John Taylor announced a forthcoming *Life*, while lawyer-poet friend J. H. Reynolds wanted to be asked to write one. Taylor, however, backed away from the task. Cowden Clarke and Leigh Hunt contented themselves with brief personal reminiscences. Severn took the view that Brown was the only man for the job. But the memory of their friendship was so raw, and the anger fostered by the belief that Keats was killed by his critics so intense, that Brown stalled for many years. He also believed that George Keats had deprived John of his inheritance, so there was no cooperation over the letters to America, which were the closest thing to a diary of Keats's inner life.

Even twenty years after Keats's death, Brown recorded that every time he set to work on his biography of his friend, 'it forcibly seems to me, against all reason . . . that he is sitting by my side, his eyes seriously wandering from me to the papers by turns, and watching my doings. Call it nervousness if you will; but with this nervous impression I am unable to do justice to his fame.' The only part of the *Life* that he saw into print was the journal of the walk north to the Lake District and the Highlands, published serially in the *Plymouth and Devonport Weekly Journal* in the autumn of 1840.

Thereafter, Brown handed over his papers to his friend Richard Monckton Milnes – flagellant, suitor of Florence Nightingale, and admirer of Keats with no first-hand knowledge. After George Keats died in 1841, probably of intestinal tuberculosis, it became possible for Monckton Milnes to bring together Brown's memories and a full range of Keats's correspondence, enabling him to publish a volume of *Life, Letters, and Literary Remains* in 1848. This self-proclaimed 'signal monument of the worth and genius of Keats' established the enduring image of the quintessential Romantic: the ultrasensitive mind revealed in the letters ('documentary evidence of his inmost life'), the beautiful language of the poetry, the damnation to consumptive death at a tragically young age. From this point forward, Keats's fame was assured, even though some of his letters – notably those to Fanny Brawne, published thirty years later – were a cause of embarrassment to Victorian sensibilities.

Facsimile of a love letter to 'My dearest Fanny', in
Letters of John Keats to Fanny Brawne (1878)

Monckton Milnes was a member of the Apostles, the elite secret society at Cambridge University that exerted strong behind-the-scenes influence on Victorian taste. Another member was the future Poet Laureate Alfred Tennyson, whose early work was deeply influenced by Keats, of whom he said 'There is something of the innermost soul of poetry in almost everything he ever wrote.' Had Keats lived, Tennyson believed, he would have become the greatest English poet since Milton. Championship of this kind was a major factor in shaping the obsession with Keats in the circle of the Pre-Raphaelite Brotherhood – Dante Gabriel Rossetti proclaimed him as the spiritual father of the group, while his brother William Michael Rossetti wrote a biography. Inspired by the medievalism, the bright colours and the sensuous details of the poetry, Arthur Hughes, John Everett Millais and William Holman Hunt all painted scenes from 'The Eve of St Agnes'. Millais and Hunt also produced their wonderfully precise visions of moments in 'Isabella'.

For Scott Fitzgerald, the most authoritative voice in raising Keats into the pantheon of English literature was – despite his own occasional marginal rebuttals of particular points – that of Matthew Arnold in his preface to an 1853 selection of the poems. The essay was reprinted in Arnold's *Essays in Criticism*, a copy of which Fitzgerald gave to Sheilah Graham. There she read:

> by virtue of his feeling for beauty and of the perception of beauty with truth, Keats accomplished so much in poetry, that in one of the two great modes by which poetry interprets, in the faculty of naturalistic interpretation, in what we call natural magic, he ranks with Shakespeare . . . No one else in English poetry, save Shakespeare, has in expression quite the fascinating felicity of Keats, his perfection of loveliness. 'I think', he said humbly, 'I shall be among the English poets after my death.' He is; he is with Shakespeare.

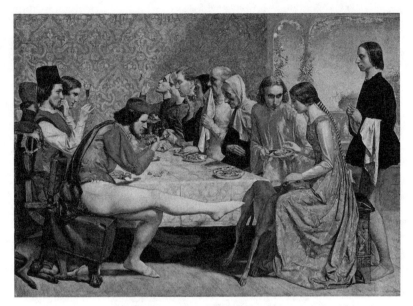

Millais, *Isabella*: the pot of basil where Lorenzo's head will end up is on the balustrade; the brothers are on the left, one contemplating a glass of blood-red wine, another stretching his foot like a knife and, to judge from the phallic shadow of the pepper pot, revealing a degree of sexual jealousy at Lorenzo's intimacy with his sister

20

THE RECORD

Lily Shiel, aka Sheilah Graham

ily Shiel was the youngest of the eight children of a Ukrainian Jewish tailor who, fleeing a Cossack pogrom, had died of tuberculosis in Berlin while she was still an infant. Her mother struggled to bring up the children alone in a basement flat in Stepney Green in the impoverished East End of London, eking out a living as a washerwoman in a public bathhouse. Lily was accordingly placed in the Jews Hospital and Orphanage in the suburb of Norwood, her golden hair shaved to prevent the recurrence of lice. She married at eighteen, became a music-hall dancer, had numerous affairs, used her looks and her personality to make her way into high society, was presented at court and courted by a marquess. When she flew to California to remake herself again, she changed her name to Sheilah Graham. She was smart, but with little formal schooling, so she felt insecure in the company of a lover who had spent his adult life absorbed in great literature.

Her literary education began on a night in May 1939, as she and Fitzgerald were driving back – at his habitual crawl of twenty miles per hour – to the cottage in Encino after one of the many film previews that they attended. Scott taught her the words of a comic popular song called 'Don't Bring Lulu': 'She's the kind of smartie / Who breaks up every party / Hullabalooloo, don't bring Lulu'. They sang at the top of their voices and collapsed into laughter. Then there was a moment of silence, Scott turning pensive. In a low voice, he started reciting something very different:

Fair youth, beneath the trees, thou canst not leave
    Thy song, nor ever can those trees be bare;
        Bold Lover, never, never canst thou kiss,
Though winning near the goal – yet, do not grieve;
    She cannot fade, though thou hast not thy bliss,
        For ever wilt thou love, and she be fair!

He took his eye from the wheel to see if she was listening. It was a kind of test: did she appreciate such poetry or was she just a good-time girl, content with 'Don't Bring Lulu'? She leaned in and asked 'Who wrote it?' They had learned a few poems at the orphanage, but nothing like this. It was so beautiful.

She had passed the test. He explained that it was from his beloved Keats. The 'Ode on a Grecian Urn'. He did not say as much to Sheilah, but in his mind's eye the lover might as well have been Jay Gatsby, looking out over the Sound from his forty-acre Long Island estate, near the goal of winning Daisy Fay, but knowing that he can never kiss her again. She cannot fade. Though Gatsby has not his bliss, for ever will he love and she be fair – within, that is, the narrative of Nick Carraway.

Scott carefully parked his battered old Ford coupé in the courtyard and led Sheilah into the living room, where a volume of Keats had pride of place on the bookshelves. 'Sitting close beside me,' she recalled, 'he read me the whole poem, savoring each word.' Then he read Andrew Marvell's 'To his coy mistress'. Sheilah was 'filled with an overwhelming sense of wonder' that people who lived so long ago should have written about love in a way that echoed her own feelings. 'Sheilo,' said Scott, 'that is part of the beauty of all literature. You discover that your longings are universal longings, that you're not lonely and isolated from anyone. You belong.'

That night, he stayed awake, far into the small hours, drawing up a syllabus for what he called his 'College of One': a programme of directed reading for Sheilah. At the heart of her education into poetry would be the close study of thirteen poems by Keats. On the flyleaf of the edition of *The Poetical Works of John Keats* that he gave her, Fitzgerald wrote, quoting from another of his favourites, 'Isabella; or, The Pot of Basil',

> For Sheilah
>   Oh misery!
> 'To take my Basil pot
>   Away from me.'
> In memory of iambic hours
>   Scott, 1940.

'Iambic hours': he had a craftsman's love for the nuts and bolts of literary construction. The 'Preliminary' to the course on poetry was 'A Discussion of Prosody and the most familiar meters':

> We break verse into 'Feet'. According to the stress, we give these 'feet' different names. The most important is the <u>iambus</u>. Âlōne is called an iambus. Also Ôh Yeāh! <u>Five</u> iambuses form a line of iambic <u>pentameter</u> (*which means five feet in Greek*)
>
> Example
>
> Bût stīll / thê hōūse / âffaīrs / woûld cāll / hêr hēnce
>
> (Othello)

> Shakespeare is all written in unrhymed iambic pentameter (except his songs). He takes liberties with it of course adding an extra syllable sometimes or dropping one or inverting a foot. At the end of a scene he sometimes rhymes a couplet (two lines).

Sheilah Graham did not record what examples he might have given of the placement of 'Alone' within lines of iambics. Perhaps the knight in 'La Belle Dame sans Merci' 'Alone and palely loitering' or the end not of a scene but of the sonnet 'When I have fears', in which Keats 'rhymes a couplet (two lines)':

>   – Then on the shore
>   Of the wide world I stand alone, and think
>   Till Love and Fame to nothingness do sink.

First metre, then form: 'Rhymed Verse' has 'metrical pattern (feet) and rhyme' versus 'Blank Verse' ('metrical pattern but <u>no</u> rhyme'). Then 'TYPES OF POEM', such as Ballad ('short narrative'), Epic ('long narrative') and Ode ('An address'). Then 'SOME USUAL FORMS', including Sonnet: 'Fourteen lines (8 and then 6) in iambic pentameter with a complete rhyme scheme'. Finally, a term for a rhetorical device of which Fitzgerald was very fond: 'Hyperbole exaggeration.'

Once the technicalities were out of the way, they could get down to the thing itself. The reading list for 'A SHORT INTRODUCTION TO POETRY (with interruptions)' begins with:

> The Eve of St Agnes (Keats)
> COLVIN'S KEATS Chaps I–VIII inc.
> The Pot of Basil (Keats)
> COLVIN'S KEATS Chaps IX to End
> Bright Star (Keats)
> When I have Fears (Keats)
> On First Looking Into Chapman's Homer (Keats)
> Chapman's Odyssey - - One Page
> Butcher and Lang's THE ODYSSEY, Books 1–3
> ARNOLD ON POETRY

The bipartite division of Colvin's life was well judged: chapter eight ends with Keats setting off for the north; chapter nine begins 'After the farewells at Liverpool were over' and proceeds to the Scottish walking tour. That summer was indeed a turning point in Keats's life and the beginning of his year of greatest creativity.

Fitzgerald's admiration for Colvin's biography knew no bounds. At the time he was putting Sheilah Graham through the 'College of One', he was also writing at length to eighteen-year-old Scottie. In late July 1940, when she was choosing courses for her sophomore year at Vassar College, he informed her in no uncertain terms that 'The only sensible course for you at this moment is the one on English Poetry – Blake to Keats (English 241).' However, he wrote again a few days later. One of the daughters of his editor Maxwell Perkins had passed through Los Angeles and happened to mention to him that she had taken the course when she was at Vassar. She informed him that the professor had prescribed a different life of Keats, that of the poet Amy Lowell. Fitzgerald considered this a severe error of critical judgment, which immediately made him much less enthusiastic about the course because Lowell's biography was 'a saccharine job compared to Colvin's'.

'ARNOLD ON POETRY' meant Matthew Arnold's *Essays in Criticism, Second Series*. Signing a copy with the inscription 'For Sheilah, with love (and annotations)', Fitzgerald directed her to the essays on Wordsworth and on Keats. He put quotation marks around a pronouncement of Arnold's:

> Yet I firmly believe that the poetical performance of Wordsworth is, after that of Shakespeare and Milton, of which all the world now recognises the worth, undoubtedly the most considerable in our language from the Elizabethan age to the present time.

And in the margin he wrote:

> This, with its following artillery, is a famous critical sentence. Why it is accepted with such authority is a mid-Victorian mystery, yet – it has effected [*sic*] everyone. I place Keats above him but I am such a personal critic & may be wrong, because of the sincerity of this God damned sentence. F.S.F.

The 'College of One' was not, however, all schoolmasterly Arnoldian judgments regarding the touchstones of 'the best which has been thought and said in the world'. There was real scholarship, too. Scott explained how 'Isabella' was adapted from Boccaccio and he was positively donnish when it came to textual details. In Sheilah's copy of the 1910 Oxford Edition of *The Poetical Works of John Keats*, he wrote in the margin beside 'La Belle Dame sans Merci', 'This is the *bad* form as edited by Leigh Hunt', adding 'See below' to indicate the variant version that he preferred.

There was playfulness, too, as in a paraphrase of the 'Ode on a Grecian Urn' in the language of hard-boiled tough guy fiction that Fitzgerald scrawled onto the inside back cover of the copy of Palgrave's *Golden Treasury* that he gave to his golden-haired lover:

A Greek Cup They Dug Up

S'as good as new! And think how long it was buried. We could learn a lot of history from it – about the rubes in ancient history, more than from any poetry about them. Those pictures on it must tell a story – about their Gods, maybe, or just ordinary people – some thing about life in the sticks at a place called Tempe. Or maybe it was in the Arcady Valley. These guys chasing the dames are either Gods or just ordinary people – it doesn't give the names on the cup. They sure are tearing after them and the dames are trying to get away. Look – this guys got a flute, or maybe its an obo and they're going to town, etc. etc.

This was not the only Keatzian inscription in the books that he gave her. The front free endpaper of her copy of *The Beautiful and Damned* carries a handwritten dedication with a line from the 'Grecian Urn':

To the Beautiful from the almost damned.
'What struggle to escape.'
With love from
Scott Fitzgerald
to Sheilah Graham
New Years 1940.

*

They were walking along Hollywood Boulevard one evening in the last year of the writer's life. He was softly reciting a poem, as he often did. He knew so many classic poems by heart. They were on their way back to the parking lot, after a preview screening of a new movie. They happened to pass a small store with a sign outside: 'Make your own records – hear yourself speak.'

In those days before the advent of the tape recorder, devices were available for self-recording via a microphone directly onto an aluminium disc that could then be played at 78 rpm on any phonograph. These do-it-yourself recordings were often used to create Valentine messages, as suggested by an advertisement placed by a Chicago supplier of the Wilcox-Gay Recordio, a model released in 1939 that reportedly sold 25,000 units in its first year of production.

1940 advertisement for a Wilcox-Gay Recordio

F. Scott Fitzgerald and Sheilah Graham went into the store on Hollywood Boulevard. Once the machine was set up, he recited three passages of poetry from memory. He began with the first half of John Masefield's double sonnet 'On Growing Old'. He was only in his early forties, but the ravages of alcohol, tuberculosis, a volatile marriage and the insecure life of the writer made him feel that he was growing old, that he was mortal. A couple of years earlier, he had lunched alone in the commissary of MGM studios. Groucho Marx, who was there, remembered him as 'A sick old man – not very funny stuff.'

His voice was soft and low, hypnotic, as he began to speak into the microphone:

Be with me, Beauty, for the fire is dying;
    My dog and I are old, too old for roving.
    Man, whose young passion sets the spindrift flying,
    Is soon too lame to march, too cold for loving.
    I take the book and gather to the fire,
    Turning old yellow leaves; minute by minute
    The clock ticks to my heart. A withered wire,
    Moves a thin ghost of music in the spinet.
    I cannot sail your seas, I cannot wander
    Your cornland, nor your hill-land, nor your valleys
    Ever again, nor share the battle yonder
    Where the young knight the broken squadron rallies.
    Only stay quiet while my mind remembers
    The beauty of fire from the beauty of embers.

There is a catch, almost a choking, in Fitzgerald's voice on that repetition of 'beauty' in the final line, as if among the embers of his own life he is trying to rekindle the beautiful times of his youth.

Masefield was the Poet Laureate of Great Britain. Born a

Victorian, he had been a sailor as a young man and had come to poetic fame with his 'Sea-Fever', published in the Edwardian first decade of the twentieth century: 'I must down to the seas again, to the lonely sea and the sky, / And all I ask is a tall ship and a star to steer her by.' Like almost every major poet of his generation, Masefield worshipped John Keats. He had contributed the introduction to the authoritative scholarly edition of Keats's works. The mood and language of 'On Growing Old' are unmistakably Keatzian: the address to Beauty with a capital B, the sense of mortality and evanescence ('thin ghost of music'), the lost freedom, the desire for quietude and remembrance, the play of light as the embers on the fire glimmer in faint answer to the bright star by which he navigated the seas of his youth.

All this spoke deeply to Fitzgerald. As did the second part of the double sonnet, in which Masefield laments that as an ageing writer he does not share the power of the strong, the wealth of the rich, or the grace of the young. He has left behind 'the glittering world with all its fashion', but if beauty is able to bequeath him 'wisdom and passion' from that lost world, then 'though the darkness close', 'Even the night will blossom as the rose'. Fitzgerald did not read this second sonnet, probably because he had not committed it fully to memory. Besides, he had already filled one minute and eleven seconds of the six minutes available on the disc, so he moved on to another favourite. He began to repeat the words that he had been reciting in the warm evening air out on Hollywood Boulevard:

My heart aches, and a drowsy numbness pains
    My sense, as though of hemlock I had drunk,
    Or emptied some dull opiate to the drains
      One minute past, and Lethe-wards had sunk:
    'Tis not through envy of thy happy lot,

But being too happy in thine happiness, –
    That thou, light-winged Dryad of the trees,
        In some melodious plot
Of beechen green, and shadows numberless,
    Singest of summer in full-throated ease.

O, for a draught of vintage! That hath been
    Cool'd a long age in the deep-delved earth,
Tasting of Flora and the country-green,
    Dance, and Provençal song, and sunburnt mirth!
O for a beaker full of the warm South,
    Full of the true, the blushful Hippocrene,
        With beaded bubbles winking at the brim,
            And purple-stained mouth;
That I might drink, and leave the world unseen,
    And with thee fade away into the forest dim:

Fade far away, dissolve, and quite forget
    What thou among the leaves hast never known,
The weariness, the fever, and the fret
    Here, where men sit and hear each other groan;
Where palsy shakes a few, sad, last gray hairs,
    Where youth grows pale, and spectre-thin, and dies;
        Where but to think is to be full of sorrow
            And leaden-eyed despairs,
Where Beauty cannot keep her lustrous eyes,
    Or new Love pine at them beyond tomorrow.

Listening to the recording, you can sense him savouring every word, measuring the iambic rhythm of the verse. He is careful to respect the extra beat of the final syllable in 'purple-stainèd'. Reciting from memory, he made a few trivial slips: 'as if of hemlock' instead of 'as though'; 'A moment since' instead of

'One minute past'; a 'drop of vintage' instead of a 'draught'; 'sunbeam' instead of 'sunburnt'; the omission of 'and leave the world unseen' at the end of the second stanza; 'fast forget' instead of 'quite forget'. Halfway through the third stanza, he seems to be distracted by a siren out in the street. The dying youth becomes 'dumb and fever-thin' instead of 'pale, and spectre-thin' and then Fitzgerald jumps to a garbled version of the last lines: 'And new love cannot live beyond tomorrow' – a moment's hesitation – 'or beauty cannot live' – a sense of tailing off.

Then he stops, the thread of memory unwound. Was it just the distraction or was he overwhelmed by the sense that Keats was speaking not only of his own sense of mortality but uncannily anticipating Fitzgerald's fear that his new love for Sheilah Graham could not live much longer? And that the beauty he was seeking to capture in his novels – one of which was lying, accusingly half-finished, on his work table back at his apartment – would also die? As with the Masefield, the idea of beauty's passing has silenced him.

*

There was still room on the aluminium disc for another three minutes. Instead of resuming the 'Ode to a Nightingale', he turned his memory to the greatest of all writers, the poet who was Keats's god, William Shakespeare. Othello, under accusation, addresses the Venetian senators. This time, Fitzgerald began in an orotund, actorly tone: 'Most potent, grave and reverend signors . . .' As he continued, just occasionally fluffing a line, he became more conversational, beginning to inhabit the being of Othello as he delivers 'the round unvarnished tale' of his 'whole course of love', 'The story of my life from year to year', the claim that the only witchcraft he has used to win his love has been the weaving of a magical web of enchanted words. Fitzgerald knew a thing or two about using beautiful words to charm a beautiful woman. He also knew that, as in *Othello*, marriage may end in tragedy: Zelda, her schizophrenia becoming ever more severe, was still confined in the Highland hospital far away in Asheville, North Carolina.

In April 1940, Zelda left hospital and went to live with her mother. The following month, still freelancing between the big five studios, Scott moved to 1403 North Laurel Avenue, just off Sunset Boulevard in West Hollywood. He set to work on a script that dramatized his story 'Babylon Revisited'. And he focused on the Hollywood novel that he had been planning for several months. He was beginning to feel that his talent as a novelist was returning. Towards the end of October, he wrote to Zelda: 'I am deep in the novel, living in it, and it makes me happy. It is a *constructed* novel like *Gatsby*, with passages of poetic prose when it fits the action, but no ruminations or side-shows like *Tender*. Everything must contribute to the dramatic movement.' He put his energy into the novel, while still churning out screenplays and short stories, notably a sequence of seventeen tales for *Esquire* in which he mocked both himself and the phoniness of Hollywood in the figure of Pat Hobby, a washed-up alcoholic screenwriter who is 'forty-nine with red-rimmed eyes and a soft purr of whiskey on his breath'. One of the stories ('Pat Hobby Does his Bit') features a cameo appearance by a British actress called Lily Keatts, a private joke that yokes Sheilah Graham's real first name to a misspelling of the poet who sparked the 'College of One'.

Methodically, he sketched out synopses, chapter summaries, notes, ideas and sample paragraphs for his novel. Like a movie, it would be episodic. On the last working day before Christmas 1940, he was at the midpoint of the story. He finished crafting the seventeenth of a proposed thirty episodes, reaching a point where Monroe Stahr, his reinvention of Irving Thalberg, meets with the communist organizer of the labour union, who is disrupting production.

That evening, he had dinner with Sheilah at a restaurant on Hollywood Boulevard and they went to the premiere of a new movie, *This Thing Called Love*. He felt dizzy as they left the theatre, stumbling on his way back to the car. 'I feel awful,' he said to Sheilah, 'everything started to go as it did in Schwab's' – the previous month, he had suffered what his doctor called a 'cardiac spasm' in the drugstore when he had gone for cigarettes. This had led him to move out of his apartment, which was up a flight of stairs, and into Sheilah's, which was at ground level. Sheilah was unsure how seriously she should worry. Scott was always a hypochondriac; obsessively taking his own temperature, he had been saying for months that he feared his tuberculosis was becoming active again. She asked him if they should call for medical help, but Scott said that his doctor was coming the following afternoon anyway.

The next day, 21 December 1940, with the early afternoon winter solstice sun beaming into the little West Hollywood apartment, Scott was sitting happily in an armchair reading the Princeton alumni magazine and annotating the details of the football team for the upcoming season. Sheilah was reading a biography of Beethoven, with the *Eroica* symphony playing on the gramophone. Scott started out of his chair, clutched the mantelpiece and fell on the floor. At first, Sheilah thought that he had fainted. But he did not stir. The cause of death was given as 'Coronary occlusion due to Arteriosclerotic Heart Disease'. The alcohol had done its toxic work upon the heart muscles.

A few days later, Sheilah Graham forced herself to go to a Christmas party hosted by Dorothy Parker. On arriving, she broke down and lay on the bed, weeping. In her own words,

I recited, 'Bold lover . . . do not grieve, She cannot fade, though thou hast not thy bliss, Forever wilt thou love, and she be fair – '

And then I wept again. 'I've had such a loss, Oh, such a terrible loss.'

And Dorothy sat with me, and wept with me.

*

His last letter to Zelda was signed off with the words 'Dearest love'; hers to him, 'Devotedly'. For all the fights and the recriminations, the drinking and the madness, the infidelity and the spectre of emotional as well as financial bankruptcy, a great love shines through their correspondence in these last years. A love more profound, indeed, than that expressed in the letters of Keats and Fanny Brawne, because Scott and Zelda had both been through the vale of soul-making. In Zelda's words,

> Dearest: I am always grateful for all the loyalties you gave me, and I am always loyal to the concepts that held us to-gether so long: the belief that life is tragic, that a mans spiritual reward is the keeping of his faith: that we shouldn't hurt each other. And I love, always your fine writing talent, your tolerance and generosity; and all your happy endowments. Nothing could have survived our life.
>
> Devotedly,
> and always with my
> deepest gratitude
> Zelda

Eight years later, having gone in and out of Highland numerous times, her condition worsened rather than improved by electroshock therapy and insulin treatment, she was sleeping under sedation on the top floor of the Central Building of the sanatorium. The room was locked even though she had always been a voluntary patient. She had been to a hospital dance that evening. According to a friend of a friend who was at the dance, her mind was 'as clear as a bell' and 'she was attractive, gracious, and charming'. At half-past eleven that night, a fire began in the kitchen. It spread up the shaft of the dumb waiter. Not all the patients escaped. Three days later, Zelda's remains were identified on the basis of the location of her room, her dental records and 'a single charred slipper beneath her burnt body'. The death certificate stated that she died of asphyxiation while trapped in a burning building.

*

Scott gave Sheilah the disc. It survives in the collection that she bequeathed to the library at Princeton University, where his manuscripts are preserved. She inscribed on its centre: 'a new and better Barrymore' (John Barrymore was America's most famous Shakespearean actor). Years later, after Fitzgerald's death, listening to the disc again, she was 'surprised at the deep professorial tone of his voice, much lower than it was in real life'. It was the Keats that she especially remembered. Masefield was the overture, Othello the coda.

Keats's name was not written on water. It lives whenever his poems are read. He spoke his last to Severn, but his written voice endures in his letters. Thanks to the record, in Scott Fitzgerald's case the actual voice has been preserved. And thanks to the Internet we can hear his reading of the opening stanzas of the 'Ode to a Nightingale'.

'My heart aches, and a drowsy numbness pains / My sense . . .'

Go now, listen.

AFTERWORD

Keats: 'I think I shall be among the English Poets after my death.'

Matthew Arnold: 'He is; he is with Shakespeare.'

F. Scott Fitzgerald: 'thinking of my ambitions so nearly achieved of being part of English literature.'

Fitzgerald's body was laid out in the William Wordsworth Room of the full-service Pierce Brothers Mortuary in downtown Los Angeles. A few friends came to pay respects. Dorothy Parker was one; she had first seen Scott and Zelda atop a taxi at the height of their New York glory days. Looking at the embalmed body of the liquor-ravaged failed screenwriter, cheeks rouged by the mortician, she spoke, without irony, the words of Owl-eyes at Gatsby's barely attended funeral: 'The poor son-of-a-bitch.' At least Scott was now, after a fashion, among the English Poets.

In the years after the Napoleonic Wars, when the literary scene was dominated by a lord (Byron) and a gentleman who became a baronet (Walter Scott), the publisher John Taylor nurtured and championed two lower-class poets: Keats, son of a livery stable keeper, was one. The other was John Clare, a farmworker. Early in the year 1821, responding to the news from Taylor that Keats had died of tuberculosis in Rome at the age of just twenty-five, Clare metaphorically elected his fellow poet to the immortal Freemasonry of literary greats. He wrote a sonnet 'To the memory of John Keats', addressing him as a 'true child of Poesy':

> Thou shalt survive – Ah, while a being dwells,
>   With soul, in Nature's joys, to warm like thine,
> With eye to view her fascinating spells,
>   And dream entranced o'er each form divine,
> Thy worth, Enthusiast, shall be cherish'd here, –
> Thy name with him shall linger, and be dear.

Clare's brave assertion is that in spite of Keats's premature death he will *survive* so long as there are beings on this planet who take joy in nature, so long as there are dreamers who are enchanted by beauty. The name of Keats lingers in his readers. Scott Fitzgerald was a being who fulfilled John Clare's prophecy. He had an eye to fascinating spells and dreamed entranced over forms divine. The name of Keats always lingered in his mind. No writer was more dear to him.

But why should we continue to read Keats 200 years after his death and Fitzgerald 100 years after he became the voice of the Jazz Age?

They are not of our time. In Keats, women are more often objects than subjects. In Fitzgerald, there is a repellent vein of racism – albeit voiced most vigorously by the hideous Tom Buchanan – and a tendency to glamorize wealth. In Hemingway's immortal riposte to Fitzgerald's story 'The Rich Boy' – 'Let me tell you about the very rich. They are different from you and me' – 'Yes, they have more money.' And yet the continuation of Fitzgerald's paragraph hardly reveals the 'romantic awe' regarding the rich of which Hemingway accused him:

> They possess and enjoy early, and it does something to them, makes them soft where we are hard, and cynical where we are trustful, in a way that, unless you were born rich, it is very difficult to understand. They think, deep in their hearts, that they are better than we are because we had to discover the compensations and refuges of life for ourselves. Even when they enter deep into our world or sink below us, they still think that they are better than we are.

His reply to Hemingway was that the only rich people who fascinated him were those who also had charm and distinction. He was not entirely joking when he described himself as essentially Marxian – his advice to young writers was to read Marx and Tolstoy. What was quasi-Marxist about him was his recognition that our human possibilities are profoundly shaped by our class status, a lesson he learned early when it was made clear to him that he was not of the right social calibre to be suitable for the girl that he loved.

One of the aims of Plutarch's parallel *Lives* was to set readers thinking about the similarities and differences between 'Greek' and 'Roman' habits, virtues and vices. So, for example, in comparing two great warriors, Alcibiades and Coriolanus, Plutarch contrasted the Greek homosexual profligacy of the former with the stiff Roman austerity of the latter. But he was writing about generals and politicians. In the Renaissance and beyond, his subjects were read as flawed exemplars of public service. It was properly assumed that leaders should be held to account for their attitudes and behaviour. But poets and novelists are not public servants. Literary biography should therefore be distinct from Plutarchan political biography. If Keats was right in his belief that '*Negative Capability*' is the quality that creates 'Achievement especially in Literature', then as literary biographers we should restrain the assumptions of our own time and seek instead to prove the work of our subjects 'upon our pulses', as if we had 'gone the same steps as the author'.

Negatively capable biography will let other pens dwell on guilt and the miseries of historical prejudice. Of Fitzgerald's racism, we can only say, as W. H. Auden wrote of W. B. Yeats's sympathy for fascism,

> Time that is intolerant
> Of the brave and innocent . . .
> Worships language and forgives
> Everyone by whom it lives . . .
> Time that with this strange excuse
> Pardoned Kipling and his views,
> And will pardon Paul Claudel,
> Pardons him for writing well.

Kipling was, of course, an imperialist; Paul Claudel was a French Catholic poet and dramatist with notoriously right-wing views. To Fitzgerald's credit, the Nazi–Soviet Pact provoked his final renunciation of communism: 'The Comrades out here are in a gloomy spot', he wrote from the Hollywood hotbed of leftism, 'the party line is to let National Socialism (Nazism) conquer us and then somehow milk Marxism out of Hitler's sterile teats!' Having recognized that there was idealism and good judgment in aspects of Fitzgerald's politics, it is up to the reader to decide whether or not to pardon him of his racism because he wrote so well.

Why should we continue to read Keats and Fitzgerald now? Because they lived by language and because they wrote well. Because the leading 'parallel' is that they crafted words and impressions of *beauty* in a world of mortality. Fitzgerald achieved fame as 'symbol and historian of the Jazz Age', but he sought to capture his world in prose unlike that of the sociologist recording the cultural changes that swept through the United States in the wake of the Great War. His original ambition was to be a poet and although his poetry is very bad his prose is more poetic than that of any of his contemporaries. The purpose of poetry, he followed Keats in believing, is to speak truth not to power but to beauty, and in so doing to stake a claim that art may cheat death.

Keats was strongly influenced by a poet who was much more popular in his own time, the Irish lyricist Thomas (Tom) Moore. Yet Keats still gives pleasure after 200 years, whereas Moore is all but forgotten. Endurance, the ability to speak from beyond the grave, is what has made Keats a 'classic'. Fitzgerald considered biography to be the falsest of the arts because 'there were no Keatzians before Keats', by which he meant that our understanding of the evolution of Keats will always be shadowed by our knowledge of the writer he became and the fate that befell him. But classic status can only be conferred posthumously: Keats's immortality was made by the Keatzians who came after him, Fitzgerald himself among them.

Like Keats, Fitzgerald died with his work neglected, but became a classic posthumously – in no small measure due to the curation of his work and celebration of his name on the part of his friend 'Bunny' Wilson. In his lifetime, Fitzgerald was acutely aware of a number of contemporary writers who were much more widely read than he was. He was envious of the success of novels that are now unread – Michael Arlen's *The Green Hat* (1924), for example, or Robert Keable's bestseller *Simon Called Peter* (1921). It is a nice irony that the latter is now known only because it is the book that Nick Carraway picks up and dismisses as trash while Tom Buchanan is having sex with his mistress. Keable is not as bad a writer as one might expect from this. But his prose lacks Fitzgerald's glow and poise; structurally, his novel is episodic whereas *The Great Gatsby*, with its symmetries and contrasts, has a formal beauty. The parallel to the scene in chapter two in which Tom and Myrtle drink whiskey and have sex in the airless little apartment in New York is the scene in chapter five in which Gatsby and Daisy drink tea and speak of romance in the flower-bedecked cottage that Nick is renting on Long Island.

This time, instead of absenting himself by way of a mildly scandalous novel, Nick goes into the garden and stares at Gatsby's house in the manner, he says, of Immanuel Kant staring at a church steeple. There is deliberate irony, at Nick's expense, in the juxtaposition of the profane and the sacred, but at the same time Nick is reaching towards an intimation of the divine, contemplating higher things than tawdry adulterous relationships. For Kant, in his *Critique of Judgment*, the truly disinterested thing, existing in a separate realm from morality, was beauty. Keats was, albeit at a remove, a Kantian when he wrote that 'The excellence of every Art is its intensity, capable of making all disagreeables evaporate, from their being in close relationship with Beauty and Truth.' Beauty as truth, truth beauty: the equation at the climax of the poem that Fitzgerald said he had read a hundred times, overwhelmed by its unbearable beauty.

Art is sometimes the handmaiden of progress and at other times the instrument of oppression, but the manifestation of beauty in great art may also be a refuge from the 'disagreeables' of life. The opening of Keats's longest poem is a manifesto for this belief:

A thing of beauty is a joy for ever:
Its loveliness increases; it will never
Pass into nothingness; but still will keep

A bower quiet for us, and a sleep
Full of sweet dreams, and health, and quiet breathing.

These lines embody the beauty of which they speak. They achieve euphony through poetic devices that Keats would perfect in his odes: internal rhyme (loveliness/nothingness; still/ will), assonance (increases/pass), incantatory repetition (and/ and/and). As his health declined with tuberculosis, 'quiet breathing' became increasingly difficult for Keats. The dream of beauty, lodged in his imagination and released in his poems and letters, gave him hope of spiritual survival even as his young body decayed.

'I felt rather lonely this Morning at breakfast', he wrote to his brothers from the Isle of Wight, 'so I went and unbox'd a Shakespeare – "There's my Comfort".' The quotation is from a moment in *The Tempest* when the drunken butler Stephano reaches for a bottle of wine salvaged from the shipwreck. For Keats, the beauties of Shakespeare offered an alternative release to that provided by the bottle. Fitzgerald destroyed himself with drink, but as he descended into alcoholism and illness, comfort still came from the books that he shared with Sheilah Graham. Among them, the most precious was his Keats. For both writers, reading was a remedy for loneliness and a tonic against despair.

Two hundred years after Joseph Severn witnessed his friend's death in the room beside the Spanish Steps, old comforts about health – personal in the wake of pandemic, social in an age of inequality, and that of the natural world in an era of unprecedented ecological change – are threatening to 'pass into nothingness'. Under the shadow cast by global damnation, the loveliness of Keats's poems and Fitzgerald's novels increases. Their beautiful works will not endure for ever, but in dark times they can at least bring moments of joy.

English Cemetery, Rome, Italy and Rockville Union Cemetery,
Maryland, USA

Sheilah Graham said that Scott had always hated California and
would not have wished to be buried there; his body was taken east by
train to Rockville, Maryland, where his parents had lived in their last
years. Since he was not practising the faith, he was not allowed a
Catholic burial. He was buried here after an Episcopalian funeral
attended by his daughter Scottie and between twenty and thirty
friends. Following Scottie's advice, Sheilah remained in California
out of respect to Zelda, who was not well enough to be there.

ACKNOWLEDGMENTS

Writers are readers before they become writers. I have been interested in this phenomenon ever since I took an undergraduate elective course on the Romantic poets as readers of Shakespeare. At the centre of that course was the figure of John Keats, with his belief that even in hard times, in poverty and in illness, he could share William Hazlitt's view that 'Shakespeare is enough for us'. This theme, animated by Keats and Hazlitt, became the subject of my doctoral dissertation and first two books. I remember with gratitude the late John Beer and Leo Salingar for starting me down this road.

Having then used Keatzian 'negative capability' as a touchstone for many of my own readings of Shakespeare, I have more recently found myself asking *which writer was shaped by Keats as Keats was shaped by Shakespeare?* My answer was partly prompted by a move to the United States – for which I thank my new colleagues at Arizona State University – that led me to reread my favourite American novelist and to see, as I had not before, how deeply Keatzian his imagination was. The unifying strand of influence study in this book thus circles back to my academic origins and is intended as a coda to my work as a purely literary biographer and critic, prior to a more sustained devotion to the wider concerns that I began to explore in my readings of Keats and his fellow Romantics in the age of climate change in *Romantic Ecology* and *The Song of the Earth*.

I am deeply grateful to my own readers: Paula Byrne, first and last as always; Merve Emre, my brilliant colleague at Worcester College, Oxford; the eagle-eyed Rob Watson of UCLA; my ASU colleague Brian Goodman for casting an Americanist's eye over the *Gatsby* chapter; my exemplary editors Arabella Pike at William Collins and Jennifer Banks at Yale University Press; and two anonymous readers for Yale. Jo Thompson and Iain Hunt guided the production process; David Milner was, once again, a superb copy-editor. Andrew Wylie was my Harold Ober, ably supported by Tracy Bohan.

Emma Sarconi provided valuable assistance with the Scott and Zelda Fitzgerald Papers in the Princeton University Library Special Collections. Thanks also to Tim Hands, headmaster of Winchester College, for inviting me to give a lecture on the 200th anniversary of the composition of the 'Ode to Autumn', which gave me the opportunity to retrace Keats's footsteps through the water meadows to the Hospital of St Cross.

The book could not have been written without the work of my subjects' editors, critics and prior biographers, notably Miriam Allott, John Barnard, Walter Jackson Bate (no relation, though he taught me at Harvard), Christopher Ricks and Nicholas Roe for Keats; Matthew J. Bruccoli, Sarah Churchwell, Arthur Mizener, James L. W. West III and Edmund Wilson for Fitzgerald. The dedication is made out of gratitude to the Department of English at the University of Liverpool, because it was there, during my thirteen-year tenure as King Alfred Professor of English Literature, that I learned how to turn my teaching and research into writing that seeks to be readable not only by students but also by lovers of literature beyond the grove of academe.

NOTES

CHAPTER 1

1   **The last days** *The Letters of John Keats 1814–1821*, ed. H. E. Rollins (2 vols, 1958), 2. 4. Cited hereafter as KL. Keats's letters are quoted from this edition, save in contexts where Fitzgerald is tracking him, in which case quotations are from the edition that he owned.

1-2 **scarce a doubt . . . as near each other**   KL 2. 4–5.

2   **time zone**   Even domestically, prior to the adoption of uniform 'railway time' in the 1840s, time differed from town to town, according to the position of the sun; international time zones were only introduced in the late nineteenth century.

2   **the mighty dead**   *Endymion: A Poetic Romance* (1818), 1. 21. On Keats and other Romantic poets in relation to 'the mighty dead', see my *Shakespeare and the English Romantic Imagination* (1986).

2   **charactered language . . . an immortal freemasonry**   'Mr Kean' (unsigned theatre review), *The Champion*, 21 Dec 1817.

2   **the name of Keats**   *Freeborn County Standard*, 24 April 1879.

3   **Academic essays**   For example, John Grube, 'Tender Is the Night: Keats and Scott Fitzgerald', *Dalhousie Review*, 44 (1964), 433–41; Richard Lehan, *F. Scott Fitzgerald and the Craft of Fiction* (1966), especially pp. 8–12; Dan McCall, '"The Self-Same Song That Found a Path": Keats and *The Great Gatsby*', *American Literature*, 42.4 (1971), 521–30; Margaret Frances Loftus, 'John Keats in the Works of F. Scott Fitzgerald', *Studies in English Literature*, 7 (1972), 17–26; George

Monteiro, 'James Gatz and John Keats', *Fitzgerald/Hemingway Annual*, 4 (1972), 291–4; Robert E. Morsberger, 'The Romantic Ancestry of *The Great Gatsby*', *Fitzgerald/Hemingway Annual*, 5 (1973), 119–30; Barry Scherr, 'Lawrence, Keats and *Tender Is the Night*: Loss of Self and "Love Battle" Motifs', *Recovering Literature*, 14 (1986), 7–17; Catherine B. Burroughs, 'Keats's Lamian Legacy: Romance and the Performance of Gender in *The Beautiful and Damned*', in *F. Scott Fitzgerald: New Perspectives*, ed. Jackson R. Bryer, Alan Margolies and Ruth Prigozy (2000), 51–62; Philip McGowan, 'Reading Fitzgerald Reading Keats', in *Twenty-First Century Readings of 'Tender is the Night'*, ed. William Blazek and Laura Rattray (2007), 204–20; and Lauren Rule-Maxwell, 'The New Emperor's Clothes: Keatsian Echoes and American Materialism in *The Great Gatsby*', *The F. Scott Fitzgerald Review*, 8 (2010), 57–78. Sarah Churchwell's fine essay 'Realms of Gold', in *Pursuit: The Balvenie Stories Collection*, ed. Alex Preston (2019), 141–57, provides a less specialized overview of the influence.

4   **whenever I can have Claret** To George and Georgiana Keats, 19 Feb 1819, KL 2. 64.

4   **stories are fit** Plutarch, trans. Sir Thomas North (1579), 'Preface to the Reader'.

5   **admirable biographers** Such as Walter Jackson Bate, *John Keats* (1963); Aileen Ward, *John Keats: The Making of a Poet* (revised edn, 1986); Andrew Motion, *Keats: A Biography* (1998); R. S. White, *John Keats: A Literary Life* (2010); and especially Nicholas Roe, *John Keats: A New Life* (2012); Arthur Mizener, *The Far Side of Paradise: A Biography of F. Scott Fitzgerald* (1951); Andrew Turnbull, *Scott Fitzgerald* (1962); Matthew J. Bruccoli, *Some Sort of Epic Grandeur: The Life of F. Scott Fitzgerald* (1981); Andre Le Vot, *F. Scott Fitzgerald: A Biography* (1983); James R. Mellow, *Invented Lives: F. Scott and Zelda Fitzgerald* (1984); and most recently David S. Brown, *Paradise Lost: A Life of F. Scott Fitzgerald* (2017). Also, the restoration of a voice to Zelda in Nancy Milford, *Zelda: A Biography* (1970), and Sally Cline, *Zelda Fitzgerald: Her Voice in Paradise* (2002). More than any other treatment, I admire Stanley Plumly's selective, angled 'personal biography' *Posthumous Keats* (2008),

the excellence of which has given me licence to write only briefly about Keats's final months in Rome.

CHAPTER 2

6   **found solace** Colvin, *John Keats: His Life and Poetry, His Friends, Critics and After-Fame* (1917), p. vii.
8   **instead of answering** Ibid., p. 7.
8   **He was when an infant** Ibid.
9   **A Man's life** KL 2. 67.
10   **we loved, jangled** Colvin, p. 11.
10   **His *penchant* . . . In all active** Ibid., pp. 11–12.
11   **One of the transports . . . It was all** Ibid., p. 13. For Charles Cowden Clarke's full account, see his *Recollections of Writers* (1878).
11   **utter unconsciousness** Ibid.
12   **What an image** Clarke, p. 126, quoted, Colvin, p. 20; quoting Edmund Spenser, *The Faerie Queene* (1590), 2. 12. 23. 6 (on the approach to the Bower of Bliss).
13   **a country of winding . . . and no youth** Colvin, p. 22.
13   **In drear-nighted December** The 'College of One' is discussed in my final chapter. Colvin (p. 159) printed the manuscript text of this poem, but Fitzgerald's edition of the *Complete Poetical Works* follows the (posthumously published) printed text, which has some variants (e.g. an indefinite article added to the first line – 'In a drear-nighted December' – and 'steal' for 'steel'). Most of my quotations from Keats's poems use the edition that Fitzgerald owned, published by Houghton, Mifflin of Boston and New York – *The Complete Poetical Works and Letters of John Keats: Cambridge Edition* (1899) – but occasionally textual variants are adopted from other editions. I have greatly benefited from the three authoritative modern editions: *The Poems of John Keats*, edited by Miriam Allott (1970), *The Poems of John Keats*, edited by Jack Stillinger (1978), and *The Complete Poems*, edited by John Barnard (1988).
14   **Ah! would 'twere so** Fitzgerald's edition of Keats, p. 34.
15   **noted as carefully . . . there was no view** Ernest Hemingway, *A Moveable Feast* (1964; repr. 1996), p. 157.
16   **1896 Sept 24th** *F. Scott Fitzgerald's Ledger: A Facsimile*, intro-

duction by Matthew J. Bruccoli (1972), p. 151. Memory and family tradition are fallible: 24 September 1896 was actually a Thursday, not a Sunday.

18 **He began to remember** Ibid., p. 157.

18 **After the wedding** Ibid. By 'black' he may have meant 'black Irish'.

19 **I He went to** Ibid., p. 160.

19 **all based on . . . kissing party** Ibid., pp. 161–2.

20 **Dancing school . . . Ginevra King** Ibid., p. 165.

20 **personality, charm** Quoted, Andrew Turnbull, *Scott Fitzgerald* (1962), p. 34.

20-1 **he had sat . . . the romantic glamour** Fitzgerald, 'Homage to the Victorians', review of Leslie's Eton novel *The Oppidan*, *New York Tribune*, 14 May 1922.

21 **He left for Princeton** Entries from her diary were printed for the first time in James L. W. West III's excellent *The Perfect Hour: The Romance of F. Scott Fitzgerald and Ginevra King, his first love* (2005), pp. 117–18, to which my account is indebted.

23 **Poor boys** *Ledger*, p. 170 (Aug 1916).

24 **symbols of ambition . . . one star** Closing paragraph of 'Basil and Cleopatra', *Saturday Evening Post*, 27 April 1929.

24 **my first girl** *These Stories went to Market*, ed. Vernon McKenzie (1935), p. xviii, quoted, *Perfect Hour* (which reprints 'Winter Dreams'), p. 91.

25 **for once, he was magnificently** 'Winter Dreams', in *The Collected Short Stories of F. Scott Fitzgerald* (1986), p. 370. Where possible, the short stories are quoted from this accessible Penguin edition.

25 **Suddenly she turned** Original version of 'Winter Dreams', written Sept 1922, published *Metropolitan* magazine, Dec 1922, quoted from reprint in *Perfect Hour*, p. 171.

26 **Her porch was bright** *The Great Gatsby* (1925), p. 179.

26 **the man who had taught me** Hemingway, *A Moveable Feast*, p. 118.

27 **The dream was gone** 'Winter Dreams', in *Perfect Hour*, p. 185. Adjacent quotations from same page.

CHAPTER 3

28   **Mr Keats** 'London Adjourned Sessions', *Morning Chronicle*, 23 April 1816. This is one of the very few genuinely new facts about Keats's life to have been discovered in recent years: the newspaper report was found by Professor Nicholas Roe of St Andrews University, and published in his essay 'Mr Keats', chapter 4 of his exceptionally valuable edited collection, *John Keats and the Medical Imagination* (2017).

29   **the jumbled heap** 'O Solitude', *The Examiner*, 5 May 1816.

30   **A tall ungainly** *Memorials of John Flint South* (1884), quoted, Colvin, p. 29.

31   **he has been . . . an Assistant Surgeon** Contemporary account quoted in John Barnard's indispensable article, '"The Busy Time": Keats's duties at Guy's Hospital from Autumn 1816 to March 1817', *Romanticism*, 13 (2007), 199–218. 'The busy time' was a phrase used by Keats in a letter, referring to one of the periods when he had to reside in the hospital and walk the wards at night.

31   **The breezes were ethereal** 'I stood tiptoe upon a little hill' (published 1817), lines 221–6.

32   **The other day . . . reflecting on what passed** quoted, Colvin, p. 29.

32   **idle loafing fellow** quoted, Colvin, p. 17.

32-3 **That breast . . . But I want** This poem was first published in 1905, so was not in Fitzgerald's 1899 Cambridge Edition; it was, however, discussed by Colvin (p. 259) and included in the 1910 Oxford Edition that Scott gave to Sheilah Graham.

33   **That breast . . . Fill me, boy** Thomas Moore, *The Odes of Anacreon translated into English Verse* (1800), p. 220, opening of Ode LXII.

33   **What wondrous beauty!** Holograph manuscript now in the Morgan Library, New York, quoting from Terence, *Eunuchus*, act 2 scene 3 (misidentified by Keats as scene 4).

34   **in my syllabus . . . Give me women** Henry Stephens, letter to Keats's friend G. F. Mathew (1847), quoted, Colvin, p. 32; this valuable memoir of Keats's time at Guy's is reprinted from the original MS in *The Keats Circle: Letters and Papers and More Letters and Papers of the Keats Circle*, ed. H. E. Rollins (2 vols,

1965), 2. 206–14, cited hereafter as KC. Stephens omitted the last two lines of the poem, presumably because of their blasphemy; they are to be found in the original MS, now at Trinity College, Cambridge.

35   **Ah! I see** 'Hadst thou lived in days of old', included in Keats's 1817 volume.

36   **Time's sea** Fitzgerald's 1899 edition, quoted here, followed the text of *Life, Letters, and Literary Remains, of John Keats*, ed. Richard Monckton Milnes (2 vols, 1848) and converted the footnote into the title 'To a Lady seen for a few moments at Vauxhall'. The poem was first published, with a few variants, in *Hood's Magazine*, Sept 1844.

37   **He was Keats's senior** Colvin, p. 41.

38   **his love of civil** Cowden Clarke, p. 124.

38   **He decorated his apartment** Colvin, pp. 42–3.

38   **In Spenser's halls** 'Written on the day that Mr Leigh Hunt left prison'.

38   **Such a prosperous opening** Cowden Clarke, pp. 135–6.

39   **O for ten years** 'Sleep and Poetry', lines 96–110.

41   **Glory and loveliness** 'Dedication. To Leigh Hunt, Esq.' in *Poems, by John Keats* (1817).

41   **Light feet, dark violet** *Poems*, p. 48.

42   **Keen fitful gusts** Sonnet IX, in *Poems*, p. 87.

42   **From mouth and nose . . . Then forth he came** Cowden Clarke, p. 130.

44   **His followers** Robertson, *The History of America* (1777), 1. 204.

44   **Scott pointed out** Sheilah Graham, *College of One* (1967; pbk 1968), p. 96.

44   **'Young Poets'** *The Examiner*, 1 Dec 1816, p. 761.

CHAPTER 4

47   **to do this . . . Almost my final memory** 'Who's Who – and Why: Serious and Frivolous Facts about the Great and the near Great: F. Scott Fitzgerald', *Saturday Evening Post*, 18 Sept 1920, pp. 42, 61.

47   **I had decided . . . a book of startling** Ibid.

47   I lie upon my heart 'Rain before Dawn', *Nassau Literary Magazine*, 72.7 (Feb 1917), p. 321. Fitzgerald's italics.

48   Thou still unravished *Nassau Literary Magazine*, 72.3 (June 1916), p. 137.

48-9 one part deadly Philistines . . . The world became *This Side of Paradise* (1920), pp. 56–7.

49   You need, at the beginning To Scottie Fitzgerald, 3 Aug 1940, in F. Scott Fitzgerald, *A Life in Letters*, ed. Matthew J. Bruccoli (1995, repr. 1998), p. 460, cited hereafter as FLL.

49   a depth and dignity . . . becoming a genuine Edmund Wilson, *Letters on Literature and Politics, 1912–1972* (1977), p. 30.

49   The last light wanes 'Princeton – The Last Day', *The Nassau Literary Magazine*, 73.2 (May 1917), p. 95.

50   I'll never be a poet *This Side of Paradise*, p. 93.

50   ecstatic hours Wilson, *Letters on Literature*, p. 30.

51   Everything was wonderful *Nassau Literary Magazine*, May 1917, p. 63.

52   I don't think Fitzgerald, *Letters to his Daughter*, ed. Andrew Turnbull (1965), p. 165.

53   She has the straightest Clipping from local newspaper in Zelda Fitzgerald's scrapbook, now held in the Princeton collection and digitized at http://pudl.princeton.edu/objects/x346d693p.

54   exuding the delicacy Zelda Fitzgerald, *Save Me the Waltz*, in *The Collected Writings of Zelda Fitzgerald*, ed. Matthew J. Bruccoli (1992; repr. 1997), p. 39.

54   If ever there was Edmund Wilson to Nancy Milford, 19 July 1965, quoted, Milford, *Zelda: A Biography* (1970), p. 25.

55   DARLING HEART *Dear Scott, Dearest Zelda: The Love Letters of F. Scott and Zelda Fitzgerald*, ed. Jackson R. Bryer and Cathy W. Barks (2002), p. 12.

55   a somewhat edited history 'Who's Who – and Why', p. 61.

56   Every Saturday Ibid.

56   We have been reading *Correspondence of F. Scott Fitzgerald*, ed. Matthew J. Bruccoli and Margaret M. Duggan (1980), p. 31.

57   trail murderers . . . complicated advertising schemes 'Who's Who – and Why', p. 61.

57   I informed family Ibid.

58   wild letters *Ledger*, p.173.

58 **relegated it** Sara Mayfield (a Montgomery friend of Zelda's), *Exiles from Paradise: Zelda and Scott Fitzgerald* (1971), p. 48.

59 **He seized her in his arms** 'The Sensible Thing', *Liberty* (15 July 1924), repr. in the short story collection *All the Sad Young Men* (1926), p. 227.

60 **thirsty first** 1 July 1919, when the Wartime Prohibition Act came into effect, preceding the constitutional imposition of the Eighteenth Amendment in January 1920 prohibiting the manufacture, transportation and sale of intoxicating liquors.

60 **a sort of substitute . . . My whole theory** 'The Author's Apology' (1920), repr. in *F. Scott Fitzgerald in his own Time*, ed. Matthew J. Bruccoli and Jackson R. Bryer (1971), p. 164.

60 **Then the postman rang** 'Early Success', in Fitzgerald, *The Crack-Up*, ed. Edmund Wilson (1945, repr. 1993), p. 86.

CHAPTER 5

63 **elegant white flannels** Jeffrey Meyers, *Scott Fitzgerald: A Biography* (1994), p. 50.

63 **wordsworthian or egotistical sublime** KL 1. 387.

63 **taking things hard** *The Crack-up*, p. 180.

64 **Isabelle and Rosalind** To Max Perkins, *Dear Scott / Dear Max: The Fitzgerald–Perkins Correspondence*, ed. John Kuehl and Jackson Bryer (1971), p. 20.

64 **There was no God** *This Side of Paradise*, p. 304.

65 **about a love affair** To Frances Turnbull, 9 Nov 1938, FLL, p. 368.

65 **It was always the becoming** *This Side of Paradise*, p. 19.

65 **MRS CONNAGE** Ibid., p. 204.

66 **Terms ect . . . Would it be utterly impossible** To Max Perkins, *Dear Scott / Dear Max*, p. 21.

67 **She is one of those girls . . . dull men** *This Side of Paradise*, p. 182.

67 **once told a roomful** Ibid., p. 183.

67 **just awake to the fact** *Dear Scott, Dearest Zelda*, p. 23.

67 **her fresh enthusiasm . . . gray eyes** *This Side of Paradise*, p. 183.

67 **I have to be won . . . selfish people** Ibid., pp. 194, 210, 198.

68 **once-in-a-century blend** Ibid., p. 184.

68 **she treats men terribly** Ibid., p. 182.

69   **Well this side of Paradise!** Brooke, closing lines of the poem 'Tiare Tahiti'. His ellipsis.

69   **What he said** *This Side of Paradise*, p. 248.

70   **The problem of evil** Ibid., p. 302.

70-1   **fiery windows . . . still ecstatic** 'Blue Evening', in *The Collected Poems of Rupert Brooke* (1916), p. 81; 'Princeton – The Last Day', as cited earlier.

71   **In its whispering embraces** *Collected Poems of Rupert Brooke*, p. xiv (introduction by George Edward Woodberry). There are copies among both Fitzgerald's books and Sheilah Graham's 'College of One' library at Princeton.

71   **Beauty that must die** Quoted, ibid., p. vii.

71   **Oh, I've read Keats** *The Collected Poems of Rupert Brooke: with a Memoir* (1918), p. xxvi.

71   ***Sinister Street*** Published in the USA in two parts, *Youth's Encounter* (1913) and *Sinister Street* (1914).

72   **the modern novel** Mackenzie, in his essay 'Poetry and the Modern Novel', *The English Review*, 11 (April 1912), p. 279.

72   **The imagination of a boy** Epigraph to *Sinister Street*. Fitzgerald may have been familiar with an essay in *The Living Age*, vol. 288 (Boston, 1916), pp. 280–8, that considered in detail the influence of Keats on *Sinister Street* and also cited Mackenzie's very Fitzgeraldian idea of the modern novel achieving universality through poetry.

72   **Fair youth . . . These lines** *Sinister Street* (1913, repr. 1960), pp. 231–2.

73   **almost every fault . . . With the seeds** Edmund Wilson, 'Literary Spotlight: F. Scott Fitzgerald' (1924), repr. in *F. Scott Fitzgerald: The Man and his Work*, ed. Alfred Kazin (1951), p. 78.

74   **Where, if not from the Impressionists** Wilde, *The Decay of Lying* (1902), p. 57.

75   **Why can't I write?** Zelda to Scott, Dec 1919, F. Scott Fitzgerald Papers (1897–1944), Department of Rare Books and Special Collections, Manuscripts Division, Firestone Library, Princeton University, CO142, Box 42.

75   **'The Iceberg'** *Sidney Lanier High School Literary Journal* (1918), rediscovered and published in the *New Yorker*, 20 Dec 2013.

75   **She danced exceptionally well** *This Side of Paradise*, p. 183.

75   **I wish that I had been able** Zelda Fitzgerald to Scottie Fitzgerald,

1944, in *The Romantic Egoists: A Pictorial Autobiography from the Scrapbooks and Albums of F. Scott Fitzgerald and Zelda Fitzgerald*, ed. Matthew J. Bruccoli, Scottie Fitzgerald Smith and Joan P. Kerr (1974), p. 237.

75-6 **but after two pages . . . And so you see** *Dear Scott, Dearest Zelda*, p. 40.

76 **There was a dusky** *This Side of Paradise*, pp. 303–4.

77 **Something in me vibrates** *Dear Scott, Dearest Zelda*, p. 26 (April 1919).

79 **a blue-grey spring suit** Sally Cline, *Zelda Fitzgerald: Her Voice in Paradise* (2002), p. 75. This is the best of the several biographies of Zelda.

79 **I married the Rosalind** To Shane Leslie, 6 Aug 1920, *The Letters of F. Scott Fitzgerald*, ed. Andrew Turnbull (1963), p. 376.

79 **no end to our delight** Unpublished autobiography of Rosalinde Fuller, p. 81, quoted, James R. Mellow, *Invented Lives: F. Scott and Zelda Fitzgerald* (1984), p. 82.

80 **fix up data** To Max Perkins, *Dear Scott / Dear Max*, p. 22.

80 **At certain moments** Notes for *The Last Tycoon*, F. Scott Fitzgerald Papers, Princeton, CO187, Box 8a.

80 **I'm sick of the sexless animals** *Shadowland*, Jan 1921, repr. in *Fitzgerald in his own Time*, p. 243.

81 **ALEC: Does Rosalind behave** *This Side of Paradise*, p. 182.

CHAPTER 6

83 **the greatest musical . . . Men of Genius** *The Notebooks of F. Scott Fitzgerald*, ed. Matthew J. Bruccoli (1978), pp. 9–10.

84 **He owned the 1899** Shortly after Fitzgerald's death, his library of about a thousand books was deposited at Princeton. About a third of them were retained, and remain there, while the other two-thirds were either dispersed or returned to his daughter Scottie, presumably because the university library already had copies. Lists of these were compiled by librarians. The 1899 Cambridge edition of Keats and a copy of Colvin's biography (distinct from the one given to Sheilah Graham) are in the list of dispersed copies, which had no annotations or markings by Fitzgerald. See John Kuehl, 'Fitzgerald's

Reading', *The Princeton University Library Chronicle*, 22.2 (1961), 58–89 (p. 79).

85   **to jump and skipp** KL 1. 99.

85   **who walks about** Ibid., 2. 360.

85   **some beautiful Scenery** Ibid., 1. 115.

86   **Great spirits** Letter of 20 Nov 1816, KL 1. 117. I quote and discuss the sonnet (and its influence on Shelley's 'Ozymandias') in my account of Keats's attitude to Wordsworth in Jonathan Bate, *Radical Wordsworth: The Poet who Changed the World* (2020), pp. 394–5 and 550.

87   **more than with any other** Quoted, Colvin, p. 66.

87   **Banish money** letter 4, to J. H. Reynolds, 17 Mar 1817, in 1899 Cambridge edition of *Complete Poetical Works and Letters of John Keats* owned by Fitzgerald. The quotation adapts *Henry IV Part 1*, 2. 4. 346–50.

88   **But the sea** To J. H. Reynolds, 17 April 1817, KL 1. 131.

88   **It keeps eternal . . . O ye!** 'On the sea', in letter to J. H. Reynolds, published in *The Champion*, 17 Aug 1817. Both the vexing and the eyeballs are echoes of *King Lear*.

89   **I find that I cannot exist** To J. H. Reynolds, 18 April 1817, KL 1. 133.

89-90 **Nothing seemed to escape him . . . Certain things affected him 90**   Severn's notes, transcribed by William Sharp, quoted in Colvin, pp. 79–80.

91   **This Oxford** To Fanny Keats, 10 Sept 1817, KL 1. 154.

91   **Do not the Lovers** To Benjamin Bailey, 8 Oct 1817, KL 1. 170.

92   **spiritualized** *Endymion*, 4. 993.

92   **A thing of beauty . . . live for ever** Ibid., 1. 1; Stephens' account was reported by Sir B. W. Richardson, *The Aesculapiad* (April 1884), pp. 148–9, quoted, Colvin, p. 176.

93   **A flowery band . . .** *Endymion*, 1. 7–13.

93   **daffodils . . . An endless fountain** Ibid., 1. 15–24.

94   *John Keats' genius!* KL 1. 203.

94   **Beauty – a living Presence** William Wordsworth, *The Excursion* (1814), 'Prospectus', lines 41–5.

95   **the desire to enjoy beauty** 'fruende pulchritudinis desiderium': Marsilio Ficino, *Opera Omnia* (1576), p. 1322. Fitzgerald did not number *Endymion* along with the shorter poems among his Keatzian favourites, but in one of his short stories there

is a glancingly suggestive allusion to an 'Indian maiden drowning herself for love', spoken by a girl called Atlanta, whose name then prompts one of Fitzgerald's several quotations of his favourite lines from Swinburne's *Atalanta in Calydon*, the epitome of late Romanticism ('When the hounds of Spring are on Winter's traces . . .'). The short story, entitled 'I'd Die for You', was about a failed actress who commits suicide. Written in 1935, Fitzgerald could not get it published – see *I'd Die for You and other Lost Stories*, ed. Anne Margaret Daniel (2017), p. 94.

95　**The great consolations . . . wrongs within the pale**　To Benjamin Bailey, 3 Nov 1817, KL 1. 179.

96　**Men of Genius**　Letter 21 in Fitzgerald's edition of Keats.

96　**If spirit of wine**　Joseph Priestley, *Heads of Lectures on a Course of Experimental Philosophy: Particularly including Chemistry* (1794), 'Of Aether'.

96　**ethereal liquor**　see further, Donald C. Goellnicht, *The Poet-Physician: Keats and Medical Science* (1984), pp. 68–70.

96　**looking upon the Sun**　Letter 8, to B. R. Haydon, 10 May 1817.

96　**the same relation to ordinary reality**　George Bornstein, 'Keats's Concept of the Ethereal', *Keats–Shelley Journal* 18 (1969), 97–106 (p. 98). See further, Earl Wasserman, *The Finer Tone: Keats's Major Poems* (1953), pp. 15–16.

96　**Things real . . . Things semireal**　Letter 40, to Benjamin Bailey, 13 Mar 1818.

97　**I am certain of nothing**　Letter 21, to Benjamin Bailey, 22 Nov 1817.

97　**Beauty is truth**　As originally published in Jan 1820 in the magazine *Annals of the Fine Arts*, the ending of the poem gives the impression that the Grecian urn says 'Beauty is Truth, Truth Beauty. – That is all / Ye know on Earth, and all ye need to know.' But in Keats's 1820 volume, there are quotation marks around 'Beauty is truth, truth beauty', implying that this is the motto of the urn and that it is Keats who says to the reader 'That is all / Ye know on earth, and all ye need to know.'

97　**he awoke and found it truth**　Letter 21, to Benjamin Bailey, 22 Nov 1817., making reference to *Paradise Lost*, 8. 460–90.

97　**have you never**　Ibid.

97   **It should strike . . . Its touches of beauty** Letter 38, to John Taylor, 27 Feb 1818.

98-9 **His every sense . . . tenderest, milky** *Endymion*, 2. 671–773. Christopher Ricks memorably defends 'slippery blisses': 'I cannot see why "Those lips, O slippery blisses" has been so scorned, except that scorn can be the recourse of embarrassment and of a timorous imagination finding itself unduly, even improperly, moved. The phrase is famous for its exultant patterning of sounds: "Those" into "O slippery," and "lips" into "slippery"; I think that the effortlessness, naturalness, and yet surprise with which "lips" slips into "slippery" is a bliss to experience. True, it insists upon the saliva which we shall meet if we kiss; but I think that a good thing to insist upon, given that Keats does not remain fixated upon it.' Ricks, *Keats and Embarrassment* (1974), p. 104.

99   **such writing** Byron to his publisher John Murray, 9 Sept 1820 (for 'frigging' Byron actually wrote 'f–gg–g'). The insult also appeared in his draft of a review of Keats, for the *Quarterly*, mercifully removed by his editor. Haydon wrote in his diary: 'Lock[h]art shewed me a review by Lord Byron of Keats's work, in which Lord Byron called him a *dirty little blackguard*. I said "This is shocking," & Lockart took his pen & scratched it out. He said he had scratched out a great deal; Lord Byron called Keats "The *Masturbater* [sic] of the *human mind* – the *Onan of Literature*."' (*The Diary of Benjamin Robert Haydon*, ed. W. B. Pope (1960–3), 3. 257).

99   **curls of glossy . . . There she lay** *Endymion*, 4. 60, 101–3.

99   **Fondling and kissing . . . O known Unknown!** Ibid., 2. 734–48.

100   **In the very deeps** Ibid., 2. 823–4.

100   **The very music** Ibid., 1. 36–7.

100   **load every rift** KL 2. 323, the phrase is itself loaded from the realm of Spenserian gold: 'load every rift' is self-consciously quoted from *the Faerie Queene*: 'with rich metal loaded every rifte' (Bk 2, canto 7, stanza 28, line 5).

100   **rain-scented eglantine** *Endymion*, 1. 100–106.

101   **I never read** To Benjamin Bailey, 3 Nov 1817, KL 1. 180.

101   **I fought under disadvantages** rejected preface of 19 Mar 1818, Keats manuscript MA 209, Morgan Library, New York.

102 **Wherein lies Happiness** To John Taylor, 30 Jan 1818, KL 1. 218, becoming *Endymion*, 1. 777–80.

102 **earthly love** *Endymion*, 1. 843–4.

102 **Into a warmer air** Ibid., 1. 664.

102 **If human souls** Ibid., 1. 842.

103 **false, delusive . . . that abominable** Benjamin Bailey to John Taylor, 29 Aug 1818, KC 1. 35.

103 **I remember Keats** Thomas Medwin, *Conversations of Lord Byron* (1824), pp. 294–5.

103 **warmed with her** KL 1. 403.

104 **Oh, breathe a word** Final stanza of 'You say you love', autograph manuscript in the hand of John Taylor, annotated 'from Miss Reynolds and Mrs Jones', Morgan Library, manuscript MA 215.79.

104 **full and fine . . . beautiful** Benjamin Bailey to R. M. Milnes, 7 May 1849, KC 2. 253.

104 **corrected the Poison . . . suffering** To Benjamin Bailey, 8 Oct 1817, KL 1. 171; 30 Oct 1817, KL 1. 175.

104 **venereal poison** Dr Solomon Sawrey, who treated the Keats brothers, was an STD specialist, author of the widely read *Inquiry into some of the Effects of the Venereal Poison on the Human Body* (1802), in which he made the then commonplace assumption that gonorrhea was an early symptom of syphilis; Astley Cooper subsequently distinguished between the two infections. Dr James Curry, under whom Keats studied medicine, was an enthusiastic prescriber of mercury.

105 **In the autumn** Sir Benjamin Richardson, 'John Keats – an Esculapian Poet', *The Aesclepiad*, 1 (1884), 143. Keats's modern biographers remain divided on this question. For the possibility that mercury poisoning contributed to Keats's premature death, see Susan L. Davis, 'John Keats and "The Poison": Venereal or Mercurial?', *Keats–Shelley Journal*, 53 (2004), 86–96.

CHAPTER 7

106 **a very pretty piece** quoted, Colvin, p. 249.

107 **who believed nothing . . . And then he and Keats** Haydon's diary, quoted, Colvin, p. 247.

107 **Do not all charms** Keats, 'Lamia', in *Lamia, Isabella, The Eve of St Agnes, and other Poems* (1820), p. 41.

108 **I HAVE SOLD** 24 Feb 1920, FLL, p. 37.

108 **I am a realist** 'Head and Shoulders' in Fitzgerald, *Flappers and Philosophers* (1920), p. 95.

108 **but audiences agreed** Ibid., p. 88.

109 **Well, Omar Khayyam** Ibid., p. 90.

109 **fiery Soul** Edward FitzGerald to the American poet James Russell Lowell, 28 Feb 1878, in *Letters and Literary Remains of Edward FitzGerald* (1903), 3. 312.

109 **a continual source** 'Head and Shoulders', p. 111.

110 **the fourth proposition** Ibid., p. 113.

110 **multiplicity** a concept that Bergson illustrated with the analogy of two spools of tape, one winding up as the other unwinds – Henri Bergson, *The Creative Mind* (1946), p. 164, English translation of his collection of philosophical essays and lectures *La Pensée et le mouvant* (1934).

112 **the life of one . . . How he and his beautiful** To Charles Scribner II, 12 Aug 1920, FLL, p. 41.

113 **Alone and palely . . . I saw pale kings** 'La Belle Dame sans Merci', in Keats's journal letter of 14 Feb–3 May 1819, printed in the 1848 *Life, Letters and Literary Remains*, having been first published in a variant version in *The Indicator*, 10 May 1820, signed 'Caviare'. In Fitzgerald's edition of Keats, p. 139.

114 **remote harmonies . . . far guitars** *The Beautiful and Damned* (1922), p. 126.

114 **She was beautiful . . . cold and full** Ibid., p. 116.

114 *la belle dame* Ibid., p. 329.

114 **absolute sway** Ibid., p. 444.

114-15 **merely antiquarian . . . all philistine** To Edmund Wilson, July 1921, FLL, pp. 46–7.

115 **Oh god, goofo** *Ledger*, p. 176, copied from a notebook that Fitzgerald had with him as he went in and out of the delivery room.

115 **I woke up** *The Great Gatsby*, p. 21.

116 **She was a complete** 'May Day', *Tales of the Jazz Age* (1922), p. 85.

116 **Afterward John remembered** 'The Diamond as Big as the Ritz', *Tales of the Jazz Age*, p. 121.

116 Friend Husband's Latest *New York Tribune*, 2 April 1922.

117 *Beauty, who was born* *The Beautiful and Damned*, p. 27.

117 the excitement of emotion S. T. Coleridge, 'On the Principles of Genial Criticism concerning the Fine Arts', *Felix Farley's Bristol Journal* (Aug–Sept 1814), essays 2 and 3.

117 hair soft-lifted 'To Autumn', stanza 2.

117-18 Written in starlight . . . The youth at once *Endymion*, 3. 1020–30.

118 She turned her face . . . Such a kiss *The Beautiful and Damned*, p. 102.

118 that cherished all beauty Ibid., p. 73.

118 There was the union Ibid., p. 148.

118 There's no beauty Ibid., p. 167.

119 And so I turned Ibid., pp. 252–3. The passage is adapted from an unpublished interview with himself that Fitzgerald wrote after the publication of *This Side of Paradise*, in which he added 'The wise literary son kills his own father': 'An Interview with F. Scott Fitzgerald', in *F. Scott Fitzgerald on Authorship*, ed. Matthew J. Bruccoli with Judith Baughman (1996), p. 34.

119 Swinburne Now hardly read, Swinburne was a huge cultural force in the late nineteenth century: I offer an overview in 'Libidinous laureate of satyrs: The importance of being Algernon', *Times Literary Supplement*, 10 July 2009, 14–15.

119-20 The arts are very old . . . You know these Ibid., p. 421.

120 cloth of Samarcand . . . spiced dainties Ibid., p. 106; 'The Eve of St Agnes', stanza XXX.

121 The breathless idyl . . . the stuff of all life *The Beautiful and Damned*, p. 156.

121 There was a kindliness Ibid., p. 417.

121 The fruit of youth Ibid.

121 In the end then . . . It cheered her Ibid., p. 393.

CHAPTER 8

125 intense power . . . Other actors 'Mr Kean', *The Champion*, 21 Dec 1817, quoted, Colvin, p. 244.

125 nothing to be intense To George and Thomas Keats, 21 Dec 1817, KL 1. 192.

126 gusto . . . to be *beside* . . . we see not Hazlitt, *The Round*

Table (1817), 'On Gusto', 'On Actors and Acting'; Keats's annotated copy of *Characters of Shakespear's Plays* (1817) is
preserved in the Houghton Library, Harvard University (the 'see
not Lear' phrase is actually Hazlitt quoting Charles Lamb).

126 **the excellence** To George and Thomas Keats, 21 Dec 1817, KL
1. 192.

126 **burn through . . . new phoenix wings** 'On sitting down to read
King Lear once again', written 22 Jan 1818, holograph in his
facsimile Shakespeare First Folio (now at Keats House,
Hampstead), published posthumously.

126 **which Shakespeare . . . would let go by** To George and Thomas
Keats, 27(?) Dec 1817, KL 1. 193–4.

127 **We hate poetry . . . Poetry should be** To J. H. Reynolds, 3 Feb
1818, KL 1. 224.

127 **to surround . . . genius shone** *Lectures on the English Poets*
(1818), pp. 104, 92.

128 **the wordsworthian . . . it is not itself** To Richard Woodhouse,
27 Oct 1818, KL 1. 387.

128 **When I have fears** Published in Keats's 1820 volume.

129 **When I have seen . . . that thou shouldst** Shakespeare, Sonnet
64; Shelley, 'To Wordsworth', in *Alastor; or, The Spirit of Solitude*
(1816), p. 67.

129 **three or four** To Scottie Fitzgerald, 3 Aug 1940, FLL, p. 460.

130 **The innumerable compositions** Letter 46, to B. R. Haydon, 8
April 1818. 'Snail-horn' is an allusion to an image in Shakespeare's
Venus and Adonis (line 1033) that he especially admired (see
KL 1. 189).

130 **a translation of some** Lecture attended by Keats on 3 Feb 1818,
English Poets, p. 158.

131 **The three Brethren** *The novels and tales of the renowned John
Boccacio, the first refiner of Italian prose containing a hundred
curious novels by seven honourable ladies, and three noble
gentlemen, framed in ten days* (1620; 5th edn, 1684), 4th Day,
5th Novel, p. 182. In Boccaccio's original Italian, the girl is
called Elisabetta.

132 **too much inexperience** KL 2. 174.

132 **to throw back** 'Isabella', lines 376.

132 **'Lorenzo!'** Ibid., lines 55–6.

132 **mawkish** KL 2. 162.

132 'Then should I be' Transcription by Richard Woodhouse of Keats's fair copy of the manuscript, Morgan Library, MA 215.78.

133 Until we are sick To J. H. Reynolds, 3 May 1818, KL 1. 279.

133-4 large Mansion . . . burden of the Mystery Ibid., 1. 281–2, citing Wordsworth, 'Lines composed a few miles above Tintern Abbey', *Lyrical Ballads* (1798).

134 Tom has spit Ibid., 1. 282–3 (medial colon mine).

134 remarkably well KL 1. 283.

135 somewhat singular KC 2. 212.

136 The different falls To Thomas Keats, 27 June 1818, KL 1. 300.

136 Silverly Shakespeare, *King John*, 5. 2. 46. Also used by Keats to describe the course of a serpentine river in *Endymion* (1. 541).

137 What astonishes me To Thomas Keats, 27 June 1818, KL 1. 301.

138 hollowing out To Thomas Keats, 26 July 1818, KL 1. 348.

138 Imagine the worst To Thomas Keats, 9 July 1818, KL 1. 321.

138 I should not have consented To Benjamin Bailey, 18 July 1818, KL 1. 342. Charles Brown wrote up an account of the first part of the tour under the title 'Walks in the North, During the Summer of 1818', for publication in a regional newspaper, the *Plymouth and Devonport Weekly*, in Oct 1840 (repr. KL 1. 421–42). See further, Carol Kyros Walker's splendid annotated and illustrated edition of both Keats's journal-letters written during the tour and Brown's account, *Walking North with Keats* (1992).

139 This young man appears John Gibson Lockhart, 'The Cockney School of Poetry. No. IV', *Blackwood's Edinburgh Magazine*, 3 (Aug 1818), 519–24.

140 It is a better Ibid.

140 our author John Wilson Croker, *Quarterly Review*, 19 (dated April, but published late September 1818), 204–8.

140 a mere matter To George and Georgiana Keats, 14 Oct 1818, KL 1. 394. The phrase 'the English Poets' was obviously inspired by Hazlitt's lectures on them.

140 Had I been nervous To James Augustus Hessey, 8 Oct 1818, KL 1. 374.

CHAPTER 9

142 **I never was in love . . . Yet the voice** To J. H. Reynolds, 22(?) Sept 1818, KL 1. 370.

142 **Poor Tom** Ibid.

142-3 **When she comes . . . You will by this time** To George and Georgiana Keats, 14 Oct 1818, KL 1. 395.

143 **rich eastern look** Ibid.

143 **I am free . . . This is Lord Byron** Ibid., 1. 396.

144 **Since I wrote . . . She has always been** To George and Georgiana Keats, 24 Oct 1818, KL 1. 402.

144 **Some times through shabby . . . As I had warmed** Ibid., KL 1. 402–3.

145 **Talking of game** To George and Georgiana Keats, 19 Feb 1819, KL 2. 65.

146 **I now claim** Blunden quoted or paraphrased the letters in *Keats's Publisher: A Memoir of John Taylor (1781–1864)* (1936), pp. 96–8; after the war, he shared his research with the biographer Robert Gittings, who became the first to write at length about Isabella Jones, putting the relationship at the centre of *John Keats: The Living Year* (1954).

146 **What will you say** Isabella Jones to John Taylor, 14 April 1821, printed in Gittings's Appendix D, *Living Year*, pp. 231–3.

146 **The Poem was written** *Commonplace book of poems, etc., mainly by John Keats, compiled by Richard Woodhouse; dated November 1818; with some notes by other hands*, MS Keats 3, 3.2, Houghton Library, Harvard University, fo. 109r. One of Isabella Jones's letters to Taylor was written while she was staying on Mount Sion in the spa town of Tunbridge Wells, at the residence of the widow of an Irish peer, Lord Lismore. This was the starting point for a story told by Gittings, whereby Mrs Jones was in Hastings under the watchful eye of an aged relative of Lady Lismore, from whom Keats allegedly stole her away for seaside intimacies. As far as I can tell from a lengthy search of the genealogies of the Irish aristocracy and gentry, this aged gentleman did not exist. Gittings' theory was based on a highly tendentious biographical reading of a short lyric beginning 'Hush, hush! Tread softly!' which Fanny Brawne copied down on St Agnes Day 1819. It seems a little unlikely that Keats

would have given her this poem if, as Gittings supposed, it was the fruit of lovemaking with Mrs Jones the previous night.

147 **What days** J. H. Reynolds to John Taylor, 31 Oct 1837, KC 2. 469.

147 *Portrait of a Lady* *The Exhibition of the Royal Academy, MDCCCXIX* (1819), p. 37. In her letter written from Tunbridge Wells, Isabella Jones asked John Taylor for his 'candid opinion' of it.

147 **killed in a duel** Her contribution is recorded in the *Morning Post*, 30 March 1821. For the duel, see chapter 19, below.

147 **'Mrs' denoted** See further Amy Louise Erickson's splendidly informative 'Mistresses and Marriage: or, a Short History of the Mrs', *History Workshop Journal*, 78.1 (Autumn 2014), 39–57.

148 **a plausible candidate** See further, my forthcoming essay 'Keats and Mrs Jones'.

149 **They told her how** 'The Eve of St Agnes', published in Keats's 1820 volume, stanza VI (Keats uses his favoured form of the Spenserian stanza, with the extra beat in the last line).

149 **Full on this casement** Ibid., stanzas XXV–XXVI.

150 **And still she slept** Ibid., stanza XXX.

150 **Beyond a mortal man** Ibid., stanza XXXVI.

151 **But, as it is now altered** Richard Woodhouse to John Taylor, 19 Sept 1819, KL 2. 163.

151 **He says he does not want** Ibid.

152 **palsy-twitched** 'The Eve of St Agnes', stanza XLII. In the original version, she has the palsy but does not die.

153 **The wind shivered** *Notebooks*, p. 29. The 'cornice' may also be a memory of 'The Eve of St Agnes'. Stanza IV, where Fitzgerald found 'The silver, snarling trumpets', ends with 'The carved angels, ever eager-eyed, / Stared, where upon their heads the cornice rests, / With hair blown back, and wings put cross-wise on their breasts.'

CHAPTER 10

155 **A Complete Novelette** cover of *The Smart Set*, June 1922.

155 **Zelda & her abortionist** *Ledger*, p. 176. Censored out of the facsimile published in 1972, but included in the online digital

transcription at https://delphi.tcl.sc.edu/library/digital/collec tions/Fitzgerald_Ledger_-_USC_Transcription_2013.pdf.

155 **His son went down** *Notebooks*, p. 244.

155 **FITZGERALD'S LATEST** Clipping from *Ralegh NC News*, pasted into the Fitzgeralds' scrapbook, repr. in *The Romantic Egoists*, ed. Matthew J. Bruccoli, Scottie Fitzgerald Smith and Joan P. Kerr (1974), p. 96. This handsome folio volume reproduces substantial portions of the scrapbooks and photo albums of Scott and Zelda Fitzgerald, which are now in the Princeton archive. The scrapbooks are digitized at http://arks.princeton. edu/ark:/88435/sf268784s and http://arks.princeton.edu/ ark:/88435/x346d693p.

155 **An Ironic Story** Scrapbook clipping, *Romantic Egoists*, p. 98.

156 **intellectual conscience** Fitzgerald's first conclusion about himself in 'Pasting it Together', Part II of 'The Crack-Up' (*Esquire*, March 1936), was 'That I had done very little thinking, save within the problems of my craft. For twenty years a certain man had been my intellectual conscience. That was Edmund Wilson.' Repr. in *The Crack-Up*, p. 79.

156 **the most enormous influence** To Edmund Wilson, Jan 1922, FLL, p. 51.

156 **he has been given** *The Bookman*, March 1922, repr. in Wilson, *The Shores of Light: A Literary Chronicle of the 1920s and 1930s* (1952), p. 27. Wilson was a great admirer of Millay, not least because she took his virginity.

156 **It seemed to Anthony** *The Shores of Light*, p. 33 (in the published version of the review, Wilson generously attributed his burlesque to Fitzgerald, praising his friend's ability to laugh at himself).

157 **How to Live on $36,000** *Saturday Evening Post*, 5 April 1924.

158 **as flat as one** Zelda Fitzgerald to her friend Xandra (Sandy) Kalman, Zelda Fitzgerald Papers (1917–1997), Department of Rare Books and Special Collections, Manuscripts Division, Firestone Library, Princeton University, CO183, II. B. 5. 5 (quoted in several biographies).

158 **Any man who doesn't** *The Vegetable* (1923), title page.

158 **Making Monogamy Work** e.g. in *Metropolitan Syndicate*, Jan 1924, and *New York American*, 24 Feb 1924. Subheadings from clipping pasted into scrapbook, misdated 1923 in *Romantic Egoists*, p. 113.

159 the mating instinct . . . decide that the only The article is reprinted in *Fitzgerald in his own Time*, pp. 179–84.

159 100 feet of copper screen To Tom Boyd, May 1924, FLL, p. 68.

159 The Big crisis *Ledger*, p. 178.

160 he is full *Save Me the Waltz*, in *The Collected Writings of Zelda Fitzgerald*, ed. Matthew J. Bruccoli (1997), p. 82.

160 He drew her body Ibid., p. 86.

160 I am very sorry Ibid., p. 94.

161 something had happened *Notebooks*, p. 113.

161 The table at Villa Marie Ibid., p. 106.

161 the loss of those illusions To Ludlow Fowler, Aug 1924, *Correspondence*, p. 145.

162 It will concern To Max Perkins, *Dear Scott / Dear Max*, p. 61.

162 It was a dark sad face Repr. in Matthew J. Bruccoli, '"An Instance of Apparent Plagiarism": F. Scott Fitzgerald, Willa Cather, and the First *Gatsby* Manuscript', *Princeton University Library Chronicle*, 39.3 (Spring 1978), 171–8.

163 When a lot of people . . . There was something 'Absolution', *The American Mercury*, June 1924. The story is readily accessible in the Penguin *Collected Short Stories of F. Scott Fitzgerald* (1986), pp. 398–412.

163 Passion is lord Hazlitt, 'Why Distant Objects Please', in *Table Talk; or, Original Essays on Men and Manners* (1824), 2. 220. Hazlitt's argument is that when the distant object is reached, touched or obtained, it ceases to please. This is the discovery and the argument of his quasi-novel *Liber Amoris* (1823), as I suggest in *The Cure for Love* (1998), a quasi-novel about his life which had the working title *Distant Objects, Please*.

163 a cloud of magic . . . April is over 'The Sensible Thing', *Liberty*, July 1924, *Collected Short Stories*, pp. 385–97.

CHAPTER 11

165 The roaring of the wind To George and Georgiana Keats, Oct 1818, KL 1. 403.

165 not live in this world . . . According to my state Ibid., KL 1. 403–4.

166 who appear to me . . . The only thing Ibid., KL 1. 404.

166 I stalk about *Troilus and Cressida*, 3. 2. 7.

166 I am giddy Ibid., 3. 2, in Keats's 1808 facsimile of the First

Folio, now in Keats House, Hampstead. His underlinings and emendation are repr. in Caroline Spurgeon, *Keats's Shakespeare* (1929), p. 164.

167 **rather more easy** To George and Georgiana Keats, 29 or 31 Oct 1818, KL 1. 405.

168 **Have nothing more** Charles Armitage Brown, manuscript 'Life of John Keats' (1841), KC 2. 64. There is no reason to doubt the veracity of the exchange, even though Brown goes on to say 'From that moment he was my inmate', whereas in fact Keats moved in some weeks later.

169 **the rapidity of the blows** Clarke, *Recollections of Writers*, p. 145.

169 **I must work** To Richard Woodhouse, 18 Dec 1818, KL 1. 412.

169 **beautiful and elegant** To George and Georgiana Keats, 16 Dec 1818, KL 2. 8.

169 **Shall I give you Miss Brawn** To George and Georgiana Keats, 18 Dec 1818, KL 2. 13.

170 **Miss Brawne and I** To George and Georgiana Keats, 14 Feb 1819, KL 2. 59.

170 **the very first week** To Fanny Brawne, 25 July 1819, KL 2. 132.

172 **Why did I laugh?** Sonnet included in letter to George and Georgiana Keats, 19 Mar 1819, KL 2. 81, reading 'Deaths is Life's' in final line. Published with minor variants in the 1848 *Life, Letters and Literary Remains*.

172 **he broached a thousand things** To George and Georgiana Keats, 16 April 1819, KL 2. 88–9.

173 **A loose, slack** Coleridge, *Table Talk* (1836), p. 184, quoted, Colvin, pp. 346–7.

174 **In the midway** Dante, *Inferno*, 1. 1–3, trans. Cary.

174 **the principle of melody** Benjamin Bailey to R. M. Milnes, Oct 1848, KC 2. 277.

175 **Deep in the shady** *Hyperion*, 1. 1–10 (published in Keats's 1820 volume).

176 **From chaos and parental darkness** Ibid., 2. 191–201.

177 **So on our heels** Ibid., 2. 212–17.

177 **the count** Ibid., 2. 723–5.

177 **How could any English poet** On this, see especially 'The Burden of the Mystery: the Emergence of a Modern Poet', chapter 13 of Walter Jackson Bate, *John Keats* (1963), a line of thinking

which stimulated Jackson Bate's *The Burden of the Past and the English Poet* (1970), Harold Bloom's *The Anxiety of Influence* (1973), and my own *Shakespeare and the English Romantic Imagination* (1986).

177 **agonies, / Creations** *Hyperion*, 3. 115–16.

CHAPTER 12

178 **tried his hand** A fragmentary 'Ode to May', written on May Day 1818; Keats intended 'to finish the ode all in good time' (to J. H. Reynolds, 3 May 1818, KL 1. 278), but never did. The surviving fourteen lines actually form an interestingly irregular sonnet, anticipating the April 1819 sonnets in which Keats sought 'to find a better sonnet stanza than we have' (KL 2. 108): 'To Sleep' innovatively begins with two Shakespearean quatrains and ends with a Petrarchan sestet. He had also written two odes to Apollo: the first, very early in his career, merely consists of a few regular stanzas; the second, written in spring 1817, was a flippant 'apology' to the god for 'having made a mockery of him at [Leigh] Hunt's' (KL 1. 170).

179 **I think it reads** To George and Georgiana Keats, 30 April 1819, KL 2. 106.

179 **I wander'd in a forest** text in letter to George and Georgiana Keats, KL 2. 106; published in 1820 volume with minor variants: 'silver-white' for 'freckle-pink' (an alternative reading in Keats's holograph now in the Pierpont Morgan Library), and 'Tyrian' (purple-coloured) for 'syrian' (a publisher's substitution for Keats's baffling word choice).

180 **odes** Woodhouse dated the 'Nightingale' and Dilke the 'Grecian Urn' to May 1819; the two other odes are merely dated 1819 in their surviving transcripts, but editors concur on a May dating, though the seed of 'Indolence' was sown in March.

180 **In the spring** Brown, 'Life of Keats', KC 2. 65.

181 **pure delusion . . . We do not** Dilke, annotation in *Life, Letters, and Literary Remains*, quoted, *The Odes of Keats and their earliest known Manuscripts*, introduced with notes by Robert Gittings (1970), p. 65.

181 **Where youth grows pale** Holograph of 'Ode to the Nightingale' (two sheets, written on both sides), Fitzwilliam Museum,

Cambridge. See *The Odes of Keats and their earliest known Manuscripts*, pp. 36–43.

181 **Haydon recorded** *Diary*, 2. 318.

181 **While Man grows old** Wordsworth, *The Excursion* (1814), 4. 757–9.

181 **Thou wast not** 'Ode to a Nightingale', opening of stanza VII.

182 **fame / Should share** Coleridge, 'The Nightingale', lines 30–4, in the anonymously published *Lyrical Ballads* (1798).

183 **I am sick . . . weary, stale** Keats's underlinings and annotations in his pocket Shakespeare are digitized at https://iiif.lib.harvard. edu/manifests/view/drs:14637636$1i.

183 **The heartache** *Hamlet*, 3. 1. 68–9.

184 *Dentes illidunt* Robert Burton, *The Anatomy of Melancholy* (1621; quoted from 1813 edition owned by Keats), 2. 296–7. This volume of Keats's copy is now in Keats House, Hampstead. He also owned an abridged edition (see KC 1. 258). See also Janice Sinson, *John Keats and 'The Anatomy of Melancholy'* (1970).

185 **Though you should build** cancelled opening stanza of 'Ode on Melancholy', Woodhouse transcript, Houghton Library, Harvard University.

185 **No, no** 'Ode on Melancholy', stanza 1, in 1820 volume. The manuscript draft reads '~~Henb~~ Wolfsbane': Keats's first thought was 'henbane', perhaps in recollection of the 'cursed hebenon' that poisons old Hamlet.

185 **Then glut thy sorrow** 'Ode on Melancholy', stanzas 2–3.

185 **Galen** The attribution of the tag to Galen is traditional but uncertain; it ended by making an exception for roosters and women (*sive gallus et mulier*).

186 **the fibres of the brain** To George and Georgiana Keats, 19 March 1819, KL 2. 78–9.

186 **demon Poesy . . . Pain has no sting** 'Ode on Indolence', first published in *Life, Letters, and Literary Remains* (1848).

187 **a sick eagle . . . a shadow** 'On seeing the Elgin Marbles', first published in *The Examiner* and *The Champion*, 9 March 1817.

189 **the sculptured forms . . . The second** Colvin, p. 417.

189 **Heard melodies** 'Ode on a Grecian Urn', stanzas 2 and 3 in Keats's 1820 collection.

190 **The Grecian Urn** To Scottie Fitzgerald, 3 Aug 1940, FLL, pp. 460–1.

CHAPTER 13

191 **I think the novel** 14 Nov 1924, *Dear Scott / Dear Max*, p. 82.

191 **André Malraux** Fitzgerald's copy of *Man's Hope* (1938), now in the Princeton archive. The list provides the structure of Sarah Churchwell's meticulously researched and highly readable *Careless People: Murder, Mayhem and the Invention of 'The Great Gatsby'* (2013), though I disagree with some of her identifications.

192 **Allan Dwan** See further, Sharon Kim's excellent article 'The Lost Tycoon: Allan Dwan in the Works of F. Scott Fitzgerald', *The F. Scott Fitzgerald Review*, 14.1 (2016), 79–109.

192 **the moving-picture director** *The Great Gatsby* (1925), p. 129.

192 **We're all white here** Ibid., p. 156. But note my subsequent discussion of the additional phrase regarding Tom in the 'Trimalchio' version of the novel.

192 **Goddards** Biographers and critics have assumed that Fitzgerald was referring to some Goddards he met at a Long Island party, but there is no record of any such meeting, no Goddard who can be mapped onto the novel from the ledger as Rumsey, Hitchcock, Dwan and Swope can.

192 **'Civilization's going to pieces'** *The Great Gatsby*, p. 16.

193 **vigorous adulterous sex** Ibid., p. 34. Fitzgerald wrote more than once to Max Perkins with the worry that this risqué scene might get him into trouble.

194 **Stoddard Lectures** Ibid., p. 55.

195 **Whoever will take the time** 'Harding Discusses Future State of American Negro', *The Evening Independent*, 27 Oct 1921.

195 **It was an age of miracles** 'Echoes of the Jazz Age', *Scribner's Magazine*, Nov 1931, *The Crack-Up*, p. 14.

195 **one Jew is all right** *The Great Gatsby: A Facsimile of the Manuscript*, ed. Matthew J. Bruccoli (1973), p. 171. The original manuscript, now at Princeton, is digitized at http://arks.princeton.edu/ark:/88435/fq977w07f.

195 **radical-Jew outfit** see Michael Yudell, *Race Unmasked: Biology and Race in the Twentieth Century* (2014), pp. 41–2.

196 **Conceive that those Christian nations** *Stoddard Lectures* (1898), 2. 220–1.

197 **a Teutonic-featured man** Arthur Mizener, *The Far Side of Paradise* (1951), p. 171. Mizener's source was Henry Dan Piper, who was also working on a Fitzgerald biography. The misspelling of Gerlach is due to Zelda's report being verbal. See further Matthew J. Bruccoli, '"How Are You and the Family Old Sport?" – Gerlach and Gatsby', *Fitzgerald/Hemingway Annual* (1975), 33–6, and Horst Kruse's fascinating investigation into all that is known about Gerlach, 'The Real Jay Gatsby: Max von Gerlach, F. Scott Fitzgerald, and the Compositional History of *The Great Gatsby*', *The F. Scott Fitzgerald Review*, 1 (2002), 45–83.

197 **he was Gatsby** Arthur Mizener Papers on F. Scott Fitzgerald, Princeton University Library, Special Collections Manuscript Division, CO634, Series 4, Box 2.

197 **Enroute from the coast** Max Gerlach to Fitzgerald, 20 July 1923, *Correspondence*, p. 134. The clipping is repr. in *Romantic Egoists*, p. 103.

197 **Wolfshiem** Perkins spelt the name 'Wolfsheim' (more appropriately Jewish), but Fitzgerald the great misspeller uses 'Wolfshiem' throughout the novel.

197-8 **extraordinary book . . . come bit by bit** Max Perkins to Fitzgerald, 20 Nov 1924, *Dear Scott / Dear Max*, pp. 82–4.

198 **walk toward the American Express** *Tender is the Night* (1934), p. 288.

199 **six weeks . . . brought Gatsby to life** Fitzgerald to Max Perkins, 18 Feb 1925, *Dear Scott / Dear Max*, p. 94.

199 **exactly . . . the thing** Fitzgerald to Max Perkins, 24 Jan 1925, ibid., p. 93.

200 **shiftless and unsuccessful** *The Great Gatsby*, p. 118.

200 **the man who fixed** Ibid., p. 88.

200-1 **would have accepted . . . intermarriage** Ibid., pp. 60, 156.

201 **curiously neglected by Fitzgerald scholars** with the partial exception of Michael Pekarofski in his excellent article 'The Passing of Jay Gatsby: Class and Anti-Semitism in Fitzgerald's 1920s America', *The F. Scott Fitzgerald Review*, 10 (2012), 52–72. In 'Gatsby, Belasco, and Ethnic Ambiguity', *F. Scott Fitzgerald Review*, 6 (2007), 105–20, Pamela A. Bourgeois and John Clendenning assert categorically that 'no one has ever argued

that Gatsby might be Jewish' (p. 111); Pekarofski (p. 57) points
out that this is not strictly true since the suggestion was made,
'albeit in a tangential, quasi-metaphorical sense', by Barry Gross
and Eric Fretz in 'What Fitzgerald Thought of the Jews: Resisting
Type in "The Hotel Child"', *New Essays on F. Scott Fitzgerald's
Neglected Stories*, ed. Jackson R. Bryer (1996), pp. 189–205.
He might have added that several other critics have considered
the possibility of Gatsby's Jewishness. See, for example, Walter
Benn Michaels, *Our America: Nativism, Modernism, and
Pluralism* (1995), especially pp. 24–5; Meredith Goldsmith,
'White Skin, White Mask: Passing, Posing, and Performing in
The Great Gatsby', *MFS: Modern Fiction Studies*, 49.3 (2003),
443–68; and Barbara Will, '*The Great Gatsby* and the Obscene
Word', *College Literature*, 32.4 (2005), 125–44; though, as far
as I am aware, the Ashkenazi Jewish community of North Dakota
has been overlooked. Despite the signal about racial 'passing'
that may be given by the overtaking of Gatsby's car on the
Queensboro Bridge (as it crosses Blackwell's Island, where
'degenerates' were incarcerated) by 'three modish negroes' who
are 'driven by a white chauffeur' (p. 83), I am unpersuaded by
the alternative account of those scholars who have suggested
that Gatsby is a black man passing as white – a reading pioneered
by Carlyle V. Thompson, 'Was Gatsby Black?' (2000), repr. in
his *The Tragic Black Buck: Racial Masquerading in the American
Literary Imagination* (2004).

201 **Jewish Agricultural Aid** See Leonard G. Robinson, 'Agricultural
Activities of the Jews In America', *The American Jewish Year
Book*, 14 (1912–13), 21–115; J. Sanford Rikoon, 'The Jewish
Agriculturalists' Aid Society of America: Philanthropy, Ethnicity,
and Agriculture in the Heartland', *Agricultural History*, 72.1
(1998), 1–32; and Carol Ascher, 'Jewish Homesteading in
North Dakota', https://www.achanceforlandandfreshair.com/
blog/2018/10/24/jewish-homesteading-in-north-dakota [accessed
3 Sept 2020].

202 **started out as one man** Fitzgerald to John Peale Bishop, 9 Aug
1925, first published in *The Crack-Up*, p. 271.

202 **an obscene word** *The Great Gatsby*, p. 217.

202 **shrill, languid . . . I almost married** Ibid., pp. 36, 41.

202 **white girlhood . . . white roadster** Ibid., pp. 24, 117. Daisy's

actual words are 'Our white girlhood . . . Our beautiful white
– – ', at which point she is cut off by Tom.

203 **knew something about breeding** Ibid., p. 42.

203 **no indication that Wilson** It is presumably a mere coincidence
that Fitzgerald's close friend Edmund Wilson, who would have
been amused to see his surname in the novel, was a notable
philo-Semite.

203 **the gardener saw Wilson's** Ibid., p. 195.

204 **'Dalrymple Goes Wrong'** published in *The Smart Set*, repr. in
Flappers and Philosophers: 'The generation which numbered
Bryan Dalrymple drifted out of adolescence to a mighty fan-fare
of trumpets. Bryan played the star in an affair which included
a Lewis gun and a nine-day romp behind the retreating German
lines, so luck triumphant or sentiment rampant awarded him a
row of medals and on his arrival in the States he was told that
he was second in importance only to General Pershing and
Sergeant York' (*Flappers and Philosophers*, p. 75). On Gatsby
and York, see further pp. 181–3 of James H. Meredith's excellent essay 'Fitzgerald and War', in the valuable collection *A
Historical Guide to F. Scott Fitzgerald*, ed. Kirk Curnutt (2004).

205 **The test of a first-rate intelligence** Feb 1936, *The Crack-Up*,
p. 69.

205 **Later ages** Matthew Arnold, *Essays in Criticism Second Series*
(1888, repr. 1898, Sheilah Graham's copy with Fitzgerald's
marginalia), p. 100; Fitzgerald's riposte quoted, *College of One*,
p. 98.

206 **the author would like . . . discrepancy from** Introduction to
Modern Library edition of *The Great Gatsby* (1934), repr. *In
His Own Time*, p. 156.

206 **We're all white here** *Trimalchio: An Early Version of 'The Great
Gatsby'*, ed. James L. W. West III (2000), p. 103. I owe this
observation to James L. W. West III, 'Jay Gatsby's Background',
Times Literary Supplement, 20 Oct 2000, p. 17.

206 **invented an entirely fictitious** Carl Van Vechten, 'Fitzgerald on
the March', *The Nation*, 20 May 1925.

207 **the theme of a soiled** Ibid.

207 **the casual watcher . . . within and without** *The Great Gatsby*,
p. 43.

207 **Part of him** Cowley, review of *Tender is the Night*, *New Republic*, 6 June 1934.

208 **His art is happy** Yeats, 'Ego Dominus Tuus', in *The Wild Swans at Coole* (1919). There is an edition of the complete poems of Yeats in the Sheilah Graham 'College of One' collection at Princeton.

208 **a thing of incomparable form** Fitzgerald to H. L. Mencken, 4 May 1925, FLL, p. 111.

208 **it has interested** T. S. Eliot to Fitzgerald, 31 Dec 1925, first published in *The Crack-Up*, p. 310.

208 **I want to write** July 1922, *Correspondence*, p. 112.

209 **All you can get** *Notebooks*, p. 161.

209 **A Romance . . . A Romance** *Notebooks*, p.158

209 **The other things** 'Friend Husband's Latest', New York *Tribune*, 2 April 1922.

209 **a bright college boy . . . it is the charm and beauty** H. L. Mencken, 'As H. L. M. Sees It', Baltimore *Evening Sun*, 2 May 1925.

209 **the richest, most sensuous** To Scottie Fitzgerald, 3 Aug 1940, FLL, p. 460.

209 **pained heart** 'The Eve of St Agnes', stanza XVI.

210 **But his heart** *The Great Gatsby*, p. 119.

210 **The lustrous salvers** 'The Eve St Agnes', stanza XXXII.

210 **give him sight of Madeline** Ibid., stanza IX.

210 **blanched linen . . . silken Samarcand** Ibid., stanza XXX.

211 **He took out a pile,** *The Great Gatsby*, p. 112. The influence of Porphyro's feast on Gatsby's shirts, and of 'The Eve of St Agnes' on *The Great Gatsby* more generally, has been noted by various critics, most recently, fully and interestingly Lauren Rule-Maxwell in 'The New Emperor's Clothes: Keatsian Echoes and American Materialism in *The Great Gatsby*', *The F. Scott Fitzgerald Review*, 8 (2010), 57–78.

211-12 **In other words . . . Daisy's a person** *Trimalchio: An Early Version of 'The Great Gatsby'*, pp. 89–90.

212 **extraordinary gift for hope** *The Great Gatsby*, p. 2.

212 **In the same stanza** 1938, either when Scottie was in her final year of high school, or in her first semester at Vassar. FLL, pp. 341–2.

213 **He lit Daisy's cigarette** *The Great Gatsby*, p. 115: Fitzgerald was precise in his reference in the letter to his daughter.

214 **What mad pursuit? . . . What was it** 'Ode on a Grecian Urn', stanza I; *The Great Gatsby*, pp. 96, 131–2.

215 **'I wouldn't ask too much'** *The Great Gatsby*, p. 133.

215 **One autumn night** Ibid., pp. 133–4.

216 **fantastic communication** *Trimalchio: An Early Version of 'The Great Gatsby'*, p. 90. In this version, the recollection comes later in the story, at the moment when Gatsby announces that Daisy wants them to run off together; in the revision, it is made more romantic and nostalgic by being removed from the act of adultery, a broken marriage, and a possible future for Gatsby and Daisy.

216 **Through all he said** *The Great Gatsby*, p. 134.

CHAPTER 14

218-19 **on the contrary . . . To be thrown** To Sarah Jeffrey, postmarked 9 June 1819, KL 2. 115.

219 **The morning is the only** To Fanny Brawne, 1 July 1819, KL 2. 123.

220 **thou art lovely** *Love's Labour's Lost*, 4. 1. 62–3; p. 32 in the text in vol. 2 of Keats's pocket edition of Shakespeare.

220 **those sweet lips** KL 2. 123, quoting Philip Massinger, *The Duke of Milan* (1. 3, from edition of Massinger's plays edited by William Gifford in 1805).

221 **I never knew before** To Fanny Brawne, 8 July 1819, KL 2. 126–7.

221 **I am in deep love** To Fanny Brawne, 25 July 1819, KL 2. 132–3.

222 **a serpent** Burton, *Anatomy of Melancholy*, 3. 2. 1. 1, quoted in Keats's note at the end of 'Lamia', the opening poem in his 1820 collection.

223 **OTHO THE GREAT** First published in 1848 *Remains*; text here from p. 159 in Fitzgerald's Keats, though there is no evidence that he read the play.

223 **to make as great** To Benjamin Bailey, 14 Aug 1819, KL 2. 139

223 **Auranthe! My Life!** *Otho the Great*, 4. 2. 19–20, 30–42.

224 **The whole town** To Fanny Keats, 28 Aug 1819, KL 2. 148.

224 **six pence a pint** To John Taylor, 5 Sept 1819, KL 2. 156.

225 **The great beauty** To George and Georgiana Keats, 20 Sept 1819, KL 2. 201.

225 **It happened that year** Mackenzie, *Sinister Street*, p. 583.

226 **Michael envied Keats** Ibid.

226 **Our health temperament** To John Taylor, 5 Sept 1819, KL 2. 156.

227 **The delightful Weather** To Fanny Keats, 28 Aug 1819, KL 2. 148–9 (two slips of pen silently corrected).

228 **I think if I had a free** To J. H. Reynolds, 24 Aug 1819, KL 2. 146.

228 **Some think I have lost** To George and Georgiana Keats, 21 Sept 1819, KL 2. 209.

228-9 **Now the time is beautiful . . . I arrive** Ibid., KL 2. 209–10.

229 **Gross mismanagement** 'Hospitals: St Cross, near Winchester', in *A History of the County of Hampshire*, ed. H Arthur Doubleday and William Page (1903), 2. 193.

230 **Being arrived** John Milner, *The History Civil and Ecclesiastical, and Survey of the Antiquities, of Winchester* (1809), 2. 199.

230 **Having attained** Ibid., 2. 200.

230 **partially under corn** Noted by Richard Marggraf Turley, Jayne Elizabeth Archer and Howard Thomas in their excellent article, 'Keats, "To Autumn", and the new men of Winchester', *Review of English Studies*, New Series, 63 (2012), 797–817: 'in recent years – due in part to the high price of corn – there had been a concerted effort to convert wasteland around Winchester into land capable of producing food' (p. 802).

230 **How beautiful the season** To J. H. Reynolds, 21 Sept 1819, KL 2. 167.

231 **Season of mists** To Richard Woodhouse, 21 Sept 1819, KL 2. 170, published in Keats's 1820 volume with regularized punctuation and hyphenation, and minor variants ('sweet kernel' instead of 'white', 'store' for 'stores', 'winnowing' for the felicitous slip 'winmowing', 'Drown'd' for 'Dased'. 'Steady' for 'Stready', 'or dies' for 'and dies', 'gathering' for 'gather'd').

233 **For awhile after you quit** To Scottie Fitzgerald, 3 Aug 1940, FLL, p. 461. For a reading of 'To Autumn' in relation to climate and the idea of poem as ecosystem, see my *The Song of the Earth* (2000), pp. 102–10. And for highly nuanced close readings of all the odes, Helen Vendler, *The Odes of John Keats* (1983).

CHAPTER 15

234 **There are no** *Notebooks*, p. 58.

235 **about Zelda** To Max Perkins, 28 Aug 1925, *Dear Scott / Dear Max*, p. 120.

235 **survive in draft** F. Scott Fitzgerald Papers, Princeton, Box 10a. See further, Matthew J. Bruccoli, *The Composition of 'Tender is the Night': A Study of the Manuscripts* (1963) and *Tender is the Night: The Melarky and Kelly Versions*, introduced and arranged by Matthew J. Bruccoli, vol. 4 of the series *F. Scott Fitzgerald Manuscripts* (1990).

235 **F. Scott Fitzgerald's Latest** *New York World*, 12 April 1925, repr. (as are the reviews quoted subsequently) in *In His Own Time*, pp. 345–65.

235 **Mencken . . . Aiken . . . Seldes** Baltimore *Evening Sun*, 2 May 1925; *New Criterion*, Oct 1926; *The Dial*, Aug 1925, *In His Own Time*, pp. 348–65.

236 **In a short career** *The Forum*, Aug 1925, *In His Own Time*, p. 358.

237 **a man . . . The mouth worried you** Hemingway, 'Scott Fitzgerald', in *A Moveable Feast*, p. 131.

237 **Here we are** Gertrude Stein to Fitzgerald, published by Edmund Wilson in *The Crack-Up*, p. 308.

238 **The teasing is tender** *Tender Buttons* (1912), repr. in *Selected Writings of Gertrude Stein*, ed. Carl Van Vechten (1962), p. 486.

238 **it is something really NEW** To Max Perkins, 1 May 1925, *Dear Scott / Dear Max*, p. 104. Later, they had Joyce round for dinner in their Paris apartment, Scott awestruck, Zelda, to her husband's annoyance, less reverential.

239 **bright tan prayer rug . . . short dazzling beach** *Tender is the Night* (1934), p. 3.

240 **Shortly before noon** Amanda Vaill, *Everybody was so Young: Gerald and Sara Murphy: A Lost Generation Love Story* (1995), p. 161. This is the best of several biographies of the couple.

241 **The novel of selected . . . He will say only** To Thomas Wolfe, July 1937, FLL, p. 332. Had Wolfe been given this advice earlier (or indeed, had he listened more to the advice of Max Perkins), his *Bildungsroman* debut *Look Homeward, Angel* (1929) would have retained its dazzle but been less of a loose baggy monster.

242 **Futile, shameful** *Ledger*, p. 180.

242 **just between . . . Its ROTTEN** Zelda's letters from California to Scottie, Zelda Fitzgerald Papers, Princeton, Correspondence II.A.4.3–10 (Jan–Feb 1927).

242-3 **moving softly . . . All the iridescence** 'My Lost City', July 1932, in *The Crack-Up*, pp. 23, 25.

245 **one of Fitzgerald's biographers** Matthew J. Bruccoli, *Some Sort of Epic Grandeur: The Life of F. Scott Fitzgerald* (1981), p. 258, citing an interview of 17 Aug 1978. My account of the relationship is based on Lois Moran's 1948–51 letters to Fitzgerald's first biographer, Arthur Mizener, in his papers at Princeton (Mizener Papers, Box 2, Folder 5) and an excellent article by Moran's biographer Richard Buller, 'F. Scott Fitzgerald, Lois Moran, and the Mystery of Mariposa Street', *The F. Scott Fitzgerald Review*, 4 (2005), 3–19.

245 **He hadn't said a word** 'Magnetism', *Saturday Evening Post*, 3 March 1928, in *Collected Short Stories*, p. 447.

246 **he wanted his child** 'Babylon Revisited', *Saturday Evening Post*, 21 Feb 1931, repr. in *Collected Short Stories*, p. 223. The story was adapted into the 1954 movie *The Last Time I Saw Paris*.

247 **The Crash!** *Ledger*, p. 184.

247 **her doctor** original Malmaison report (in French), F. Scott Fitzgerald Papers, Princeton, Box 42, Folder 57.

248 **A Year in Lausanne** *Ledger*, p. 185.

248 **You're not so bad** 'Red-Headed Woman', carbon copy of typescript, 3 Dec 1931, F. Scott Fitzgerald Papers, Princeton, Box 32b.

249 **as he finished** 'Crazy Sunday', *The American Mercury*, Oct 1932, repr. in *Collected Short Stories*, p. 560.

249 **Darling my own** Dec 1931, *Dear Scott, Dearest Zelda*, p. 143.

249 **My God** Fitzgerald to Dr Mildred Squires of the Phipps Clinic of Johns Hopkins (Zelda's doctor and the dedicatee of *Save Me the Waltz*), 14 March 1932, headed by Squires 'Letter from husband', FLL, p. 209.

CHAPTER 16

250 **Night lends enchantment** Tony Buttita, *Lost Summer: A Personal Memoir of F. Scott Fitzgerald* (2003; original edition 1974), p. 12.

251 **At fifteen she was raped** 'GENERAL PLAN' for *Tender is the Night*, F. Scott Fitzgerald Papers, Princeton, transcribed in Bruccoli, *Composition of 'Tender is the Night'*, p. 80.

251 **Your mother took such** To Marjorie Sayre Brinson, Dec 1938, F. Scott Fitzgerald Papers, Princeton, Box 53.

252 **she was so miserable** *Caesar's Things*, Zelda Fitzgerald Papers, Princeton, I.A.2.a, quoted in Sally Cline's excellent *Zelda Fitzgerald: Her Voice in Paradise* (2002), p. 41. There is a strong reading of *Caesar's Things* in Deborah Pike, *The Subversive Art of Zelda Fitzgerald* (2017), chapter 4.

252 **I don't think it's true** Zelda in the Phipps Clinic at Johns Hopkins, quoted, Nancy Milford, *Zelda: A Biography*, p. 286.

252 **had magic** *Tender is the Night*, p. 4.

253 **They have to like it . . . so that his eyes** Ibid., p. 22.

254 ***Wire, wire, wire!*** Ibid., pp. 123–4.

254 **This corner of Europe** Ibid., p. 320.

255 **He turned away** Ibid., p. 352.

255 **Let him look at it** Ibid., p. 362.

255 **She sat upon the low wall** Ibid., p. 357.

257 **by Sara and you** Quoted, Calvin Tomkins, 'Living Well is the Best Revenge', *New Yorker*, 21 July 1962, based on an interview with the Murphys conducted the previous year. Available online at https://www.newyorker.com/magazine/1962/07/28/living-well-is-the-best-revenge [accessed 8 Sept 2020].

257 **often altered or distorted** Gerald Murphy, as reported by Tomkins, ibid.

257 **'When I like men'** Tomkins, ibid.

258 **People were always . . . person after person** quoted, ibid.

258 **All my beautiful lovely** *Tender is the Night*, p. 75.

258 **A 'schizophrêne'** Ibid., p. 250.

258 **This took religion** Ibid., p. 75

259 **He knelt on the hard soil** Ibid., p. 267.

259 **The Divers' day** Ibid., p. 26.

260 **he picked a fig . . . He had smashed** Tomkins, 'Living Well'.

261-2 **several times in the mouth . . . since sometimes beauty** *Tender is the Night*, p. 138.

262 **Do you not see** To George and Georgiana Keats, 21 April 1819, KL 2. 102.

262 **On an almost parallel** *Tender is the Night*, p. 391.

CHAPTER 17

264 **lost caviare . . . bouillabaisse . . . colored beads** *Tender is the Night*, pp. 19, 344, 71.

264 **Along the walls** Ibid., p. 32.

264 **Into the dark** Ibid., p. 69.

265 **this moment I was writing** To Charles Dilke, 22 Sept 1819, KL 2. 179.

266 **Thou hast felt** 'The Fall of Hyperion. A Dream', canto 1, lines 141–5. First published in 1857 by Richard Monckton Milnes, editor of the 1848 *Remains*, under the title 'Hyperion, A Vision' in the curious venue of *Miscellanies of the Philobiblon Society*, 3 (1856–7), 5–24. This periodical brought a wide range of manuscript materials into print – shortly before the Keats, it included a selection of hitherto unpublished poems by John Donne.

266 **None can usurp this height** Ibid., 1. 147–9. 'Hyperion: A Vision' was included among Keats's 'Supplementary Verses' in Fitzgerald's edition. There is no firm evidence that Scott read it through. This text, following Milnes, omitted a sequence (1ines 187–210 in modern editions) which, according to Woodhouse's notes on his transcript of the holograph, Keats intended to erase: the first-person narrator challenges Moneta with the claim that 'a poet is a sage, / A humanist, a physician to all men'; she replies that he is 'of the dreamer tribe' and that 'The poet and the dreamer are distinct, / Diverse, sheer opposite, antipodes'. One 'pours out a balm upon the world', while 'The other vexes it'. But it is not entirely clear which is which: Keats is asking himself whether he is poet or dreamer.

266 **I have given up Hyperion** To J. H. Reynolds, 21 Sept 1819, KL 2. 167. See further, my essay 'Keats's two *Hyperion*s and the problem of Milton', in *Romantic Revisions*, ed. R. A. Brinkley and K. Hanley (1992), 321–38.

267 **wise passiveness** Wordsworth, 'Expostulation and Reply', in *Lyrical Ballads* (1798).

267 **I will write** To Charles Brown, 22 Sept 1819, KL 2. 176.

267 **brought to his mind** And that of Brown when he too was in Winchester – he claimed that he gave Keats the idea for the play (KC 2. 67).

268 **neither finished nor published** According to Brown, the plan was to publish it 'under the feigned authorship of Lucy Vaughan Lloyd' with the title of either *The Cap and Bells* or *The Jealousies* (KC 2. 71). Leigh Hunt published the amusing hackney-coach sequence in his essay 'On Coaches' in *The Indicator*, August 1820. Keats's political commitments are discussed at length by his biographers Andrew Motion and Nicholas Roe; see also Roe's pioneering *John Keats and the Culture of Dissent* (1997). It is, however, noteworthy that the most astute literary editor of the day, John Scott, stated categorically in his review of the 1820 volume that Mr Keats was 'not a political writer' – *London Magazine*, 2 (Sept 1820), p. 315.

268 **This living hand** fragment first published in 6th edition (1898) of H. B. Forman's *Poetical Works of John Keats*.

268 **much possessed by death** T. S. Eliot's memorable characterization of Webster in his 'Whispers of Immortality' (*Poems*, 1920).

268 **My sweet Girl** To Fanny Brawne, 11 Oct 1819, KL 2. 222.

269 **Sweet voice** 'The day is gone', probably written 10 Oct 1819, immediately after seeing Fanny for the first time on his return to London. Included in 1848 *Remains*.

269 **let me feel . . . Touch has a memory** 'What can I do to drive away', dated Oct 1819 in *Remains*, given the title 'Lines to Fanny' in Fitzgerald's edition.

269 **Oh, let me have thee** 'I cry your mercy', dated 1819 in *Remains*, given the title 'To Fanny' in Fitzgerald's edition.

270 **infidelity of Chaucer's and Shakespeare's Cressida** 'the fear of you being a little inclined to the Cressid': to Fanny Brawne, Feb(?) 1820, KL 2. 256. The poem, probably written in Feb 1820, begins 'Physician Nature! Let my spirit blood'. Published in the 1848 *Remains* as 'Ode to Fanny', it was assumed in early editions, including Fitzgerald's, to belong to the earlier phase of Keats's relationship with Fanny.

270 **We also took it** *Audubon and his Journals*, ed. Maria Audubon (1897), 1. 34. For more on George Keats, see Denise Gigante's splendid parallel life, *The Keats Brothers: The Life of John and George* (2011).

271 **From imprudently leaving off** To Fanny Keats, 6 Feb 1820, KL 2. 251.

271 **I know the colour** Brown, manuscript 'Life of John Keats', KC 2. 73–4.

271 **with bobbins . . . his hands joined** To Fanny Keats, 8 Feb 1820, KL 2. 253.

272 **nervous irritability . . . years addicted** To Fanny Keats, 21 Apr 1820, KL 2. 287; Clare's admission papers to the Northampton General Lunatic Asylum (1841), quoted and discussed, Jonathan Bate, *John Clare: A Biography* (2003), pp. 466–8.

272 **like the radiance** Lamb, review in *New Times*, 19 July 1820, repr. the following month by Leigh Hunt in *The Indicator*. Lamb thought 'Isabella' was the best poem in the collection. For comprehensive collections of contemporary reviews of all Keats's poems, see *John Keats: The Critical Heritage*, ed. G. M. Matthews (1971) and *The Romantics Reviewed: Contemporary Reviews of British Romantic Writers. Part C: Shelley, Keats and London Radical Writers*, ed. Donald H. Reiman (1972).

272 **one of the most extraordinary** Scott, review in *London Magazine*, 2 (Sept 1820), 315–21.

273 **the most beautiful passages** To Fanny Brawne, 4 July(?) 1820, KL 2. 302. The copy of Spenser does not survive.

273 **conviction of the ultimate** *Remains*, 1. 281.

275 **A poem for Fanny** There can be no doubt of this, despite Gittings' suggestion that it was written for Mrs Jones: Fanny lovingly transcribed it in the copy of Cary's translation of Dante that Keats gave her before he left England.

276 **On his way to Italy** Fitzgerald's Cambridge Edition, p. 232.

276 **I will imagine you** To Fanny Brawne, 25 July 1819, KL 2. 133.

276 **Bright star** text from Fitzgerald's edition; first published by Brown in the *Plymouth and Devonport Weekly Journal*, 27 Sept 1836, repr. in 1848 *Remains*.

277 **the silver pepper . . . a single green light** *The Great Gatsby*, pp. 25–6.

277 **seen for the first time** Ibid., p. 82.

277 **drove on toward death** Ibid., p. 163.

278 **Until gradually . . . for a transitory** Ibid., pp. 217–18.

278-9 **when he first . . . it was already** Ibid., p. 218.

CHAPTER 18

281 **For the psychiatrist** *Journal of Nervous and Mental Disease,*
July 1935, pasted into Scrapbook 5, Fitzgerald Digital Collection,
Princeton. http://pudl.princeton.edu/viewer.php?obj=sf268784s
&vol=v5phys&log=v5log#page/88/mode/2up\ [accessed 9 Sept
2020].

282 **Books are like brothers** *Notebooks,* p. 158.

282-3 **Debts terrible . . . Zelda very bad** *Ledger,* p. 189. The ledger
ends in March 1935.

283 **There are emotions** To Beatrice Dance, summer 1935, *Letters,*
ed. Turnbull, p. 530.

283 **a romantic sap . . . a worthless woman** Buttita, *Lost Summer,*
p. 73. 'Lottie Stephens' was the pseudonym that he gave her in
this book; her real name is unknown.

284 **fun and exciting** Ibid., p. 134.

285 **He talked . . . a white boy** Ibid., pp. 171–2. She used a different
word, the toxic one, of course, to taunt him all the more.

285 **collection of short stories** Entitled *Taps at Reveille,* published
March 1935; eighteen stories, including 'Crazy Sunday' and
'Babylon Revisited', as well as two series with the respective
protagonists 'Basil' and 'Josephine'.

286 **Of course all life** 'The Crack-Up', *Esquire,* Feb 1936, repr. as
the title-essay of the posthumous collection edited by Edmund
Wilson, *The Crack-Up,* p. 69.

287 **Scott who?** reminiscence of Edwin Knopf, reported in Aaron
Latham, *Crazy Sundays: F. Scott Fitzgerald in Hollywood* (1971),
p. 102. My account of Fitzgerald's screenwriting career is much
indebted to this book, which is based on a wealth of primary
sources and interviews.

288 **Don't rub the sleep** To Mrs Sayre, Zelda's mother, 23 April
1938, *Correspondence,* p. 498. On Yanks in Oxford after the
Great War, see Christopher A. Snyder's lively and wide-ranging
*Gatsby's Oxford: Scott, Zelda, and the Jazz Age Invasion of
Britain: 1904–1929* (2019).

289 **Taking things hard** *Notebooks,* p. 163.

289 **At least they've kept** Sheilah Graham, with Gerod Frank, *Beloved
Infidel: The Education of a Woman* (1958, repr 1959), p. 176.

290 **Sex** *The Production Code of the Motion Picture Producers and*

Distributors of America, Inc (devised 1930, enforced from 1934, known popularly as the Hays Code), Particular Application II.

291 **I have been playing** Fitzgerald, notes in MGM archive, dated 3 Feb 1938, quoted, *Crazy Sundays*, p. 160.

291 **the Moor** Ibid.

291 **infinite disappointment . . . It won't be Joan's** To Scottie Fitzgerald, spring 1938, FLL, p. 357. The unproduced script of *Infidelity* was published in *Esquire*, Dec 1973.

291 **About adjectives** Ibid.

292 *swimming under water* Undated fragment of letter to Scottie Fitzgerald, *Letters*, ed. Turnbull, p. 101.

292 **don't depress the clutch** To Scottie Fitzgerald, 11 Apr 1940, FLL, p. 441.

292 **Poetry is either something . . . In themselves** To Scottie Fitzgerald, 3 Aug 1940, FLL, pp. 460–1.

293 **It's news** Carbon copy typescript of *Gone with the Wind* script, with Fitzgerald's holograph corrections (11–24 Jan 1939), F. Scott Fitzgerald Papers, Princeton, Box 31.

294 **They were all nice kids** *Beloved Infidel*, p. 163.

295 **She is of the movies** To Kenneth Littauer of *Collier's* magazine, copied to Max Perkins, 29 Sept 1939, FLL, p. 409.

295 **It's more than possible** *The Last Tycoon* (1941), p. 18.

295 **to get the verisimilitude** To Kenneth Littauer and Max Perkins, FLL, p. 410.

295 **This is Cecilia** Ibid., p. 77. She is 'Cecelia' in the typescript (Fitzgerald's usual bad spelling), corrected by Wilson to Cecilia in the published text.

296 *The Last Tycoon* Wilson's exceptionally well-judged choices for the five short stories were 'May Day', 'The Diamond as Big as the Ritz', 'Absolution', 'The Rich Boy' and 'Crazy Sunday' (it is a shame that 'Winter Dreams' was lacking).

296 **STAHR** F. Scott Fitzgerald Papers, Princeton, Box 8b, repr. in *The Love of the Last Tycoon: A Western*, ed. Matthew J. Bruccoli, in *The Cambridge Edition of the Works of F. Scott Fitzgerald* (1993), p. xv (an edition of the typescript, together with a fuller selection of the working notes than that provided by Wilson).

296 **starry veiled expression** *Last Tycoon*, p. 59.

297 **like a constellation** Ibid., p. 127.

297 **because she is slipping** *Love of the Last Tycoon*, p. 166.

297 **Stahr's eyes** *Last Tycoon*, p. 64.

297 **wild surmise . . . the man named Dick** *Correspondence*, p. 517; *Last Tycoon*, p. 9.

297 **Anything added . . . glad that there was beauty** *Last Tycoon*, pp. 66, 168.

297-8 **He led pictures . . . I'm the unity** Ibid., pp. 28, 58 (the typescript has 'before the censorship in 1933' – *Love of the Last Tycoon*, p. 28).

298 *Tout passe* Gautier's poem 'L'Art', in his *Émaux et camées* (1872), p. 225.

298 **his apprehension of splendor** *Last Tycoon*, p. 62.

298 **would be short** To Beatrice Dance, 11 Oct 1938, *Correspondence*, p. 517.

298-9 **Suddenly outdated . . . There was a flurry** Typed working note for episode 28, repr. in facsimile, *Love of the Last Tycoon*, p. 190.

299 **new British stage play** Emlyn Williams, *The Light of Heart* (1940). Fitzgerald's script of the play is in the F. Scott Fitzgerald Papers, Princeton, Box 32a.

299 **a Broadway play** A flop, which closed within a week. The author, Philip Barry, was better attuned to romantic comedy – his play *The Philadelphia Story* was turned into a film and nominated for six Oscars (winning two) in the year of Fitzgerald's death. Fitzgerald's script of the play is in the F. Scott Fitzgerald Papers, Princeton, Box 29b.

CHAPTER 19

301 **I wish for death . . . I eternally see** To Charles Brown, 28 Sept 1820, KL 2. 345.

302 **the drawing** Caroline Spurgeon, author of *Keats's Shakespeare*, believed she had found it, and included it as frontispiece to the book, but the attribution was false: 'The watercolour drawing called "Keats on board the brig *Maria Crowther*", repr. in Caroline Spurgeon, *Keats's Shakespeare*, 1928, frontispiece in colour, is actually of Garret Lansing drawn by Alexander Anderson, see B. J. Lossing, *Memorial of Alexander Anderson MD . . .* , 1872' (https://www.npg.org.uk/collections/search/ personExtended/mp02480/john-keats?tab=iconography).

302 **Byron's poetry** Severn to Monckton Milnes, KC 2. 134.

302 **seeming close . . . lay entranced** Severn's words, in William Sharp, *The Life and Letters of Joseph Severn* (1892), p. 58.

303 **Every thing I have** To Charles Brown, 1 Nov 1820, KL 2. 351.

303 **buried amid a people** Sharp, *Joseph Severn*, p. 63 (the last word in Severn's original manuscript was unclear).

303 **literally filled** Ibid., p. 64.

304 **mental exertions** Clark to unidentified recipient, 27 Nov 1820, KL 1. 358.

304 **There is one thought . . . I always made** To Charles Brown, 30 Nov 1820, KL 360.

304 **Not a moment** Severn to Charles Brown, 17 Dec 1820, KL 1. 361.

305 **Poor Keats** Severn to William Haslam, dated 15 Jan 1821, KL 2. 367.

305 **Why is this** Ibid., KL 2. 368.

305 **Another week** Severn to John Taylor, 25 Jan 1821, KL 2. 371.

306 **Four days previous** Severn to John Taylor, 6 March 1821, KL 2. 378.

306 **23 February 1821** The Roman calendar was reckoned differently, so the cemetery register and gravestone give the date as 24 February.

306 **an immense sweat** Severn to John Taylor, 6 March 1821, KL 2. 378.

306 **Severn – I – lift me up** Severn to Charles Brown, 27 Feb 1821, KC 2. 94, first published in Sharp, *Joseph Severn*, p. 94.

307 **I know my Keats** 27 March 1821, *Letters of Fanny Brawne to Fanny Keats 1820–1824*, ed. Fred Edgcumbe (1937), p. 25.

307 **the worst possible** Severn to Charles Brown, 27 Feb 1821, KL 2. 379.

308 **HERE LIES ONE** Severn to Charles Brown, 8 Feb 1821, KC 2. 91.

309 **four days after Keats** I write about the duel at greater length in *Radical Wordsworth*, pp. 407–11. There is a full account in Leonidas M. Jones, 'The Scott–Christie Duel', *Texas Studies in Literature and Language*, 12 (1971), 605–29.

309-10 **noteless blot . . . Peace, peace!** Shelley, *Adonais* (1821), stanzas XXXVII, XXXIX, XLIII.

310 **it forcibly seems to me** Charles Armitage Brown, *Life of John Keats*, ed. Dorothy H. Bodurtha and W. B. Pope (1936), p. 24.

311 **signal monument . . . documentary evidence** Monckton Milnes's preface to *Remains*, 1. 8–9.

311 **a cause of embarrassment** But then, as Keats's best modern critic notes, he was the great poet of the expression of embarrassment in the flush, the blush, the self-consciousness (about kissing, for example) and the half-stammer: Christopher Ricks, *Keats and Embarrassment*.

312 **There is something** Tennyson, quoted in his son Hallam Tennyson's *Alfred Lord Tennyson: A Memoir* (1898), 2. 286.

312 **Championship of this kind** George H. Ford, *Keats and the Victorians: A Study of his Influence and Rise to Fame 1821–1895* (1944; repr 1962), is a thorough study of this subject; the cultural politics of Keats's Victorian reputation are explored in Jonah Siegel, 'Among the English Poets: Keats, Arnold, and the Placement of Fragments', *Victorian Poetry,* 37 (1999), 215–32.

312 **by virtue of his feeling** Matthew Arnold, 'John Keats', in *Essays in Criticism: Second Series*, p. 119.

CHAPTER 20

314 **Lily Shiel . . . Sheilah Graham** She told the story of her life and her affair with Fitzgerald in a string of autobiographies, beginning with *Beloved Infidel* (1958). By far the best account of her life, and the relationship, is that of her son, who had the benefit of a copy of *Beloved Infidel* in which his mother had annotated all the things that she had exaggerated or made up: Robert Westbrook, *Intimate Lies: F. Scott Fitzgerald and Sheilah Graham* (1995).

315 **Fair youth** From the second stanza of 'Ode on a Grecian Urn'.

316 **Sitting close** Sheilah Graham, *College of One* (1967; pbk 1968), p. 69.

316 **filled with an overwhelming . . . Sheilo** *Beloved Infidel*, p. 196.

316 **For Sheilah** Inscription in 1910 Oxford University Press edition (ed. H. Buxton Forman), now in the Rare Books collection of Princeton University Library.

317 **We break verse** 'SOME TERMS' in typed 'College of One' curriculum (my italics indicate a handwritten insertion), repr. in

College of One, p. 211. Fitzgerald is forgetting that Shakespeare's early plays include much more frequent use of rhyme – and that many of his scenes are in prose.

317	**Then on the shore** 'When I have fears that I may cease to be'.

317	**Rhymed Verse . . . Hyperbole** typed curriculum repr. in *College of One*, pp. 211–12.

318	**A SHORT INTRODUCTION . . . The Eve** Ibid., p. 209.

318	**The only sensible course** To Scottie Fitzgerald, 29 July 1940, FLL, p. 457.

319	**a saccharine job** FLL, p. 460.

319	**Yet I firmly believe** Sheilah Graham's copy, now at Princeton, of *Essays in Criticism, Second Series* (1898 edn), p. 132.

319	**This, with its following** Repr. in *College of One*, p. 99.

319	**the best which has been** Arnold's famous definition of culture in the preface to his *Culture and Anarchy* (1875).

320	**This is the *bad* form** *Beloved Infidel*, p. 196. As noted earlier, 'La Belle Dame' was first published in Leigh Hunt's *Indicator*. This version begins 'Ah, what can ail thee, wretched wight', and has many variants from the original holograph of 21 April 1819 in Keats's long journal-letter to his brother and sister-in-law, which Fitzgerald was quite right to prefer.

320	**A Greek Cup** Repr. in *College of One*, pp. 104–5.

320	**To the Beautiful** 'College of One Collection', Call Number: Rare Books (Ex) College of One – 62, Princeton University Library.

322	**'On Growing Old'** Masefield, *Enslaved and other Poems* (1920), pp. 123–4.

322	**A sick old man** Quoted, Latham, *Crazy Sundays*, p. 8.

322	**Be with me** Audible on the Internet at, for example, https://www.brainpickings.org/2013/09/24/f-scott-fitzgerald-reads-john-masefield-on-growing-old/.

323	**I must down** 'Sea-fever' in *Salt-Water Poems and Ballads* (1902), opening later revised to 'go down to the sea again'.

323	**My heart aches** Audible on the Internet at several sites, including https://youtu.be/fMKHwMGIVI8.

325	**Most potent** Audible on the Internet at, for example, https://youtu.be/wwo-qiJP4co.

326	**big five studios** Columbia, Twentieth-Century Fox, MGM, Paramount and Universal.

326 **I am deep** To Zelda Fitzgerald, 23 Oct 1940, *Dear Scott, Dearest Zelda*, p. 373.

326 **forty-nine with red-rimmed eyes** 'Fun in an Artist's Studio' in Fitzgerald, *The Pat Hobby Stories*, with an introduction by Arnold Gingrich (1962), p. 128. Gingrich was the editor of *Esquire*.

327 **I feel awful** *Beloved Infidel*, p. 248.

328 **I recited** Ibid., p. 254.

328 **Dearest love . . . Devotedly** Scott's: 18 Dec 1940; Zelda's: undated, Nov/Dec 1940, *Dear Scott, Dearest Zelda*, pp. 383, 380.

328 **Dearest: I am always grateful** March 1939, *Dear Scott, Dearest Zelda*, p. 277.

329 **as clear as a bell** Sara Mayfield, *Exiles from Paradise: Zelda and Scott Fitzgerald* (1971), p. 285.

329 **a single charred slipper** Sally Cline, *Zelda Fitzgerald: Her Voice in Paradise* (2002), p. 402.

329 **surprised at the deep** Sheilah Graham, *The Real F. Scott Fitzgerald: Thirty-five Years Later* (1976), p. 208.

329 **Go now, listen** at https://granta.com/john-keats-ode-nightingale-read-f-scott-fitzgerald/ [accessed 6 Sept 2020]. Having listened, readers might also like to watch four gallant cinematic attempts at recreating the worlds of Keats and Fitzgerald, all of which contain many authentic details as well as the usual Hollywood embroidery: *Bright Star* (2009), director Jane Campion's rendition of Keats and Fanny Brawne; *Beloved Infidel* (1959), starring Gregory Peck and Deborah Kerr, a remarkably faithful dramatization of Sheilah Graham's first book about her affair with Scott Fitzgerald; *Midnight in Paris* (2011), Woody Allen's fantasia on the American writers in Paris in the 1920s, with Tom Hiddleston as Fitzgerald and Kathy Bates delivering a bravura adaptation of Gertrude Stein's verdict on *The Great Gatsby*; and, for Max Perkins as visionary literary editor, *Genius* (2016), mostly about Perkins (Colin Firth) and Thomas Wolfe (Jude Law), but with a Fitzgerald cameo by Guy Pearce. None of the films of Fitzgerald's novels has been entirely satisfactory: *The Great Gatsby* remains elusive despite the best efforts of Robert Redford and Mia Farrow (1974, directed by Jack Clayton

from a screenplay by Francis Ford Coppola) and Leonardo DiCaprio and Carey Mulligan (2013, adapted and directed by Baz Luhrmann).

AFTERWORD

331 **The poor son-of-a-bitch** *The Great Gatsby*, p. 211; Dorothy Parker, quoted, Marion Meade, *Dorothy Parker: What Fresh Hell is This?* (1989), p. 299. In her interview, 'The Art of Fiction No. 13', *Paris Review*, 13 (Summer 1956), Parker confirmed that she did say this and that it was her true feeling, not one of her wisecracks.

332 **Thou shalt survive** Clare, *The Village Minstrel, and other Poems* (1821), 2. 207.

332 **voice of the Jazz Age** Serendipitously, Keats died in 1821, Fitzgerald reached Keats's age at death in 1921, and this parallel life was written for publication in 2021. The title of Fitzgerald's 1922 short-story collection does seem to be the earliest usage of the actual phrase 'The Jazz Age', though newspapers in late 1920 began talking about living in *a* jazz age. In the explanatory notes appended to the contents list of *Tales of the Jazz Age*, Fitzgerald wrote of his story 'May Day', 'This somewhat unpleasant tale, published as a novelette in the "Smart Set" in July, 1920, relates a series of events that took place in the spring of the previous year . . . In life they were unrelated, except by the general hysteria of that spring which inaugurated the Age of Jazz' (p. viii).

332 **Let me tell you** 'The Rich Boy', in *All the Sad Young Men* (1926), p. 1.

332 **Yes, they have more** Ernest Hemingway, 'The Snows of Kilimanjaro', *Esquire*, August 1936.

333 **They possess and enjoy early** 'The Rich Boy', p. 2.

334 ***Negative Capability* . . . gone the same steps** KL 1. 193, 279.

334 **Time that is intolerant** 'In Memory of W. B. Yeats' (Feb 1939), in W. H. Auden, *Another Time* (1940).

334 **The Comrades out here** To Scottie Fitzgerald, 7 June 1940, FLL, p. 449.

335 **symbol and historian** Buttita, *Lost Summer*, p. 5. I am not denying that Fitzgerald's *oeuvre*, in both fiction and non-fiction,

was a remarkably insightful commentary, both direct and indirect, on those changes – as is shown illuminatingly throughout the most recent biography of him, David S. Brown, *Paradise Lost: A Life of F. Scott Fitzgerald* (2017).

335 **Keats was strongly influenced** See my essay 'Tom Moore and the Making of the "Ode to Psyche"', *Review of English Studies*, 41 (August 1990), 325–33.

336 **Kant staring at a church steeple** Fitzgerald was writing *The Great Gatsby* at a time when newspaper and magazine articles were celebrating the bicentenary of Kant's birth; an essay called 'Kant after Two Hundred Years' by the distinguished philosopher John Dewey appeared in the *New Republic* of 30 April 1924, immediately after an 'Imaginary Conversation' between Van Wyck Brooks and Scott Fitzgerald, written by Edmund Wilson. See further, Horst Kruse, '*The Great Gatsby*: A View from Kant's Window – Transatlantic Crosscurrents', *The F. Scott Fitzgerald Review*, 2 (2003), 72–84. Fitzgerald knew about Kant's ideas and his influence on Romanticism primarily through chapters 10 and 11 of vol. 2 of Herbert Ernest Cushman's *Introduction to Philosophy* (1911), a book which he bought when taking Philosophy 301 at Princeton and gave to Sheilah Graham as a textbook in the 'College of One'.

336 **The excellence of every Art** To George and Tom Keats, 21 Dec 1817, KL 1. 192.

336 **A thing of beauty** *Endymion*, 1. 1–5.

337 **I felt rather lonely** To George and Tom Keats, 15 April 1817, KL 1. 128.

INDEX